CAMBRIDGE STUDIES IN PHILOSOPHY

The Metaphysics of Mind

CAMBRIDGE STUDIES IN PHILOSOPHY

General editor SYDNEY SHOEMAKER

Advisory editors J. E. J. ALTHAM, SIMON BLACKBURN,
GILBERT HARMAN, MARTIN HOLLIS, FRANK JACKSON,
JONATHAN LEAR, WILLIAM G. LYCAN, JOHN PERRY,
BARRY STROUD

The Metaphysics of Mind

Michael Tye
Temple University

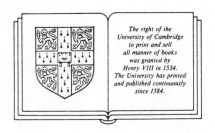

The right of the
University of Cambridge
to print and sell
all manner of books
was granted by
Henry VIII in 1534.
The University has printed
and published continuously
since 1584.

Cambridge University Press

Cambridge
New York   New Rochelle   Melbourne   Sydney

Published by the Press Syndicate of the University of Cambridge
The Pitt Building, Trumpington Street, Cambridge CB2 1RP
32 East 57th Street, New York, NY 10022, USA
10 Stamford Road, Oakleigh, Melbourne 3166, Australia

First published 1989

Printed in Canada

Library of Congress Cataloging-in-Publication Data
Tye, Michael.
The metaphysics of mind / Michael Tye.
p.   cm. – (Cambridge studies in philosophy)
ISBN 0 521 35470 6
1. Mind and body – Philosophy.   2. Psychology – Philosophy.
I. Title.   II. Series.
BF161.T94   88–15301
128'.2 – dc19   CIP

British Library Cataloguing in Publication Data
Tye, Michael
The metaphysics of mind – (Cambridge studies in philosophy)
1. Mind – Philosophical perspectives
I. Title
110

ISBN 0 521 35470 6

For my mother and Mary

Acknowledgments

Many philosophers have in one way or another provided invaluable stimuli for the views presented in this book. I would like to mention Simon Blackburn, Romane Clark, Frank Jackson, William Lycan, Wilfrid Sellars, and William Tolhurst. I am especially indebted to Terence Horgan, with whom Chapter 1 was co-written.

I have drawn on several of my published articles in various parts of the book. Chapter 1 is a minimally revised version of "Against the Token Identity Theory," which appeared in *The Philosophy of Donald Davidson: Essays on Actions and Events*, edited by Ernest Le Poré and Brian McLaughlin (Oxford: Blackwell Publisher, 1985). Parts of Chapter 4 draw on "Pain and the Adverbial Theory," *American Philosophical Quarterly*, 21 (1984). Chapter 5 incorporates material from "The Adverbial Approach to Visual Experience," *The Philosophical Review*, 93 (1984). And Chapter 6 is a virtual reprint of "The Subjective Qualities of Experience," *Mind*, 95 (1986). I am grateful to the editors and publishers of the sources given for permission to make use of previously published work.

Introduction

The metaphysical theory of mind I advocate has three primary component theses:

1. Psychological statements are frequently true.
2. The only entities required for the truth of psychological discourse are persons and other sentient creatures together with sets built up out of such entities.[1]
3. Collectively, the various generalizations of a psychological theory, be it folk or scientific, implicitly define the psychological predicates occurring within that theory.

There are also five subsidiary negative theses that figure in the development of my overall position:

4. There are no mental events.
5. Sensation is not relational: There are no sensory objects.
6. The propositional attitudes are not relational: There are no objects of the attitudes, be they abstract propositions or sentences in an inner or an outer language.
7. Cognitive psychology is not committed to the existence of mental representations.
8. Neither modal arguments nor the argument from knowing 'what it is like' establish that anything is left out by a physicalist approach to the subjective aspects of sensory experience.

Of the eight theses, the first is given the least defense. This is because I believe that most philosophers do not need to be convinced of its truth and also because I have little to add to standard criticisms of eliminative materialism, that is, the view that present-day psychological statements are infected with radical error.

The structure of my argument is basically as follows. It is widely held that there really are such entities as mental events – for example, beliefs and desires. At the beginning of Chapter 1 (which is written

1 This is to oversimplify a little; in certain cases space–time regions are also required.

1

	Psychophysical event dualism	Token identity theory	Eliminative materialism	Operator theory
Psychological statements are frequently true	Yes	Yes	No	Yes
There are mental events	Yes	Yes	No	No
There are nonphysical mental events	Yes	No	No	No

jointly with Terence Horgan) it is shown that this view generates a problem: that of finding a satisfactory niche for mental events in nature as a whole. Many philosophers solve this problem by endorsing the token identity theory (the theory that every mental event is strictly identical with some physicochemical event). However, in Chapter 1, it is argued that the token identity theory is false (as is the closely related materialist view that mental events are complex entities that are composed of physicochemical events but that are nonetheless distinct from the aggregates or fusions of their parts). What to do? There are only two courses of action left open: Become a psychophysical event dualist or deny that mental events really exist. In Chapter 2, I argue for the latter alternative. This smacks strongly of eliminative materialism, a view I reject. So the argument appears to lead nowhere. But there is a way out, I suggest, since the claim that mental events do not exist does not *entail* that eliminative materialism is true. Rather it entails only that *either* eliminative materialism is true *or* psychological statements have a misleading grammatical form and, contrary to appearances, do not require for their truth the existence of mental events (just as 'Paul died for the sake of his country' does not require for its truth that there really exist such an entity as a sake). In Chapter 3, I embrace the second of these disjuncts, and I present the outline of a metaphysical theory of mind that has the commitments expressed in thesis 2. For reasons that will become clear later, I call this theory the "operator theory." The table above summarizes how the operator theory resembles and differs from the usual three alternative theories on the issues of truth and mental events.

The operator theory repudiates not only mental events but also mental objects – for example, pains and images. These entities face the same sort of problem as the one presented in Chapter 1 for mental events. They also encounter all sorts of well-known philosophical puzzles of their own. The underlying reason for these puzzles, according to the operator theory, is straightforward enough: Psychological statements putatively about mental objects are, in reality, free of any such commitment. There are no mental objects, just as there are no mental events. This point is given a preliminary defense in Chapter 3.

Chapters 4, 5, and 7 are concerned primarily with the detailed development of the operator theory in the context of the statements of folk psychology. I begin with statements "about" bodily sensations such as pain; I proceed next to statements "about" perceptual sensations; and I continue on in Chapter 7 to statements "about" belief, desire, and other propositional attitudes. I argue that all of these statements can be regimented in the same general way and that there is no need to invoke such entities as sense data, mental sentences, or abstract propositions in order to account for the truth of folk psychological discourse.

So far in my explanation of the operator theory I have said nothing about the meaning of psychological discourse and the status of sensory qualia. Nevertheless, as I indicated at the beginning, I have definite views on these matters. On the issue of the status of qualia, I offer, in Chapter 6, what I hope is a compelling defense of thesis 8. On the issue of meaning, I opt for a broadly functionalist approach to psychological predicates. My primary concern here is to show how a version of conceptual functionalism can be developed that goes hand in hand with my general semantical views and that also avoids any metaphysical commitment to events (including states and conditions) or even to properties. This seems to me worthwhile in part because conceptual functionalism sometimes seems to be an isolated position set apart from other views on the semantics of everyday nonpsychological language, and in part because it is not obvious what a satisfactory reconstruction of functionalism would look like (or even whether it is possible) within the metaphysical confines of my position. Parts of Chapters 4, 5, 7, and 8 address these topics.

In the concluding chapter, my discussion of the operator theory moves from folk psychology to cognitive psychology. It is widely held that cognitive psychology is committed to the existence of mental representations (be they quasi-linguistic, quasi-pictorial, or

3

otherwise). In opposition to this view, I present an interpretation of cognitive psychology that avoids any commitment to mental representations, and I maintain that from the point of view of metaphysics this interpretation is preferable to the standard one.

The view that emerges from my discussion is a form of physicalism with respect to the mental in that it denies that there are any nonphysical mental entities. But it is a physicalism that avoids both the radical extremism of eliminative materialism and the pitfalls of the token identity theory. Admittedly the truth conditions I state for psychological discourse involve sets, and this may not sit well with physicalists who are die-hard nominalists. Still, as Quine has stressed, sets do at least have the virtue of clear, uncontested identity conditions. Moreover, they seem needed in formal treatments of truth conditions generally. My hope, I should add, is that this commitment is merely apparent and that sets are ultimately eliminable both in the truth conditions for psychological discourse and elsewhere.[2] However, I make no attempt to argue for this view in the present book. Overall, it seems to me, the operator theory has great systematic unity and great simplicity. For these reasons, it is, I believe, the most promising metaphysical theory of mind available to the physicalist.

The metaphysical views presented in this book rest on an important background assumption. Space limitations prevent me from offering a full defense of this assumption here. But I think I ought to explain what the assumption is and, in general terms, why I make it.

With one qualification to be stated shortly, I assume that the existential quantifier is a constant indicator of reference that provides us with the means to determine the ontological commitments of what we say. This view of metaphysics is, of course, that of Quine.[3] The reasoning behind it can be summarized as follows. Everyday English is full of expressions that appear to be singular terms but that are not used referringly, for example, 'the average family', 'Pegasus', 'the behalf of Amy', 'the equator'. So the or-

---

2 For a promising account of how such an elimination might go, see Terence Horgan, "A Nominalistic Theory of Truth," *International Logic Review*, forthcoming.

3 See W. V. O. Quine, "On What There Is," in *From a Logical Point of View* (New York: Harper & Row, 1963); idem, *Word and Object* (Cambridge, Mass.: MIT Press, 1960).

dinary assertion of an English sentence containing an apparent singular term does not commit its speaker to the existence of an entity corresponding to that term. How, then, are we to determine the ontic commitments of given utterances? Quine's position, in essence, is that we must translate the utterances into a formal language incorporating the existential quantifier '$(\exists x)$'. We then commit ourselves ontologically by asserting sentences that contain '$(\exists x)$' or that logically imply sentences containing '$(\exists x)$'. In taking this view, Quine makes no attempt to explicate or analyze the ordinary term 'exist'. Quine's strategy is rather to introduce a symbolic expression, namely the existential quantifier, which formally captures the standard existentially committing use of this term without further illuminating its meaning. The test of a set of translations of a given body of discourse, θ, into the language of quantification is simple enough: Since the formalized sentences are intended to represent perspicuously the truth conditions of the informal sentences making up θ, any proposal that fails to preserve any of the various logical entailments and nonentailments that obtain between the members of θ must be rejected as unsatisfactory.

The qualification I referred to earlier pertains to any existential quantifier having a component variable the substitution instances for which are linguistic items other than singular terms. I hold that such a quantifier is not an indicator of reference, and hence I also hold that its use need not be existentially committing. In the case of the quantifier '$(\exists x)$', the substitution instances for the variable 'x' are usually taken to be genuine singular terms, that is, expressions that *refer* to entities in the world. It is in virtue of this fact that the use of '$(\exists x)$' is taken to indicate ontic commitment. In the case of '$(\exists F)$', however, in, say, '$(\exists F)Fa$', the substitution instances for the variable 'F' are *predicates*, and predicates are obviously *not* singular terms. This point is discussed further in Chapter 3, where it is suggested that quantifiers such as '$(\exists F)$' and '(G)' be read substitutionally.

It may be objected that once '$(\exists F)$' is interpreted substitutionally there is nothing to prevent us from interpreting any quantifier we wish substitutionally, in which case the sometimes complex analyses of logical form presented in this book become otiose. However, the attempt to interpret '$(\exists x)$' substitutionally is fraught with difficulty. One major problem is this: If we hold that '$(\exists x)Fx$' is true just in case some instance of 'Fx' is true, then not only is it difficult to grasp what the right side of the biconditional asserts if it does not involve objectual quantification over linguistic items, but there also remains the task of spelling out adequate truth conditions for atomic sentences of the form 'Fx'. This task, moreover, is decidedly nontrivial; for the truth conditions will have to show how the world makes the atomic sentences true, and they will have to do so without reintroducing an ontological commitment to the entities that the substitutional approach is trying to avoid. In particular, the truth conditions cannot take the substitution instances of 'x' in sentences of the form 'Fx' to be names so that 'Fa', say, is true if, and only if, some individual named by 'a' belongs to the satisfaction set of 'F'.[4]

I do not claim that these difficulties *cannot* be overcome. But I do not myself see how to overcome them. And minimally I think they make it clear that a glib appeal to a substitutional interpretation of the quantifier '$(\exists x)$' *whenever* there appears to be unwanted ontic commitment carries no weight.

In concluding this introduction, I want to show how the approach to metaphysics I have sketched undercuts two general criticisms of my views that have cropped up in conversation. I have been asked repeatedly what relevance my views have for cognitive psychology. Even if I repudiate events, it has been said, cognitive psychologists, under the influence of the computer model, certainly do posit information-bearing events in people and other cognitive systems. And why shouldn't they? Why, from their own point of view and for scientific purposes, should cognitive scientists and researchers in artificial intelligence engage in the logical maneuvers I defend in an attempt to avoid metaphysical commitment to information-bearing states and events?

This criticism rests on a serious misunderstanding of what I am doing. First, my views are metaphysical. They are intended to have absolutely no relevance to the day-to-day practices and assertions of cognitive scientists. I am happy to grant that such scientists have nothing at all to learn from what I say that could or should influence their methods or theories. To suppose otherwise would be just as absurd as supposing that an ordinary person should change his or

---

4 For more on the problems associated with a substitutional interpretation of all quantifiers, see Dale Gottlieb, *Ontological Economy* (New York: Oxford University Press, 1980), pp. 48–50.

her day-to-day assertions about the mind in the light of my discussion. Second, the fact that cognitive psychologists propound theories that appear from their superficial grammatical form to be committed to the existence of representations, events, states, and so on does not entail that those theories really are so committed. That issue – the metaphysical issue – is *not* one for the cognitive scientist but rather for the philosopher. The scientist interested in the mind presents theories of how we perceive, how we remember, how we understand, and so on, which he or she believes to be true. The descriptive metaphysician, in my view, then, regiments these theories (in the manner I have indicated) in an attempt to discover what there must be in the world *in order for* them to be true. Third, the empirical evidence for the claim that cognitive scientists posit information-bearing events or states is really only evidence for the claim that cognitive scientists propound theories that putatively refer to or quantify over information-bearing events or states. Putative reference is not the same as genuine reference. Whether the cognitive theories must be interpreted as really referring to (or quantifying over) events and states is not an issue that can be settled by examining the intentions, assertions, or scientific procedures of cognitive scientists. Instead it is an issue for logical analysis.

The second criticism I want to address is that the operator theory, as I elaborate it, is merely a linguistic dodge that reveals nothing about the mind in particular and is subject to no significant constraints. This criticism reveals another serious misunderstanding. The operator theory does *not* consist of purely syntactic, formal analyses; it has an important *semantic* dimension. In this respect, it is like any other metaphysical theory (given my conception of metaphysics). Moreover, the semantic aspect of the operator theory places well-defined constraints on its applicability. If there are logical entailments among psychological sentences that the theory cannot justify via the truth conditions it assigns to those sentences, then the theory is just plain wrong. If there are nonentailments among psychological sentences that the theory converts into entailments via its assigned truth conditions, then again the theory is wrong. As to whether the strategies the theory employs may be applied elsewhere, outside of either the mind or the realm of events, I regard that as an open question. It seems to me that the operator theory provides us with a well-motivated and cohesive view of the mind and that the strategies it rests on find their natural home in

1

An objection to
the token identity theory

with TERENCE HORGAN

Philosophers have generally agreed that there are concrete mental events, for example, my now thinking of England, your remembering your last meal, my feeling pain, your desiring a week in the sun. There has been considerable disagreement, however, about where to locate mental events in nature as a whole. The modern debate on this issue originates, of course, with René Descartes.[1] According to Descartes, mental events take place in spiritual substances that are unextended, nonspatial, and immaterial. Minds, on Descartes's view, just are these spiritual substances, and though they are nonphysical, they are related in a special and close way to the physical bodies with which they are associated via a two-way causal interaction between mental events and bodily changes.

Descartes defended this view of the mind by appeal to famous arguments from doubt and possibility, arguments that need no repetition here. The view has been influential in philosophy mainly because of these arguments, but also to a lesser degree because historically many philosophers have shared the intuition that the mind and its contents are somehow intrinsically different from the rest of nature.

Today Cartesian dualism has diminishing support. Its decline can be traced to a number of factors, central among which have been a skepticism about the intelligibility of the concept of an immaterial substance and a growing belief, fostered by recent work in the physical sciences, that the physical world is causally closed. This last belief, if true, precludes any causal interaction between spirit and matter.

1 See, e.g., *Meditations on First Philosophy*, first published in 1641.

9

But if the physical world *is* causally closed, then where within it are mental events to be found? One straightforward and widely accepted answer is that every concrete mental event is strictly identical with some concrete physicochemical event. The view expressed in this answer, which has come to be called the "token identity theory," has no difficulty in explaining the special nature of the connection between a person's mind and a person's body; furthermore, it sidesteps worries about the intelligibility of the concept of a spiritual substance, and it has the immediate advantage of ontological simplicity. Nonetheless, we believe that it should be rejected. The purpose of this chapter is to present and defend our major objection.

I

In accordance with common recent practice, we shall use the rubric 'event' in a broad sense, to include not merely changes but also states, processes, and the like. Events, as we shall here construe them, are concrete entities, or tokens. If we mean to speak of the types of which events are tokens, we shall explicitly use the term 'event-type'. (Occasionally we shall use the term 'event/state' rather than 'event', in order to emphasize that the entities we are speaking of can have longer than momentary duration and that these entities can be – or have parts that are – relatively static during their duration.)

Now if mental events exist, then for any creature c who has mentality, there is a nonempty set $M(c)$ containing all and only the mental events of which c, at one time or another during the creature's lifetime, is the subject; we shall call this c's mentality set. We shall take the contents of $M(c)$ to include not only events of the kind that are apparently posited by common-sense psychology ("folk psychology"), but also mental events of any additional kinds that would be posited by an ideal theoretical psychology.

For any creature c with a nonempty mentality set $M(c)$, we shall say that a set of events $P(c)$ is a physical causal isomorph of $M(c)$ (for short, a PCI) if, and only if, (1) every member of $P(c)$ is a physicochemical event of which c is the subject, and (2) there is a one-to-one relation R between the events in $P(c)$ and the events in $M(c)$ such that (a) each event in $P(c)$ is simultaneous with its R

correlate in $M(c)$ and (b) the events in $P(c)$ collectively conform to all the causal principles of common-sense psychology and theoretical psychology that govern their respective R correlates in $M(c)$.

Our argument against the token identity theory is as follows. First premise: For any creature c with a nonempty mentality set, $M(c)$ is likely to have several distinct PCIs. Second premise: If $M(c)$ has several distinct PCIs, then some events in $M(c)$ have no unique correlate among those PCIs. Third premise: If a mental event e in $M(c)$ has no unique correlate among $M(c)$'s PCIs, then e is not identical with any of its PCI correlates [and hence $M(c)$ is not identical with any of its PCIs]. Fourth premise: If a mental event e in $M(c)$ is not identical with any of its PCI correlates, then e is not a physicochemical event. Conclusion: Any creature with a nonempty mentality set is likely to be the subject of mental events that are not identical with any physicochemical events.

The second premise, we take it, is true by definition: If $M(c)$ has several distinct PCIs, then at least one mental event in $M(c)$ has to have more than one PCI correlate. The fourth premise, too, is unproblematic: A physicochemical event that lacks the causal properties of a given mental event e cannot be identical with e. Hence, if e is identical with any physicochemical event at all, that event will have to be one of e's PCI correlates.[2] So the key premises, the ones that require defending, are the first and the third. Let us consider them in reverse order, since the third can be dealt with more briefly.

II

In defense of the third premise, we would claim that mental events can be individuated only by means of their causal roles, as specified by the causal principles that constitute the bulk of folk psychology

2 A radical psychophysical event dualist who claims that some mental events not only are distinct from physical events but also have their efficacy in a way that does not depend on the efficacy of any "underlying" physical events might conceivably claim that certain other mental events are identical with physical events but are not identical with their PCI correlates. He or she might claim that a creature's mentality set simply has no purely physical causal isomorphs. But although this is a logically possible position, it is hard to see why anyone would adopt it. Why would anyone who espouses radical dualism regarding some mental events espouse a token identity theory regarding others?

and theoretical psychology.[3] Mental events are the events that "physically realize" those principles, in a creature's head. So if there often occur "simultaneous multiple realizations" in a single creature's head at a single time, then there simply are no further, nonfunctional principles that could be used to determine which physicochemical event is really identical with a given multiply realized mental event.[4]

It should be stressed that the claim that mental events are functionally individuated is weaker than full-fledged functionalism; the latter is the view, roughly, that mental terms can be exhaustively analyzed functionally. Since we are not assuming full-fledged functionalism, our defense of the third premise actually applies to token phenomenal mental states, or token 'qualia', as they are sometimes called, even if one rejects the claim that phenomenal terms can be given exhaustive functional analyses. Our central claim is that if a certain psychological theory is true of a given creature c (something that may well depend on the nature of c's "neural hardware," and not merely on the functional organization of c's internal events/states), then the causal principles of that theory fix the extensions of its mental terms, relative to c. Qualia lovers should not object to the claim as thus interpreted; for it does not conflict with their main contention, namely that mental events in creatures whose physical constitution is radically different from ours would not necessarily have the same qualitative content as the functionally equivalent mental events in humans. (Martian pain would not nec-

3 The relevant causal roles, however, evidently will have to include certain causal connections with what goes on within the creature's social environment; they cannot merely involve causal linkages among sensory inputs, behavioral outputs, and internal events. Our doppelgangers on Putnam's famous planet Twin Earth do not undergo tokens of the type believing that water is good to drink, even though we do and even though their internal neural activity is indistinguishable (in its intrinsic features) from ours. The trouble is that the stuff they call 'water' is not water at all. See Hilary Putnam, "The Meaning of 'Meaning,'" *Minnesota Studies in the Philosophy of Science*, Vol. 7, ed. K. Gunderson (Minneapolis: University of Minnesota Press, 1975); and Tyler Burge, "Individualism and the Mental," *Midwest Studies in Philosophy*, Vol. 4, ed. P. French, T. Uehling, and H. Wettstein (Minneapolis: University of Minnesota Press, 1979).

4 This point, we might add, is not threatened by the claim that mental events have genuinely teleological functional properties that are not identical with any of their causal functional properties. Advocates of the view that there are such teleological properties must surely grant that any two physical events that play the same causal role, as specified in the preceding footnote, also have the same teleological psychological function.

essarily feel like human pain. Perhaps it would feel like a tickle, or like nothing we can imagine.)[5]

We claim that even qualia-loving token identity theorists must concede that the only way to find the neural event that is allegedly identical with a particular mental event *e*, in a creature who has the neural hardware to subserve such a mental event, is to locate the neural event having all the causes and effects that the correct psychology of that creature attributes to *e*. So even qualia lovers must concede that, if there are several neural events that fit the bill, there will be no basis for saying that one of them rather than another is identical with *e*.

III

We turn now to the first premise. We want to defend this premise on the basis of the following general thesis about causation. Quite often there is no such thing as "the cause" (at a given time) of a particular event; rather, there are a variety of events, some being proper parts of others, which all can legitimately be called "the cause." Which event one calls "the cause" is normally a contextually determined affair, having to do with such matters as the pragmatics of explanation.

This claim is not as new or radical as it might seem. Mill, for instance, held that what we normally call "the cause" is usually only a part of "the cause, philosophically speaking" – where the latter is a relatively complex event/state the occurrence of which is sufficient, given the laws of nature, for the effect.[6] If one holds Mill's view, it is natural to add that different parts of the genuine cause can be called "the cause" in a particular context – depending on which parts of the genuine cause are most naturally treated, in context, as "background conditions."

Mackie, who is critical of Mill's view that a genuine cause must

---

5 For a defense of this claim, see Chapter 4, especially Section II.
6 Hume, in a well-known passage in *A Treatise of Human Nature*, ed. L. A. Selby-Bigge (Oxford: Clarendon, 1888; 2nd ed. as revised by P. H. Nidditch, 1978), writes, "We must reject the distinction betwixt *cause* and *occasion*, when suppos'd to signify any thing essentially different from each other" (p. 171, emphasis in original). Mill's answer is that "the real Cause is the whole of these antecedents; and we have, philosophically speaking, no right to give the name of cause to one of them exclusively of the others." See John Stuart Mill, *A System of Logic* (London: Longmans, 1961), Book 3, Chap. 5, Sec. 3, p. 214.

be sufficient for its effect, claims instead that a cause is an "INUS" condition of its effect; that is, a cause is an insufficient but necessary component of a condition that is unnecessary but sufficient for the effect.[7] On Mackie's view, too, it is natural to say that more than one INUS condition can properly be called "the cause" and that which INUS condition one should pick is often a context-relative affair.

Davidson, however, in his well-known essay "Causal Relations," will have none of this:

Mill . . . was wrong in thinking we have not specified the whole cause of an event when we have not wholly specified it. And there is not, as Mill and others have maintained, anything elliptical in the claim that a certain man's death was caused by his eating a particular dish, even though death resulted only because the man had a particular bodily constitution, a particular state of present health, and so on. On the other hand Mill was, I think, quite right in saying that "there certainly is, among the circumstances that took place, some combination or other with which death is invariably consequent . . . the whole of which circumstances perhaps constituted in this particular case the conditions of the phenomenon . . . " (*A System of Logic*, book III, chap. v., 3). Mill's critics are no doubt justified in contending that we may correctly give the cause without saying enough to demonstrate that it was sufficient; but they share Mill's confusion if they think that every deletion from the description of an event represents something deleted from the event described.[8]

Davidson's view, of course, is that the man's eating the dish and his subsequent death have descriptions that instantiate a law; hence, the eating of the dish is a full and complete cause of the death. The relevant description of the cause is likely to be quite complex; in particular, it will have to include a description of the man's state of health and bodily constitution. (Either that, or it will include a complete physicochemical description of the man, specifying properties on which his state of health and bodily constitution are supervenient.)[9]

7 J. L. Mackie, "Cause and Conditions," *American Philosophical Quarterly*, 2 (1965): 245–64; idem, *The Cement of the Universe* (New York: Oxford University Press, 1974).
8 Donald Davidson, "Causal Relations," *Journal of Philosophy*, 64 (1967): 691–703.
9 In order for there to be any plausibility in Davidson's claim that causally related events have descriptions that instantiate a law, we must understand the rubric 'law' as including not only the relatively simple nomic principles that are ordinarily called the laws of a scientific theory, but also any arbitrarily complex logical

But we maintain that this treatment of such cases of causation, far from undermining our claim that several distinct events often can legitimately be called "the cause," actually supports this claim; for if the crucial factor in causation is the fact that cause and effect have descriptions that instantiate a law, and if we are allowed to make our description of the cause–event so complex that it includes a substantial amount of relevant information about the event's environment (information like the fact that the eating of the dish was an eating by a man with such and such bodily constitution and so and so state of health), then it seems quite clear that in many cases a variety of events or states can legitimately qualify as "the cause" of a particular effect.

Suppose, for instance, that one is asking why a particular man, Smith, died as a result of eating the dish when several others who ate the dish did not die. In such a context, one might choose to relegate the eating itself to the role of a "background condition," since the others ate the dish too. And against the relevant background conditions, one might pinpoint Smith's state of health as "the cause."

As far as we can tell, such an approach would be perfectly legitimate, given Davidson's treatment of causality; for when one constructs the relevant description of Smith's state of health at the time in question, one can build into the description the fact that this event/state is the state of a man who is ingesting thus and such a substance. This description-expanding move is quite parallel, it seems, to Davidson's move of building a description of Smith's state of health into a description of Smith's eating the dish. In neither case are we describing an event/state whose occurrence is itself irrelevant to the effect. Rather, we are describing two different components of the complex event/state that Mill would have called "the cause, philosophically speaking." Thus, if Smith's eating the dish and his death have descriptions that instantiate a law, presumably his being in such and such a state of health and his death also have descriptions that instantiate a law. Hence, if Smith's eating the dish can properly be called "the cause" of his death in certain

consequence of these principles. The "laws" that underlie garden-variety macro-level causal statements are likely to be very complex indeed; for garden-variety macrolevel objects and events have a vast number of microphysical components, and it is plausible to conjecture that the only truly "homonomic" science is physics.

15

contexts of inquiry, then Smith's state of health also can properly be called "the cause" in other such contexts.[10]

Perhaps it will be objected that we have misrepresented Davidson's treatment of causation. One might construe him as claiming that two events are related as cause and effect only if they have purely intrinsic descriptions that instantiate a law – that is, descriptions that refer to the events solely in terms of their nonrelational features, rather than in terms that include aspects of the events' surroundings. One might then argue as follows.

Since Smith's eating the fish causes his subsequent death, these two events have intrinsic descriptions that instantiate a law. But there is no causal connection between his state of health antecedent to eating the fish and his death; for the former event simply has no intrinsic description that, together with some intrinsic description of the death, instantiates a law. (If it did, we would have a case of causal preemption or causal overdetermination; but ex hypothesi we do not.) So even though several different events can perhaps be called "the cause" relative to different contexts of inquiry, it does not follow, on Davidson's picture, that the various events really are causes; for genuine causes and their effects must have intrinsic descriptions that instantiate a law, whereas what are *called* causes need not satisfy this condition. This is because we sometimes single out events that interest us in the circumstances, not bothering to locate the events that are the causes more accurately. Thus, there is no real context relativity about genuine causation.

Our own interpretation of Davidson is different from the one motivating this objection. We take him to be allowing that the relevant descriptions under which a cause and its effect instantiate a law can be partially nonintrinsic; that is, these descriptions can cite features of the described event's surrounding environment, in addition to any purely intrinsic features of the event itself. Our point was that, once one allows reference to nonintrinsic features into one's event-descriptions, it seems that Smith's state of health,

---

10 One might object that only momentary changes, and not longer-lived states, can be causes. But many of our ordinary causal judgments seem to contradict this claim. One highly relevant counterexample is the causation of human actions by wants and beliefs. No doubt "the cause, philosophically speaking," must include some element of change. Otherwise, why would the effect occur at just the moment it does? But in certain contexts the relevant change elements are evidently relegated to the background conditions, rather than being included in the event/state we call the cause.

immediately before his eating the dish, does indeed have a description that, together with some appropriate description of the death, instantiates a law. (Also, the event described is no mere causally extraneous one, whose connection to the death is solely a matter of the nonintrinsic information packed into its description. Rather, this event is a bona fide component of the complex event that does have a purely intrinsic description under which it is nomically linked to the death.)

We do not insist that our interpretation represents Davidson's actual position. As far as we know, he nowhere explicitly says whether or not law-instantiating event-descriptions must be purely intrinsic in order for the events described to be genuinely causally related to one another. Consequently, either interpretation seems consistent with his published discussions of causation.

We do contend, however, that his position must be interpreted our way if it is to be at all plausible. To see this, consider an often-cited garden-variety example of causation: a short circuit causing a fire. As Mackie would emphasize, it is most implausible to suppose that the short-circuit-event has a purely intrinsic description that, together with a purely intrinsic description of the fire, instantiates a law. On the contrary, another short-circuit-event, intrinsically indistinguishable from the given event, will be followed by a fire only if it too is embedded in an appropriate surrounding environment – an environment in which the electrical insulation is faulty, in which flammable material is present, in which a suitable supply of oxygen is present, and so forth.

Or consider Smith, who died from eating the fish. Another eating-event, intrinsically indistinguishable from the one involving Smith, will be followed by a death only if the relevant surrounding events/states are again present: a certain state of health and constitution on the part of the person eating, the person's subsequent failure to consume an antidote, and so forth. (Admittedly, things are less clear-cut in this case than in the short-circuit case. One might try arguing that this particular eating by Smith includes, among its intrinsic components, not merely such events as chewings and swallowings, but also certain fatally abnormal digestive processes that would not have occurred but for Smith's constitution and state of health. But such a move, whatever its plausibility, cannot accommodate such blatantly nonintrinsic events/states as Smith's failure to consume an antidote after eating the fish.)

In the face of these considerations, which are easily multiplied with other examples, an advocate of a nomic-regularity view of causation evidently has three alternatives: (1) denying that the short circuit (or Smith's eating the dish) really causes the fire (or Smith's death) and claiming that the genuine cause is a complex event/state that includes the relevant surrounding events/states as components (the 'Millian move'); or (2) claiming that, in the present context, the term 'the short-circuit' (or 'Smith's eating the dish') really denotes the relevant complex event, rather than the short-circuit proper (or the eating proper); or (3) allowing that the descriptions under which the short circuit and the fire (or the eating and the death) instantiate a law can mention nonintrinsic features, features of the event's environment.

Alternative (1), the Millian move, is prima facie highly objectionable, because it forces us to say that most garden-variety singular causal sentences are literally false. Furthermore, as the earlier-quoted passage from Davidson makes clear, he himself thinks that Mill was mistaken in denying that the events we ordinarily call causes are genuine causes. Alternative (2) is also prima facie highly objectionable, for it forces us to say, counterintuitively, that terms like 'the short-circuit' denote different events within causal contexts than they normally denote. (In the relevant causal context, the short-circuit-event evidently must include, as intrinsic components, the surrounding presence of oxygen, the surrounding presence of flammable material, the surrounding presence of faulty electrical insulation, and so on. Similarly, mutatis mutandis, for Smith's eating the dish.) Surely Davidson would not wish to be saddled with this claim. Thus, the only viable alternative, for someone who wishes to hold that causally related events must have descriptions that instantiate a law, is (3). But once (3) is adopted, Davidson's approach becomes vulnerable to our earlier argument for the context relativity of causation. The reply cited six paragraphs ago becomes unavailable, because that reply rests on the untenable contention that causally related events must have purely intrinsic descriptions that instantiate a law.

So under Davidson's own treatment of causation, as well as under Mill's or Mackie's, it appears that any of several different events/states can legitimately be called "the cause" (at a time t) of a given effect and that matters of context will normally dictate the appropriate event to receive this designation. We submit that any adequate treatment of the notion of cause should yield this consequence, because it is a feature of our ordinary concept of causation itself.

This feature, not surprisingly, also manifests itself in the domain of the mental. For example, suppose that a subject s in a psychological experiment has been instructed to watch a panel with one green light and one red light and to say "red" whenever the red light flashes and "green" whenever the green light flashes. The red light flashes, and he promptly says "red." What event/state would we call "the cause" of his behavior, at the level of folk psychological explanation? It depends on the context of inquiry. In one context we might take for granted that s understands his instructions and wants to cooperate, and so we would most naturally describe "the cause" as his noticing that the red light has just come on. But in another context we might be interested in providing a more complete folk psychological explanation; here we would more naturally describe "the cause" as including not only the noticing-event, but also s's current desire to cooperate and his current belief that in order to cooperate he must say "red" when he sees the red light flash. There is no single, context-independent answer to the question of which folk psychological event/state constitutes "the cause" of s's behavior.

Let us now consider the relevance of context relativity to the first premise of our argument against the token identity theory. That premise can be established on the basis of two subsidiary claims. First, if one decides to say that a set of physicochemical events within a creature c is a genuine PCI of $M(c)$ provided only that the events in the set satisfy all context-independent conditions on the causal relation that must be met in order for the set to count as a PCI of $M(c)$, then there is every reason to believe that $M(c)$ will have numerous PCIs. Second, it is very unlikely that there exists any such thing as a "general context of psychophysical inquiry" that can narrow down to one the class of genuine PCIs – that is, a context that, independently of any specific explanatory question or problem, generates criteria that tell us which neural event to count as "the cause" of a given neural event or piece of behavior. If both of these claims can be made good, we think there is no avoiding the first premise of our original argument. Let us consider the claims in turn.

The first claim is rendered plausible by the lately noted principle that, in general, there is no single event that can properly be counted as "the cause," at a given time, of a particular effect. This principle is dramatically relevant to the human central nervous system, because of its extreme complexity. The nervous system contains tens of billions of neurons and thousands of billions of synaptic junctures. Thus, at any moment there are vast numbers of neuron excitation states, neuron firings, intersynaptic transfers of electrical energy, and the like; and there is an even greater number of complex event/states that are "fusions" of these simpler event/states.[11] Hence, it is most unlikely that, for any given behavioral or neural event, there will be only one event/state that meets all the formal, context-independent conditions for counting as a cause (at a given time) of that effect. On the contrary, often there are likely to be any number of ways to draw the line between the neural activity that belongs to the cause and the neural activity that belongs to the "background conditions." Accordingly, when we consider a person's mentality set as a whole, there are likely to be any number of corresponding sets of physicochemical events that meet all the context-independent conditions for counting as PCIs.

Moreover, the problem of where to draw the line between the cause and the background conditions is exacerbated when one considers the diachronic dimension of complexity. The causal principles of common-sense psychology and theoretical psychology often do not seem up to the task of precisely pinpointing the temporal instant, or temporal interval, when a posited mental event takes place. Thus, the range of potential "physical realizations" of the mental event must be expanded still further, to include events that occur during a variety of eli-

11 For a discussion of event-fusions, see Judith Jarvis Thomson, *Acts and Other Events* (Ithaca, N.Y.: Cornell University Press, 1977). Thomson is quite liberal in the principles of event-construction she adopts and in the range of events she is willing to call causes of any given event.

One might construe complex events as entities distinct from the fusions of simpler events – for reasons analogous to those that have led some philosophers to claim that an entity like a ship is not identical with the fusion of its parts, but instead has different intraworld and transworld identity conditions. The points we shall make in the text concerning event-fusions will be equally applicable to these putatively different kinds of complex events. [An example of a physicalist theory that appeals to such events is Richard Boyd's "compositional materialism." See his "Materialism without Reductionism – What Physicalism Does Not Entail," in *Readings in the Philosophy of Psychology*, Vol. 1, ed. N. Block (Cambridge, Mass.: Harvard University Press, 1980).]

gible instants or intervals.[12] (When exactly does subject s in the above-described experiment notice that the red light has flashed? We know that this event occurs after the light flashes and before he says "red," but these temporal limits are quite broad in relation to the time scale of neural activity.)

Yet another exacerbating consideration is the relatively rough-and-ready nature of psychological causal generalizations, particularly those of folk psychology. It is one thing for these generalizations to be specific enough to allow us to distinguish mental events from one another. But it is quite another thing for them to allow us to make fine-grained distinctions among neural events. We can think of a person's mentality set, together with the causal principles of folk psychology and theoretical psychology, as specifying a "causal grid" that is somehow instantiated by the person's neural activity, sensory inputs, and behavioral outputs. This is a coarse-grained grid; that is, relatively few intermediary events are posited between sensation and behavior, in comparison with the vast range of intervening neural events. Now, presumably the token identity theorist is prepared to acknowledge that the strictly internal features of the causal grid can be multiply realized within a person's head; he or she believes, however, that there is only one total realization – that is, one realization with the right internal–external causal connections (over and above the right internal–internal causal connections). But in light of the context relativity of what counts as "the cause," it is unlikely that this will be so – at least, not as long as we impose no context-specific parameters onto allowable causal relations. Hence, the coarse-grained nature of the grid makes it all the more likely that the grid can be fit onto neural activity in various ways – that is, that a person's mentality set will have multiple PCIs.[13]

12 Jennifer Hornsby makes a similar point in "Which Physical Events Are Mental Events?" in *Aristotelian Society Proceedings*, 81 (1980–1): 73–92; see especially p. 81. Hornsby's attack on the token identity theory is similar in spirit to ours, although her views on the consequences for physicalism are very different from those presented in the remainder of this book. For another sort of argument against psychophysical token identities see John Haugeland, "Weak Supervenience," *American Philosophical Quarterly*, 19 (1982): 93–103.
13 This point is not affected by the fact, pointed out in note 3, that the causal grid will likely involve certain kinds of causal connections with events in the creature's social environment – features of the kind that distinguish the creature's mental life from that of his doppelganger on Twin Earth, for example.

This brings us to our second claim. Is there such a thing as a psychophysical "context of inquiry" that yields parameters restrictive enough to always pick out some single neural event as "the cause" (at a given time, or approximate time) of a particular neural or behavioral effect? We submit that there is not.

The most plausible candidate for such a context is something like "the context of neurophysiological explanation." One envisions asking an ideally well informed neurophysiologist to determine the cause of the particular effect; and one imagines her doing so in light of whatever contextual parameters govern her ordinary day-to-day causal attributions.

But there is little reason to believe that she could not do what we ask, because the context dependence of causal attributions is likely to be as much a factor within neurophysiology as it is anywhere else. The neurophysiologist's day-to-day decisions about what counts as part of the cause, and what counts instead as part of the background conditions, normally occur in much more specific investigative contexts; hence, she will probably be at a loss if we simply ask her, *qua* neurophysiologist, to tell us "the cause" of a particular neural or behavioral event.

But suppose, just for the sake of argument, that for any particular neural event or piece of behavior, our ideal neurophysiologist actually could tell us – independently of any specific context of inquiry – which neural event/state she would consider "the cause." (We shall use the term 'context N' for the putative general neurophysiological context in which she makes these judgments.) Even if we make this dubious assumption, there are still reasons to think that context N would not narrow down to one the class of event-sets that would count as allowable PCIs of a person's mentality set.

For one thing, our neurophysiologist might well focus exclusively, or almost exclusively, on so-called precipitating causes – that is, instantaneous or short-lived changes – as against more enduring states. But if so then it is implausible to suppose that the events she picks out as causes will always be the right ones to identify with mental events/states; for many of the events/states posited by folk psychology seem clearly to have the status of temporally extended states, rather than instantaneous changes. (This is why we find it more natural, in prephilosophical usage, to call beliefs and desires 'states' rather than 'events'.)

Furthermore, it is entirely possible that the events our neurophysiologist identifies as causes simply will not possess all the causal properties that folk psychology and theoretical psychology attribute to mental events/states. Often our psychological causal principles will attribute several distinct effects to a given mental event/state; and yet it is entirely possible that the ideal neurophysiologist would attribute these effects to different neural events – particularly if the events she is focusing on are momentary changes rather than more complex events that include ongoing states as parts.

One might think that, if this last possibility came to pass, then the mentality set we attribute to a person simply will not have any PCIs among that person's neural events. But this is not so, because even if someone's mentality set has no PCI among the neural events that the neurophysiologist picks as causes (in context N), that mentality set can still have numerous PCIs among other neural events – events that include ongoing states as well as instantaneous changes and that might be rather complex "fusions" of simpler kinds of neurophysiological events.

But if we must turn to these other neural events in order to find a PCI of someone's mentality set, this will mean that we were not able, after all, to pare down effectively the range of genuine PCIs by appealing to the putative context N. Rather, we will again face the likelihood that there will be many PCIs rather than just one.

This idea that the neurophysiologist might often find distinct causes, where folk psychology posits a single cause of two different effects, is not just conjectural. Even in our present state of relative ignorance about the neural basis of cognitive and volitional features of mentality, there is reason to suspect that, in many cases where we would attribute two different effects to a single mental cause, the neurophysiologist would find it natural to posit distinct neural causes; for there is reason to suspect that talk of distinct causes will already become appropriate when we drop from the explanatory level of folk psychology to that of cognitive science. Stephen Stich has pointed out that in recent years several leading cognitive scientists have become skeptical about the possibility of identifying particular memories and beliefs with "naturally isolable" parts of the cognitive system – largely because cognitive models that make such identifications do not seem capable of handling the vast amount of nondeductive inference involved in the use and comprehension of language. Stich cites Minsky as an example:

In a . . . recent paper Minsky elaborates what he calls a "Society of Mind" view in which the mechanisms of thought are divided into many separate "specialists that intercommunicate only sparsely." On the picture Minsky suggests, none of the distinct units or parts of the mental model "have meanings in themselves" . . . and thus none can be identified with individual beliefs, desires, etc. Modularity – I borrow the term from Minsky – is violated in a radical way since meaning or content emerges only from "great webs of structure" and no natural part of the system can be correlated with "explicit" or verbally expressible beliefs.[14]

Suppose Minsky's picture is along the right lines. Then in many cases where folk psychology would appeal to a single belief (say) as the cause of two distinct effects, the cognitive psychologist would be likely to appeal instead to two somewhat different subcomponents of the "great webs of structure." She would be especially likely to do this if she were operating in a context of inquiry where it is appropriate to focus on relatively narrow "precipitating causes" and to relegate much of the relevant cognitive structure to the role of background conditions. And if the cognitive psychologist posits distinct causes where the folk psychologist posits only one, then the neurophysiologist is likely to do so as well – especially if she too is focusing on relatively narrow precipitating causes.

To summarize, in general any of various events/states can properly be considered "the cause," at a given time, of a particular effect; normally a particular event/state will receive this designation on the basis of contextually specific parameters involving such matters as the pragmatics of explanation. Consequently, if one considers only the context-independent features of the causal relation, it is very likely that, for any creature c with a nonempty mentality set $M(c)$, there will be numerous sets of physicochemical events that qualify as PCIs of $M(c)$. Furthermore, it is most implausible to suppose that there is such a thing as a general "context of psychophysical inquiry" – a context that would restrict allowable causes in such a way as to pare down to one the class of genuine

---

14 Stephen P. Stich, *From Folk Psychology to Cognitive Science: The Case Against Belief* (Cambridge, Mass.: Bradford, 1983), p. 241. Stich infers, directly from the premise that beliefs and desires (probably) cannot be identified with "naturally isolable" parts of the cognitive system, that they (probably) do not exist at all. But this inference is made too quickly, because it ignores the possibility that folk psychological events are complex fusions of simpler events. For further discussion of this and related arguments in Stich's book, see Terence Horgan and James Woodward, "Folk Psychology is Here to Stay," *Philosophical Review*, 94 (1985): 197–226.

PCIs of $M(c)$. Moreover, even if an ideally well informed neuro-physiologist could make the relevant causal judgments within some "general neurophysiological context," it might well turn out that the events she picked as causes would not jointly constitute a PCI of $M(c)$ at all. This could happen if she usually picked out momentary events, rather than relatively long lived events/states that have the same duration as the more long lived propositional attitudes in $M(c)$; it could also happen if she sometimes attributed two effects to different neural causes in cases where folk psychology (or theoretical psychology) attributes both effects to a single psychological cause. And if it did happen, the putative "general neurophysiological context" would not be of any use in the attempt to pare down to one the class of genuine PCIs of $M(c)$.[15]

The upshot, then, is that, for any creature c with a nonempty mentality set, $M(c)$ is likely to have several – even many – distinct PCIs. And this is the principal premise of our argument against the token identity theory.

IV

Someone might reply to our argument as follows. If a creature's mentality set has more than one PCI, we can still adhere to the token identity theory. We can simply stipulate that $M(c)$ is to be identified with some specified PCI, and not with any others. Such a move, it might be claimed, is comparable to the stipulative identification of numbers with certain specified sets in the reduction of number theory to set theory; here too there are numerous potential identifications that will work, and we simply pick one by fiat.

One problem with this reply is that no disciplined method has been specified for determining which PCI of a creature c's mentality

15 James Woodward points out to us that one might attempt to sidestep this argument by making the 'Millian move' – i.e., by taking the cause, in the strict and philosophically relevant sense, to be the mereological sum of all those events that would be cited as cause in various contexts of inquiry. But the Millian move is particularly inappropriate with respect to the problem of finding the "right" PCI with which to identify a creature's mentality set; for it seems clear that the Millian cause of a particular effect – say, a particular piece of behavior – often will include a vast array of relatively permanent standing conditions, over and above the temporary neural events/states that identity theorists want to focus upon. (In order for beliefs and desires to generate actions, for instance, the neural linkages between the motor cortex and the muscles must be in good working order; and the muscles themselves must be in good working order; etc., etc.)

set is to be stipulatively identified with $M(c)$. By contrast, when one reduces number theory to set theory, one is explicit about one's stipulative identities.

Furthermore, this reply is not at all in the usual spirit of the token identity theory. The theory's advocates, like Davidson, think of the relevant psychophysical identities as objective facts about the world – facts that involve no element of stipulation or decision on our part. Indeed, this view of the matter is so deep-seated that it probably should be considered partially constitutive of the token identity theory. Thus, the identity-by-fiat approach is better viewed as a new theory rather than as a version of the original one.

How plausible is this non-Davidsonian identity theory? This depends partly on the alternatives. If those alternatives include only psychophysical event dualism, on the one hand, and views like psychological instrumentalism or eliminative materialism, on the other hand, then the identity-by-fiat view does have its attractions – notwithstanding the nontrivial problem of specifying which PCI of $M(c)$ is to be the one that will be identified with $M(c)$. After all, it would be nice to be able to say that mentality is something real, and it also would be nice to avoid dualism. But in the following chapters a theory will be sketched that has these advantages and that also has the advantage of avoiding any appeal to arbitrary stipulation.[16]

Another possible reply to our argument might be this. All the argument really shows is that there is an indeterminacy associated with a mental event's being identical with a certain neural event (n, say). From this it does not follow that the mental event is different from n. Rather, at best our argument merely demonstrates that token–token mental–physical identities are vague.

This reply is entirely unsatisfactory. If anything is clear, it is clear that every object is determinately identical with itself. Now, if a mental event m is only indeterminately identical with n, obviously it is not determinately identical with n. Since n is determinately identical with n, it follows that n has a property that m lacks. Hence, by Leibnitz's law, m is not identical with n. Generalizing, we reach

16 Paul Benacerraf, in his well-known "What Numbers Could Not Be," *Philosophical Review*, 74 (1965): 41–73, argues that the availability of numerous possible set-theoretic reductions of number theory shows that numbers cannot be identical with sets at all. If his argument is sound, presumably a similar argument can be deployed against the psychophysical identity-by-fiat theory.

the conclusion that an appeal to vagueness in mental–physical identities is tantamount to a rejection of those identities.[17]

Furthermore, it seems that the reasoning of the previous section can be harnessed to argue that, if a mental event m is "indeterminately identical" with its correlate in any one PCI of a creature's mentality set, then m is indeterminately identical to each of its other PCI correlates as well. So since m can be indeterminately identical with several events that are not identical with each other, one can only conclude, once again, that the putative relation of indeterminate identity is not a species of identity at all.

Perhaps, though, the idea that m is "indeterminately identical" with n should be taken to mean this: It is indeterminate which physicochemical event is identical with m, and one way of resolving this indeterminacy is by stipulating that m and n are identical. Thus understood, the "indeterminate identity" view is really just the identity-by-fiat view considered already.

A third possible reply would be to claim that mental events are to be identified with "fuzzy" or "indeterminate" neural events – that is, "fuzzy fusions" of smaller, nonfuzzy neural events. The idea here is that with respect to any given fuzzy neural event n there will be at least one neural event n_k such that it is indeterminate whether n_k is a part of n. The events of the token identity theory, then, will have both determinate and indeterminate parts. This position, it may be argued, permits token identity theorists to sidestep the problem of multiple PCIs of a creature's mentality set; they can claim that $M(c)$ has only one PCI composed of fuzzy physical events and that this is the PCI that is identical with $M(c)$.

It is worth stressing that this approach is not committed to the view, lately dismissed, that psychophysical identity statements rest on a vague or indeterminate species of identity relation. Vagueness, on the present proposal, attaches to the part–whole relationship and not to the identity relation. Thus, token mental events are held to be determinately identical with indeterminately constructed neural events.

One might question whether there could be fuzzy entities generally, and fuzzy events in particular; but we will not press this point here. Even if the existence of fuzzy events is granted, we

17 This argument derives from Gareth Evans, "Can There Be Vague Objects?" *Analysis*, 38 (1978): 208.

think that they cannot be invoked to avoid the reasoning we used in the preceding section. Consider a particular fuzzy event n with which a given mental event/state is to be identified. Consider now a different fuzzy event n', which has the same determinate parts as n plus one more determinate part n_k, which had indeterminate status for n. This event n' is different from n since it has a property that n lacks, namely having n_k as a determinate part. Nonetheless, all things considered, the difference between n and n' is quite minimal. Hence, given (1) the context dependence of what counts as "the cause" of a particular effect and (2) the extreme improbability that there exists any such thing as a "context of psychophysical inquiry" that will effectively restrict the range of allowable causes for any given behavioral or neural effect, there is no reason to suppose that n' is any less worthy a candidate than n for identification with the original mental event.

The thrust of this chapter has been negative: The token identity theory is false.[18] Where, then, do mental events fit within reality as a whole? In the next chapter, this question is answered in a seemingly radical way.

18 As is the closely related physicalist view commented on in note 11.

2

Against mental events

The argument so far appears to leave open only two views of the mental: Either mental events are classified as nonphysical events, or mental events are held not to exist. In this chapter I defend the latter view. The structure of my discussion is as follows. In Section I, I take a further look at the dualist's position. This position, I might add, need not be as extreme as that of Descartes: One can, like Kim, for example, be a psychophysical event dualist without being a Cartesian substance dualist.[1] Still, I argue that dualism, whatever its variant, should be rejected. In Section II, I briefly criticize the position of the eliminative materialist, and I argue that a rejection of mental events does not automatically support eliminative materialism. In Section III, I turn to a variety of general arguments for the existence of mental events. I maintain that none of these arguments carries any real weight.

I

One prominent difficulty for all versions of psychophysical event dualism – a difficulty I raised briefly at the beginning of Chapter 1 – is that of finding a satisfactory causal role for the mental. It is basic to our conception of the mind that mental states be causally efficacious. We take it for granted, for example, that beliefs and desires cause actions; that thoughts give rise to desires (as when thinking about writing a book makes one want to); and that thoughts sometimes cause other thoughts, thereby constituting thinking processes that culminate in beliefs. But if the physical

1 See Jaegwon Kim, "On the Psycho-Physical Identity Theory," *American Philosophical Quarterly*, 3 (1966): 227–35; idem, "Causality, Identity, and Supervenience in the Mind–Body Problem," *Midwest Studies in Philosophy*, 4 (1979): 31–49.

world is causally closed and mental events are nonphysical, it is difficult to see how these commonplace observations about the mind can be true. Difficult but not impossible, according to some philosophers. What is needed, we are told, is an account of *supervenient* causation whereby (i) mental events are supervenient upon underlying physical events, and (ii) mental events inherit the causal efficacy of the physical events on which they supervene. Such an account has been developed in detail by Jaegwon Kim.[2] But however the details go, I am skeptical about any dual-cause approach. David Lewis expresses well the grounds of my skepticism:

The position exploits a flaw in the standard regularity theory of cause. We know on other grounds that the theory must be corrected to discriminate between genuine causes and the spurious causes which are their epiphenomenal correlates. (The "power on" light does not cause the motor to go, even if it is a lawfully perfect correlate of the electric current that really causes the motor to go.) Given a satisfactory correction, the nonphysical correlate will be evicted from its spurious causal role.[3]

There is another difficulty for any version of event dualism that appeals to the supervenience of the mental on the physical. If, as Kim asserts, mental events supervene on physical events so that no two creatures could be alike in every physical respect and yet differ in some mental respect, an awkward question immediately arises: How is this supervenience or determination brought about?[4]

This question can be answered by advocates of mental–physical supervenience in one of two ways: Either they declare the determination an inexplicable mystery which there is no alternative but to accept, or they offer an explanation as to how the determination obtains. But what explanation is possible? If psychological types are identical with certain physicochemical properties, there is clearly no difficulty in seeing how the physicochemical events determine

---

2 See his "Causality, Identity, and Supervenience"; idem, "Epiphenomenal and Supervenient Causation," *Midwest Studies in Philosophy*, 9 (1984); idem, "Supervenience and Supervenient Causation," *Southern Journal of Philosophy*, 22 (1984): 45–56.

3 David Lewis, "An Argument for the Identity Theory," *Journal of Philosophy*, 63 (1966): 17–25.

4 This question has worried several philosophers. See, e.g., Colin McGinn, *The Character of Mind* (New York: Oxford University Press, 1982), p. 30; also Terence Horgan, "Supervenience and Cosmic Hermeneutics," *Southern Journal of Philosophy*, 22 (1984): 19–38.

the mental events. Since the latter are simply a subclass of the former, once the physicochemical events are fixed, the mental events are thereby fixed too. Similarly, if psychological types are identical with certain functional properties, the determination is easy to comprehend: On the functionalist view, a given physicochemical event m will determine a given psychological event p if, and only if, m has a physicochemical property that occupies the causal role definitive of the psychological property tokened in p. Since there is no difficulty in grasping how a physicochemical property can occupy a particular causal role, there is no difficulty in understanding how the physicochemical events determine the psychological events.

The problem here is that neither of these two alternatives is open to the event dualist. In the case of the former alternative, this point is obvious. In the case of the latter, since an event e will instantiate a psychological property if, and only if, e instantiates a physical propery that plays the causal role definitive of that psychological property, it follows that e will itself be a physical event, and not a nonphysical one, as the event dualist requires.

The only remaining alternative open to the event dualist who advocates supervenient mental–physical causation is to say that psychological properties are entirely nonphysical. But then how are they physicochemically determined? I see no answer to this question. But without any answer the event dualist must declare that the determination of psychological events by physical events is an enigma. And such a declaration clearly threatens the event dualist's position, for as we have just seen, there are alternative accounts within which mental–physical supervenience is not at all puzzling.

It appears, then, that event dualists are impaled on the horns of a dilemma. Either they hold that mental–physical causation is impossible, in which case they are compelled to adopt the highly counterintuitive position of epiphenomenalism, or they hold that mental–physical causation is a species of supervenient causation, in which case they are open to the charge that their view is now a covert version of epiphenomenalism and, moreover, they must concede that mental–physical supervenience is itself an inexplicable mystery.

Another problem for event dualism derives from a desire to understand the *emergence* of mental states in the history of evolution.[5] This problem can be brought out by raising a question: Given that mental states were first tokened when matter had reached a level of organization complex enough to sustain mental life, just how did the tokening of mental states result from the material configurations? In other words, what was it about matter and its organization that was responsible for the production of distinctively mental events?

If mental types just *are* certain physicochemical properties, the explanation is straightforward. As the brain evolved, more and more complex physicochemical properties were instantiated until eventually mental types (and hence tokens) themselves came on the scene. Similarly, if mental types just *are* certain functional properties, again there is no conceptual difficulty. With the evolution of the brain, overt behavior changed and grew more sensitive to incoming stimuli with the result that physicochemical properties instantiated in the brain came to occupy new and more complicated causal patterns with respect to other such properties, stimuli, and behavior. Thus, mental life itself emerged whenever physicochemical properties were tokened that occupied the causal patterns or roles definitive of specific mental states.

No satisfactory explanation is forthcoming, however, if we take the line that mental types are properties that lie altogether outside the physical realm. Admittedly, we can still say that distinctively mental events emerged in virtue of their supervening on certain physicochemical events, but this merely shifts the problem back to the one addressed before.

The final objection I have to dualism is that it has an unnecessarily complex ontology. The point here is the straightforward one that there is, in my view, no clear theoretical need to posit nonphysical mental events. So since their elimination produces a significant simplification in ontology, by an application of Occam's razor we should banish them from existence.

II

The conclusion we arrive at once we reject both the token identity theory and dualism is that mental events do not exist. This con-

5 The problem of emergence is discussed in a general way by Keith Campbell in his *Body and Mind* (Garden City, N.Y.: Anchor, 1970), pp. 48–9. It is also raised by Colin McGinn in *Character of Mind*, p. 31.

clusion smacks of eliminative materialism. Let us, then, take a brief look at the position of the eliminative materialist.

According to this version of materialism, the ordinary psychological statements we make from day to day are no more to be trusted than the statements our predecessors made "about" witches, caloric fluid, and phlogiston. Radical error infects the former talk just as it does the latter. Thus, mental events do not exist, according to the eliminative materialist, for the simple reason that the everyday statements of our folk psychology are, one and all, false.[6]

I reject this version of materialism. One standard objection that seems to me to carry significant weight is this: If folk psychology is, as a matter of fact, not true, why does it work so well? Consider, for example, explanations of behavior via beliefs and desires. There can be no denying that the attribution of the appropriate beliefs and desires frequently leads to substantiated behavioral predictions. Why? What accounts for the widespread success of belief–desire psychology? After all, in general isn't predictive success evidence for the truth of a theory, particularly when that theory is without competitors in its own area? Eliminative materialists such as Rorty and Churchland have not satisfactorily answered these questions. Instead, they have focused on what they take to be the "stagnancy" of folk psychology. Their view is that folk psychology is a *bad* theory without *any* successes worth mentioning. This seems to me to be a decidedly skewered description of the facts.

One philosopher who, at least sometimes and in some of his writings, seems to agree with Rorty and Churchland that the statements of everyday belief–desire psychology are one and all literally false, is Daniel Dennett. Like Rorty and Churchland, Dennett holds that, *within any ideal science*, the propositional attitudes must disappear. But unlike Rorty and Churchland, Dennett is an instrumentalist; belief–desire psychology, in his view, is an extremely useful, indeed vital, instrument for predicting behavior in practical contexts.[7] Still, why is this instrument so very useful? Dennett's

6 See, e.g., Paul Feyerabend, "Materialism and the Mind–Body Problem," *Review of Metaphysics*, 17 (1963): 49–66; Richard Rorty, "Mind–Body Identity, Privacy, and Categories," ibid., 19 (1965): 24–54; Paul Churchland, *Scientific Realism and the Plasticity of Mind* (Cambridge University Press, 1979); and idem, "Eliminative Materialism and Propositional Attitudes," *Journal of Philosophy*, 78 (1981): 67–90.
7 See Daniel Dennett, *Brainstorms* (Cambridge, Mass.: Bradford, 1978), esp. the essay "Intentional Systems."

answer[8] seems to be something like this: Belief–desire explanations are not really true, because they are grounded on extremely general and powerful assumptions of rationality, assumptions that, generally speaking, are not satisfied in actual fact. Nonetheless, such explanations tend to work well because the "systems" we apply them to have evolved successfully (or have been "designed" by us), and if these systems had not behaved in ways that came *close* to rationality, they *would not have* evolved successfully in the first place.

This view has various shortcomings. First, it is not at all obvious that belief–desire explanations are grounded on rationality assumptions so powerful that they are clearly false.[9] Admittedly, if we are to predict a creature's behavior on the basis of attributed beliefs and desires, we have to assume *some* degree of rationality. But why shouldn't the creature just *have* that much rationality? Furthermore, if, as Dennett says, successful evolution itself generates a significant degree of rationality (in the evolved creatures), how can the attribution of rationality *always* be purely instrumental? Relatedly, what could possibly account for the significant degree of rationality to be found in successfully evolved creatures other than the presence of an appropriate internal network of beliefs and desires?

For these reasons, I am skeptical about the viability of Dennett's instrumentalism. I should also add that I, like other critics, find eliminative materialism in all its variants highly counterintuitive, and I am unpersuaded by the positive arguments Rorty and Churchland give for their noninstrumental eliminativist view.[10]

Still, if we are to reject mental events, as I am urging we should, how can we avoid the claim that the statements of folk psychology are false? The answer is straightforward enough: The claim that there really are no mental events no more entails that the statements

---

8 This answer is given in his "True Believers: The Intentional Strategy and Why It Works," in *Scientific Explanation: Papers Based on Herbert Spencer Lectures Given in the University of Oxford* (Oxford: Clarendon, 1981). I should perhaps add that it is no simple matter to peg a definite view on Dennett, since there are tensions in his work on the issue of the truth of everyday psychological discourse that are not easy to reconcile. These tensions are especially evident in his "Three Kinds of Intentional Psychology," in *Reduction, Time, and Identity* (Cambridge University Press, 1981).

9 Cf. J. A. Fodor, "Fodor's Guide to Mental Representation: The Intelligent Aunties's Vade Mecum," *Mind*, 94 (1985): 80.

10 For a good critique of these arguments, see Terence Horgan and James Woodward, "Folk Psychology Is Here to Stay," *Philosophical Review*, 94 (1985): 197–226.

of folk psychology are false than does the claim that there really are no families having 1.2 children entails that the statement

(1) The average British family has 1.2 children

is false. The point here is the familiar one that grammatical form need not coincide with logical form. Thus, in the case of (1), the grammatical subject is the expression 'the average British family'. But the logical subject is a number,[11] and what (1) says is that this number, 1.2, is the result of dividing the number of British children by the number of British families.

The task, then, as I see it, if we are to steer a safe course between the Scylla of event dualism and the Charybdis of eliminative materialism, is to reconstruct the statements of folk psychology so that they have a logical form that requires no reference to, or quantification over, events. I also take this task to extend to the theoretical statements of cognitive psychology. The reconstruction I shall elaborate and defend is rooted in a view that has come to be called the "adverbial theory." I shall introduce my version of this theory, a version that is much more general than any hitherto proposed, at the beginning of Chapter 3. For the moment I want to postpone any discussion of the adverbial theory and to concentrate instead, in the remainder of this chapter, on a critical examination of a number of arguments *for* the existence of mental events.

III

The first argument I want to examine has to do with mental–physical causation. It is widely supposed that causal statements involving psychological terms, for example,

(2) Smith's having a pain at time t causes Smith's taking some aspirin at time t',

show that mental events exist. The standard view is that statements like (2), in Donald Davidson's words, "more or less wear their logical form on their face"; that is, they have the logical form of a two-place predication, with the gerundives functioning as event-denoting singular terms.[12] Under this approach, statements like (2),

---

11 Assuming *arguendo* that there are numbers.
12 See Donald Davidson, "Causal Relations," *Journal of Philosophy*, 64 (1967): 691–703.

if we accept them, immediately commit us to the existence of mental events; and insofar as we reject nonphysical particulars, they are thus at the heart of the problem presented in Chapter 1, namely finding the "right" neural events with which to identify mental events.

My proposed way out of the problem is to give up the token identity theory and further to reject the standard construal of statements like (2). On my view, (2) is to be analyzed as

(2a) *The fact that* Smith is pained at *t causes it to be the case that* Smith takes some aspirin at *t'*,

where '*the fact that* _____ *causes it to be the case that* _____' is a non-truth-functional sentential connective. Given (2a), no mental pain-event of Smith's is needed.[13]

One well-known objection to this proposal, that of Davidson (see note 12), is that the causal connective would have to be truth functional. But it has been argued persuasively elsewhere that Davidson's argument for this conclusion amounts to a reductio ad absurdum of his premises and that one can block the argument by means of plausible restrictions on substitutivity within causal contexts.[14]

What other difficulties are there for analyses of causal statements along the lines of (2a)? To begin with, it might be pointed out that there remains the nontrivial task of formulating satisfactory truth conditions for the causal connective. This is certainly true, but there are any number of analyses of causation that can be utilized within the proposed connective approach. Indeed, even Davidson's analysis itself can be modified so as to become applicable. To see this point, consider the Davidsonian view.[15] According to Davidson, an ordinary, everyday causal statement such as (2) is true just in case there are events described by the gerundives in that statement that are redescribable in precise, scientific vocabulary in such a way that their redescriptions instantiate a general, scientific causal law. The spirit of this account can be preserved without the postulation

---

13 For a detailed analysis of the logical form of pain statements from my perspective, see Chapter 4.

14 See Terence Horgan, "The Case Against Events," *Philosophical Review*, 87 (1978): 28–47; idem, "Substitutivity and the Causal Connective," *Philosophical Studies*, 42 (1982): 47–52.

15 See, e.g., "Causal Relations"; idem, "Mental Events," in *Experience and Theory*, ed. L. Foster and J. Swanson (London: Duckworth, 1970).

of events in the following statement of truth conditions for (2a). There are true scientific sentences 'C' and 'E' and a general scientific law 'L' such that (i) 'C' and 'L' together entail 'E'; (ii) 'C' alone does not entail 'E'; (iii) 'C, and thereby Smith is pained at t' is true; and (iv) 'E, and thereby Smith takes some aspirin at t'' is true.[16]

The truth conditions proposed here make us another non-truth-functional sentential connective 'and thereby', which we may call the 'generative connective'. This connective needs a word or two of explanation. Advocates of events have often supposed that events are not only causally related, but also upon occasion generatively related in a noncausal manner. For example, it is sometimes maintained that certain distinct simultaneous actions performed by one and the same person are connected by an asymmetric generative relation as, say, when a man salutes (at time t) by raising his hand (at t). It is also often maintained, for example, that certain micro-events in a person or an inanimate physical object generate or determine certain simultaneous macroevents in that person or object. My use of the sentential connective 'and thereby' is intended to retain the notion (or notions) of generation at work in such contexts without the postulation of events.

Of course, ultimately truth conditions will have to be supplied for the generative connective. One possible formal account of these conditions is as follows. Let statements flanking the generative connective have the canonical form 'Fxt', where 'x' is a singular term designating a spatiotemporal individual (other than an event) and 't' is a time-designating singular term. Further, let $\underset{\rightarrow}{g}$ symbolize the generative connective. Then '$Fxt \underset{\rightarrow}{g} F'x't'$' is true if, and only if, (i) 'Fxt' is true; (ii) '$F'x't'$' is true; (iii) 'x' = 'x''; (iv) 't' = 't''; (v) there is a set of true statements 'P' such that (a) 'Fxt' and 'P' together entail '$F'x't'$' but neither 'Fxt' nor 'P' alone entails '$F'x't'$'; (b) if 'Fxt' were not true then '$F'x't'$' would not be true; and (c) if the statements in 'P' were not all true then, even though 'Fxt' is true, '$F'x't'$' would not be true.

Conditions (iii) and (iv) are perhaps too strong: In some cases, we may wish to assert that two sentences are generatively connected, although they contain either different singular terms for the same individual or different singular terms for the same time. Another potential problem is that it may turn out that there are really

16 These truth conditions are proposed by Horgan, "The Case Against Events."

several different noncausal generative connectives that are expressed by the phrase 'and thereby'. For example, it could be the case that the connective representing micro–macro generation is not the same as the one representing act generation. If this is so, the above analysis, which derives (with minor changes) from a systematic transformation and generalization of Alvin Goldman's definition of what it is for one action to be generatively related to another,[17] will not be applicable to the generative connective made use of in my earlier statement of the truth conditions for (2a), and further truth conditions will have to be formulated for that connective. There is no reason to suppose, however, that the task of formulating these truth conditions would present any special difficulty. Hereafter, in order to simplify my exposition, I shall ignore the possibility that there are several different generative connectives, and I shall speak as if it is settled that there is just one.

Returning now to Davidson, I think that enough has been said to make it clear that much of Davidson's view of causation can be retained within the proposed connective approach. Once we introduce a generative link between sentences, we can connect common or garden-variety statements such as (2) with precise scientific causal laws without the postulation of events.

Perhaps some philosophers will object that, under the proposed truth conditions, ordinary causal statements are committed to the existence of sentences, and this is not only implausible but also no simpler ontologically than an approach that appeals directly to events. My reply is that there is no such commitment. To begin with, consider how truth conditions are given for truth-functional sentential connectives, 'or', say. What we do is to specify how the truth value of sentences of the type 'P or Q' is determined by the truth values of 'P' and 'Q': Thus, we say that " 'P or Q' is true" if, and only if, " 'P' is true or 'Q' is true." Now, obviously the fact that sentences of the type found on the right side of this biconditional are committed to the existence of sentences does not show that sentences of the type 'P or Q' are also so committed. Analogously, the fact that in giving the truth conditions for the causal connective we present an analysis of the metalinguistic interpretation of causal sentences that is itself committed to the existence

17 See his *Theory of Human Action* (Englewood Cliffs, N.J.: Prentice-Hall, 1970), p. 45.

of sentences does not demonstrate such a commitment in the causal sentences themselves.

I am not denying, of course, that any philosopher who accepts the modified Davidsonian proposal I present above must also accept that the associated metalinguistic statement of truth conditions for the causal connective is *true*. And I am certainly not denying that *this* statement, taken literally, is committed ontologically to the existence of sentences. But the appeal to sentences *here* is surely no more problematic than it is in giving the truth conditions for, say, 'Snow is white and grass is green'.

A second, and frequently voiced, objection to the general view that causal statements can be analyzed via the use of a non-truth-functional sentential connective is that this view cannot provide a satisfactory understanding of extensional causal contexts.[18] Suppose, for example, the following statements are true:

(3) Reagan's election to the presidency caused the sharp stock market increase.

(4) Reagan's election to the presidency occurred while James was in Europe.

From (3) and (4), we may surely infer

(5) Reagan's election to the presidency, which occurred while James was in Europe, caused the sharp stock market increase.

How are we to explain this inference? The assumption that (3) is an extensional causal statement, within which 'Reagan's election to the presidency' designates an event, permits substitution of the coreferential event-designating singular term 'Reagan's election to the presidency which occurred while James was in Europe'. So given (3) and (4), (5) certainly follows.

But if (3) and (5) are analyzed as

(3a) *The fact that* Reagan was elected to the presidency *caused it to be the case that* the stock market increased sharply

and

(5a) *The fact that* Reagan was elected to the presidency while James was in Europe *caused it to be the case that* the stock market increased sharply,

---

18 See, e.g., J. L. Mackie, *The Cement of the Universe* (New York: Oxford University Press, 1974); also John Searle, *Intentionality* (Cambridge University Press, 1983), pp. 116–17.

then the inference seems invalid. For whatever truth conditions we ultimately adopt for the sentential connective '*the fact that* _____ *causes it to be the case that* _____', we must surely agree that (3a) and (5a) are logically equivalent to

(3b) The stock market increased sharply *because* Reagan was elected president

and

(5b) The stock market increased sharply *because* Reagan was elected president while James was in Europe,

respectively. And clearly both (4) and (3b) could be true while (5b) remained false. Thus, on the causal connective view, we cannot read (3) and (5) extensionally, and this has highly counterintuitive consequences.

This objection is unsuccessful. Statement (5) need not be analyzed as (5a) within the confines of a causal connective approach. An alternative analysis for (5) is

(5c) Reagan was elected president while James was in Europe, and *the fact that* Reagan was elected president *caused it to be the case that* the stock market increased sharply.

On this analysis the clause 'while James was in Europe' lies outside the scope of the causal connective with the result that the content of the clause plays no role in explaining why the stock market increased. Given this analysis, it is easy to show that (5) does indeed follow from (3) and (4). As before, (3) is analyzed as (3a). Statement (4) becomes

(4a) Reagan was elected president while James was in Europe.

Since (5c) is a simple logical consequence of (3a) and (4a), the argument from (3) and (4) to (5) is validated.

The conclusion I reach, then, is that the causal connective view does not *automatically* fail to handle so-called extensional causal statements. One putatively event-denoting singular term *will* sometimes be substitutable *salva veritate* for another in a causal statement, even though, on the connective view, there are no events. I admit, however, that the situation is sometimes less straightforward than that presented in the above example. On occasion we use causal descriptions in which we pick out features of causes, *all* of which are irrelevant to explaining why the effect occurred. Thus, consider the following two statements:

(6) What surprised James caused the stock market to increase sharply.
(7) What surprised James was Reagan's election to the presidency.

Given (6) and (7), it seems that we may infer (3). In this case, (6) presents problems of a sort that did not arise earlier; for unlike both (3) and (5), there is nothing *at all* in the description of the cause in (6) that is relevant to explaining the occurrence of the effect. It appears, then, that here considerations of scope cannot be used to preserve the inference from (6) and (7) to (3) on an event-free approach.

Other parallel cases are easy to construct. Smith died because he ate a poisoned steak but not because he signaled Jones to leave the restaurant. Even so Smith's eating the steak was his signal to Jones to leave, and if the former event caused Smith's death, so too did the latter. In this case, as in the one about James, it may be urged that the causal connective view I am advocating is altogether unsuitable; for it appears that these intuitively reasonable cases are unintelligible, unless there are events that are subject to widely different descriptions.

I am unpersuaded that these examples present any real difficulty. On my view, statements that appear to identify events under different descriptions are best taken as compound generative statements about the concrete subjects of those events.[19] Thus, I maintain that (7) is equivalent to

(7a) Reagan was elected president *and thereby* he surprised James.

Similarly, the statement

(8) Smith's eating a steak was his signal to Jones

is recast, on my view, as

(8a) Smith ate a steak *and thereby* he signaled Jones.

Given these analyses, neither (7) nor (8) is committed to the existence of events.

It must be conceded that there are 'event identity' statements that require slightly more complicated analyses. Suppose that Smith's

19 This proposal was first made by Terence Horgan. See his "The Case Against Events," pp. 36–8. Horgan, however, does not discuss the complications I consider below.

eating a steak was not only a signal to Jones, but also a warning to Brown. Then the ordinary statement

(9) Smith's signaling to Jones was the same event as his warning Brown

seems true. But given the earlier possible analysis of the generative connective, we cannot preserve the truth of (9) if we reparse it as a compound sentence in which the sentences 'Smith signaled Jones' and 'Smith warned Brown' flank 'and thereby'. Moreover, intuitively we do not want to say either that Smith signaled Jones *by* warning Brown or that Smith warned Brown *by* signaling Jones. How, then, is (9) to be handled? Well, Smith both signaled Jones and warned Brown *by* eating a steak. Hence, commonsensically there is a property (eating a steak) such that (i) Smith had that property *and thereby* Smith signaled Jones, and (ii) Smith had that property *and thereby* Smith warned Brown. Formally, we can now regiment (9) as follows (letting 's', 'j', and 'b' name Smith, Jones, and Brown; letting '$\overset{g}{\rightarrow}$' formalize the generative connective; and letting 'Sxy' and 'Wxy' mean 'x signaled y' and 'x warned y'):

(9a) $(\exists F)[Fs \,\&\, (Fs \overset{g}{\rightarrow} Ssj) \,\&\, (Fs \overset{g}{\rightarrow} Wsb)]$.

It is clear that (9a) involves no commitment to the existence of events. Whether (9a) really involves any commitment to the existence of properties, as it appears to do, is a question I propose to leave unanswered until we have first seen how the inference from (6) and (7) to (3) can now be reconstructed.

It seems to me that (6) has the force of

(6a) One or more happenings surprised James and moreover whatever surprised James caused the stock market to increase sharply.

On the present proposal, (6a) can be partially formalized as

(6b) $(\exists x)(\exists F)(Fx$ and thereby x surprised James$) \,\&\, (y)(G)[(Gy$ and thereby y surprised James$) \supset ($the fact that Gy caused it to be the case that the stock market increased sharply$)]$.

Statements (7) and (3) are given the same analyses as earlier, namely

(7a) Reagan was elected president *and thereby* he surprised James

and

(3a) *The fact that* Reagan was elected president *caused it to be the case that* the stock market increased sharply, respectively. We can now prove that the inference from (6b) and (7a) to (3a) is valid as follows. Simplification of the second conjunct in (6b), followed by replacement of the variables '*y*' and '*G*' with 'Reagan' and 'was elected president' via applications of universal instantiation, gives us that, if Reagan was elected president *and thereby* he surprised James, then *the fact that* Reagan was elected president *caused it to be the case that* the stock market increased sharply. From this result together with (7a), (3a) immediately follows via *modus ponens*.

I conclude that inferences about causation involving descriptions of causes in which none of the causally relevant features of those causes are cited can be explained satisfactorily on a no-events theory. Nor relatedly is there any difficulty, on this theory, in understanding what Davidson calls "talk of one and the same event under different descriptions." Such talk, I maintain, is not to be taken literally. Rather it is to be spelled out via the use of the generative connective. This claim, I might add, has negative consequences for another of Davidson's arguments for the existence of events. I have in mind the argument that since any adequate theory of action must employ *literal* talk of a single action under different descriptions it follows that actions, that is, events of a certain sort, must exist.[20] I see no reason at all to grant Davidson's premise. Once we have at our disposal the generative connective, we can reconstruct all the relevant talk without supposing that there are events.

I want now to return to the question I left unanswered earlier. If (9) is analyzed as (9a) and (6) is analyzed as (6b), it appears that (9) and (6) are committed to the existence of nonlinguistic properties. Are these commitments genuine? If so, it can be argued that the price of an event-free view of the mental (and the world generally) is too high on the grounds that its ontology is no longer any simpler than an ontology that countenances events.

My reply is that there is no real commitment. As I noted in the introduction, standardly the substitution instances for the variables in objectual quantifiers are singular terms, that is, expressions that refer to objects in the world. It is precisely because of this fact that the use of objectual quantifiers is taken to indicate ontic commitment. However, in (9a) and (6b) the substitution instances for the

20 See Donald Davidson, "The Individuation of Events," in *Essays in Honor of Carl G. Hempel*, ed. N. Rescher (Dordrecht: Reidel, 1969), pp. 217–18.

component variables 'F' and 'G' are *predicates*, and predicates are certainly *not* singular terms. In making this claim, incidentally, I am not presupposing that there are no properties, for I am not presupposing that all genuine singular terms refer to individuals. My point is simply that predicates do not *refer* to anything.

My suggestion, then, is that the quantifiers '(∃F)' and '(G)' be read *substitutionally*.[21] On this interpretation, (9a) and (6b) are *not* committed ontologically to the existence of properties. Thus, in the case of (9), for example, there *really* is no nonlinguistic property *x* such that Smith had *x and thereby* Smith signaled Jones. Still, it is true that Smith ate a steak and also true that there is a property that Smith had. No inconsistency arises since 'there really is' in the last sentence but one is objectual whereas 'there is' in the last sentence is not.[22]

It may perhaps be objected that the proposed regimentations of (9) and (6) do not really enable us to avoid properties, since there are plenty of other everyday sentences that appear to require the existence of nonlinguistic properties for their truth and that cannot be regimented via the use of substitutional predicate quantifiers. Consider, for example,

21 I shall later propose that sets be assigned to predicates for certain semantical purposes. The sets so assigned are not referred to by the predicates, on my view. Rather they are *expressed* by the predicates. Since I introduce sets, it may be wondered why I do not propose some nonstandard objectual interpretation for the predicate quantifiers. My primary reason is this: If the predicate quantifiers are so interpreted that their use automatically carries ontic commitment, anyone who argues that sets and other abstracta are ultimately eliminable will have to show how sentences such as (6) and (9) can be regimented without predicate quantifiers. Since I have some sympathy for extreme nominalism, although I make no attempt to argue for this view in the present book (see the Introduction), I would prefer not to make even harder the already difficult task of extreme nominalists by requiring them to produce the alternative regimentations. Another reason for adopting an interpretation of the predicate quantifiers that permits them to play a metaphysically neutral role is that such an interpretation yields overall linguistic simplicity. This is because there are certain psychological contexts in which substitutional quantifiers must be employed if further metaphysical baggage is to be avoided, or so I maintain (see Chapter 7). So the use of predicate substitutional quantifiers introduces no *new* linguistic complexity, whereas the use of nonstandard objectual quantifiers does.

22 I should perhaps stress here that my proposed use of substitutional predicate quantifiers is not to be generalized to my use of quantifiers of the type '(∃x)' and '(x)'. I discussed this issue in the Introduction, and, as I noted there, my use of these quantifiers *is* intended to carry ontological commitment.

(10) Wisdom is a virtue[23]

and

(11) Jane's face has a striking color.

There are two points I want to make in response to this objection. First, if (10) and (11) did require the existence of properties for their truth, it could not be argued that a regimentation of (9) that invokes properties is no better than one that appeals to events on the grounds that the former regimentation is no simpler than the latter. In these circumstances, (9) would only introduce entities already required elsewhere. Second, it seems to me that (10) and (11) are not committed to properties. In the case of (10), one possible analysis that avoids properties is

(10a) All who are wise are thereby virtuous

or, more precisely,

(10b) Each person x is such that *if it were the case that x* is wise *then it would be the case that* (x is wise *and thereby* x is virtuous).[24]

Statement (10b) will not quite do as it stands, however. For there are certainly wise people who are not completely virtuous. Still, all who are wise are thereby partly virtuous or virtuous in at least one respect. I propose, therefore, that (10) can be analyzed as (10b), provided that the predicate 'is virtuous' in (10b) is replaced by the structured predicate 'is virtuous in at least one respect'. The latter predicate is to be taken to contain a predicate operator 'in at least one respect', which operates on the predicate 'is virtuous'. Later, in Chapter 3, I shall discuss the semantics of predicate operators.

23 Michael Loux argues that statements like (10) present insuperable difficulties for the nominalist. See his *Substance and Attribute* (Dordrecht: Reidel, 1978). Stephen Schiffer also claims that statements like (10) have no nominalistically palatable paraphrases. See his *The Remnants of Meaning* (Cambridge, Mass.: MIT Press, 1987). I might add here that there are many points of agreement between Schiffer's views (ibid.) and my own (as well as some substantial disagreements). Schiffer's overall position deserves detailed discussion. I do not address it in the text, since the present work was completed before Schiffer's book appeared.
24 An alternative account of (10) that is consistent with my overall metaphysics is to take 'wisdom' as a name for the set of wise people and 'is a virtue' as a predicate expressing the set of entities that are virtues. On this proposal, (10) will be true just in case the set named by 'wisdom' is a member of the set expressed by 'is a virtue'.

Suffice it to say for now that no properties are required by the semantics I advocate. In the case of (11), it obviously will not do to adopt the following regimentation:

(11a) $(\exists F)(F$ is a striking color & Jane's face has $F)$;

for F takes predicates as instances so that (11a) is ill-formed. My proposal for (11) is rather

(11b) Jane's face is colored strikingly.

In (11b) 'strikingly' is a predicate operator that operates on the predicate 'is colored' to form another predicate. On this proposal, no quantifier at all is needed in the analysis of (11). Thus, neither (10) nor (11) is committed to the existence of a nonlinguistic property.

It may now be objected that if we analyze (9) as (9a), and we take the quantifier in (9a) to be substitutional, we must be prepared to accept the implausible view that (9) is committed to the existence of linguistic items; for the interpretation of a substitutionally quantified sentence of the form

(12) $(\exists F)(Fa)$

is

(12a) $(\exists x)(\exists y)(x$ is a linguistic predicate & y is a true sentence & y results from substituting x for the variable F in $Fa)$.

However, insofar as (12a) is seen as a metalinguistic sentence that stands in the same relation to (12) as metalinguistic sentences of the type " 'P' is true or 'Q' is true" stand to corresponding sentences of the type 'P or Q', then the fact that (12a) has certain ontic commitments to linguistic entities does not show that these commitments are made by the object language sentence (12).

I turn now to another type of argument for the existence of mental events. There are various sorts of inferential relationships involving sentences that contain definite and indefinite descriptions putatively about events. For example, 'The F is G' entails 'An F is G'; and 'The F is G' and 'The F is H' together entail 'The F is both G and H'. Where 'the F' is putatively an event-denoting singular term, it can be argued that, on an event-free approach, these sentences cannot be paraphrased in a way that preserves the validity of those inferences. Since such inferences are to be found in connection with singular terms both for mental events and for other events having

46

nothing to do with the mind, the conclusion we are led to is that events, both mental and nonmental, exist. I shall argue against this conclusion by showing how the inferences can be handled without events.

The inference I shall focus on is as follows:

(13) The eruption of Vesuvius occurred during A.D. 79.
(14) The eruption of Vesuvius was violent.
(15) An eruption of Vesuvius that was violent occurred during A.D. 79.[25]

It is evident that (15) is a consequence of (13) and (14). But how is the validity of this inference to be sustained under event-free paraphrase? One proposal, based on a discussion by P. T. Geach,[26] is to reconstruct the inference as

(13a) Vesuvius erupted during A.D. 79.
(14a) Vesuvius erupted violently.
(15a) Vesuvius erupted violently during A.D. 79.

Unfortunately, this reconstruction makes the inference patently invalid. Another possibility is to introduce explicit quantification over times. This will not work either, however, because the claim that there is a unique time at which Vesuvius erupted does not entail that Vesuvius erupted just once and hence it does not guarantee that the eruption of Vesuvius occurred. To see this point, it suffices to note that Vesuvius might have had two craters in each of which there occurred simultaneous violent eruptions.

The proposal I favor is to introduce explicit quantification over space–time regions rather than simply over times. This proposal can be implemented as follows:

(13b) There is exactly one continuous space–time region x, which is such both that Vesuvius erupted at x and that Vesuvius did not erupt at any other continuous space–time region containing x, and Vesuvius erupted at x during A.D. 79.

(14b) There is exactly one continuous space–time region x, which is such both that Vesuvius erupted at x and that Vesuvius did not erupt at any other continuous space–time region containing x, and Vesuvius erupted violently at x.

(15b) There is at least one continuous space–time region x, which is such that Vesuvius erupted violently at x and Vesuvius erupted at x during A.D. 79.

25 B. D. Katz argues that this inference cannot be validated under event-free para-phrase. See his "Perils of an Uneventful World," *Philosophia*, 13 (1983): 1–12.
26 P. T. Geach, *Logic Matters* (Oxford: Blackwell Publisher, 1972).

In this analysis, the space–time regions quantified over are required to be continuous, since without this condition it could be said that, if Vesuvius had erupted at the space–time regions occupied by two different craters, there would have been a single "scattered" space–time region at which Vesuvius erupted consisting of those former regions. The other condition requiring comment is the condition in (13b) and (14b) that Vesuvius did not erupt at any other space–time region containing x. This condition is included because, if the eruption of Vesuvius had taken place all across the face of a single crater A, there would have been many different space–time regions at which Vesuvius erupted *within* the one occupied by A.

I believe that any full formalization of (13b)–(15b) requires the introduction of iterated predicate operators.[27] But we can reveal enough of the structure of (13b)–(15b) to show that the inference is valid without resort to such operators. Let 'Sx' mean 'x is a (continuous) space–time region'; let 'Ex', 'Dx', and 'Vx' mean 'Vesuvius erupted at x', 'Vesuvius erupted during A.D. 79 at x', and Vesuvius erupted violently at x', respectively; further, let 'Cx' abbreviate 'Vesuvius erupted at some (continuous) space–time region (other than x) which contains x'. We can now formalize the analysis in this way:

(13*) $(\exists x)\{Sx \;\&\; Ex \;\&\; {\sim}Cx \;\&\; (y)\,[(Sy \;\&\; Ey \;\&\; {\sim}Cy) \supset y = x] \;\&\; Dx\}$.
(14*) $(\exists x)\{Sx \;\&\; Ex \;\&\; {\sim}Cx \;\&\; (y)\,[(Sy \;\&\; Ey \;\&\; {\sim}Cy) \supset y = x] \;\&\; Vx\}$.
(15*) $(\exists x)(Sx \;\&\; Vx \;\&\; Dx)$.

Since (15*) follows from (13*) and (14*) via standard logical rules, the validity of the inference from (13) and (14) to (15) is preserved.

There is one remaining problem for the above analysis. The fact that there is a unique largest space–time region at which an individual x V-ed (where 'V' is any verb) does not clearly ensure that *the* V-ing of x occurred, as the analysis presupposes. Suppose, for example, that I have agreed with Smith that my jumping off the floor in the kitchen will be the signal for him to douse the lights, and I have agreed with Jones that my turning full circle will be my signal to him to cut the phone lines. I end up jumping and rotating all at once. Here, it may plausibly be claimed, I have signaled twice; but both signalings involve the same space–time region, namely the one taken up by my body while I simultaneously jump and rotate.

27 See Chapter 3, Section II.

One could reply that really only one complex action was performed here, namely a twisting jump, and that this one action was in the circumstances both a signaling to Smith and a signaling to Jones. Some philosophers are likely to find this reply unconvincing. I therefore propose to handle this counterexample and others like it by introducing quantification apparently over properties as well as quantification over space–time regions. The former quantification, I hasten to add, is introduced solely in order to simplify the statement of my position and should be replaced by substitutional predicate quantification in any fully formalized account. Specifically, my proposal is this: 'The V-ing is G' is true (where 'V' is a verb and 'the V-ing' is a singular term putatively denoting an event involving an object o) if, and only if, there is exactly one continuous space–time region x such that (i) o Vs at x, (ii) o Vs G-ly at x, and (iii) for any two distinct properties, y and z, if o has y at x, o has z at x, o Vs by having y, and o Vs by having z, then either o has y by having z, or o has z by having y.[28] 'The V-ing takes place' is analyzed in the same way, except that 'o Vs G-ly at x' is deleted. The 'by' locutions used here may themselves appear to indicate relations among events. But on my view, it should be clear that they do not really indicate any such thing. I maintain, as I did earlier, that object o Vs by having property y if, and only if, o has y *and thereby o Vs*. The phrase '*and thereby*' is once again the generative sentential connective. Hence, I deny that my proposed analysis involves any covert reference to events.

The signaling case is now unproblematic. Since I signal by jumping and I also signal by rotating, but I do not jump by rotating or rotate by jumping, my analysis entails, via (iii), that the sentences 'A single signaling took place' and 'My act of signaling was successful', for example, are both false (even if I did signal successfully). Furthermore, in the Vesuvius case, it should be clear that the extra conjuncts that will now be added to the formalized statements (13*) and (14*) will not change the validity of the inference from these statements to (15*).

There is one other standard argument for the existence of mental events that merits discussion. This argument, which again can be

---

28 On a substitutional reconstruction of this analysis, instead of requiring that property y is distinct from property z, it will suffice to require in clause (iii) that predicate F is not necessarily coextensive with predicate G.

generalized to events of any kind, is basically that events are needed in order to give an account of the logical form of sentences involving adverbial modification.[29] Consider, for example, the following sentences:

(16) In his study, at 10 p.m., Leopold thought about his misspent youth.
(17) At 10 p.m. Leopold thought about his misspent youth.
(18) Leopold thought about his misspent youth.

Statements (18) and (17) follow from (16), and (18) also follows from (17). Given an ontology that includes events, we can analyze (16) as

(16a) There is an event x such that x is a thinking about Leopold's misspent youth, Leopold underwent x, x took place in Leopold's study, and x was going on at 10 p.m.

Clearly, the above inferences now go through without any difficulty.

This argument loses its force if an alternative account of the logical form of adverbially modified statements can be provided that does not quantify over events. There already is such an account: the predicate-operator theory of adverbs.[30] I shall discuss the metaphysical and semantic foundations of this theory in the next chapter. For the moment, I merely wish to point out that there are plenty of inferences involving adverbially modified statements that present severe difficulties for the event theory. For instance,

(19) Leopold almost believed Julia's story

logically entails

(20) Leopold did not believe Julia's story;

and

(21) Leopold ran very quickly

logically entails

(22) Leopold ran quickly.

---

29 See Davidson, "The Individuation of Events," pp. 218–20.
30 There are several versions of this theory. See, e.g., Romane Clark, "Concerning the Logic of Predicate Modifiers," *Nous*, 4 (1970): 311–35; also Terence Parsons, "Some Problems Concerning the Logic of Grammatical Modifiers," in *Semantics of Natural Language*, ed. D. Davidson and G. Harman (Dordrecht: Reidel, 1972).

But it is hard to see how any appeal to events in the analyses of (19) and (21) will help to explain these inferences. I might add that, on the predicate-operator approach, inferences like the ones above are entirely unproblematic.[31]

I have tried to show that the major arguments for the existence of mental events are unsuccessful. In my view, there is no genuine theoretical need to posit mental events (or events of any kind for that matter).[32] Occam's razor, therefore, dictates that we should banish events from our ontology. This conclusion is bolstered by my earlier arguments against the token identity theory, event dualism, and eliminative materialism. These arguments themselves led us to a rejection of mental events. We now have independent support for this conclusion. The task that lies ahead is more positive: It is that of elaborating an alternative theory of mind that is compatible both with a rejection of mental events and with my contention that psychological statements are frequently true.

There remains one criticism I should like to answer in an attempt to avoid any misunderstanding of my strategy up to this point. If the arguments I have given in the final section of this chapter against events are correct, then it may be thought that the token identity theory itself can be analyzed as a theory that is not really about events at all. And if this is the case, then my arguments in Chapter 1 against the token identity theory are irrelevant to my project of

31 Barry Taylor, in *Modes of Occurrence* (Oxford: Blackwell Publisher, 1985), has argued that the predicate-operator approach, unlike Davidson's event view, has difficulty in handling the ambiguous sentence 'Henry gracefully ate all the crisps'. Taylor is mistaken, however. See Chapter 3, note 27. I might add that Terence Parsons has recently argued that there are certain inferences for which events are needed. See his "Modifiers and Quantifiers in Natural Language," *Canadian Journal of Philosophy*, supp., 6 (1980): 29–60; also his "Underlying Events in the Logical Analysis of English," in *Actions and Events*, ed. E. Le Pore and B. McLaughlin (Oxford: Blackwell Publisher, 1985). For an account of how these inferences can be handled *without* events, see my "Events and Logical Form" (with Terence Horgan), forthcoming.

32 One recent argument, which I have not taken up above, is that events are needed in order to dissolve Forrester's "paradox of gentle murder." See Walter Sinnott-Armstrong, "A Solution to Forrester's Paradox of Gentle Murder," *Journal of Philosophy*, 82 (1985): 162–8. Sinnott-Armstrong's argument for events is interesting, but it is very far from compelling. For an alternative way of handling the paradox, which avoids events, see Romane Clark, "Murderers Are Not Obliged to Murder: Another Solution to Forrester's Paradox," *Philosophical Papers*, 15 (1986): 51–7.

51

defending a metaphysical theory of mind that avoids events. So it may appear that the issues addressed in Chapter 1 have little or nothing to do with the rest of the book.

This criticism is based on certain misunderstandings. I believe that psychological statements have a misleading grammatical form and, contrary to appearances, do not require for their truth the existence of mental events. Now, the psychological statements I am interested in are those found in ordinary, everyday contexts and also those found in the theories of cognitive psychology. The statement that every mental event is identical with some neurophysiological event, however, is not happily located in either of the above contexts. Its home is really in philosophy. And I do not believe that this statement, as it is understood and used by professional philosophers, can be analyzed without any appeal to events; for the token identity theory, considered as a philosophical theory, requires that *there really be* mental events that are strictly identical with physical events. At least, that is how I and its major proponents (e.g., Davidson)[33] understand it. The falsity of this theory, so understood, is an important part of the motivation for my view of the mind. Admittedly, *if* my arguments in this chapter are sound, the token identity theory, considered in the usual way as a theory that requires the existence of mental events, is false anyway, since those arguments entail that there are no mental events. But that does not make Chapter 1 superfluous. Rather it adds *independent* support to a conclusion already reached via Chapter 1.

I might add finally that, in light of what I say in this chapter, I believe that I *can* give an event-free analysis of the statement 'Every mental event is strictly identical with some neurophysiological event' that captures one possible meaning of this statement. But this analysis certainly will *not* capture what the statement normally means in the writings of philosophers.

33 Donald Davidson, "Mental Events," in *Experience and Theory*, ed. L. Foster and J. Swanson (London: Duckworth, 1970), pp. 79–101.

3

The foundations
of the operator theory

In this chapter, I lay out the basic framework of the theory of mind that I accept. This theory, which I call the "operator theory," derives its inspiration from the adverbial approach to sensory experience favored by Sellars,[1] Chisholm,[2] and others. I shall begin my discussion by examining the theory of experience to which adverbialists have been most strongly opposed: the sensory object theory. I shall argue that this theory fares no better than the more general theories I have criticized in Chapters 1 and 2. I shall then sketch an operator-based adverbial account of sensory experience that avoids both mental events and sensory objects. In the course of presenting this sketch, I shall develop a detailed analysis of the metaphysical and semantic foundations of the linguistic category central to this theory – that of the predicate operator. Finally, I shall explain in a preliminary way how I propose to extend the operator theory beyond the sensory realm without any expansion in its metaphysical commitments.

I

The sensory object theory is the theory that sensory states are really *relational*, having as relata persons or other sentient creatures, on the one hand, and concrete sensory objects, on the other. On this theory, statements like

(1) Tom feels an intense pain

---

1 Wilfred Sellars, "Phenomenalism," in *Science, Perception, and Reality* (London: Routledge & Kegan Paul, 1963), pp. 92–5; idem, *Science and Metaphysics* (London: Routledge & Kegan Paul, 1968), pp. 9–28.
2 R. M. Chisholm, *Perceiving* (Ithaca, N.Y.: Cornell University Press, 1957), pp. 115–25; idem, *Person and Object* (La Salle, Ill.: Open Court, 1976), pp. 46–52.

and

(2) Paul has a visual sensation of a red square

are analyzed as

(1a) There is an object x, such that x is a pain, x is intense, and Tom stands in the relation of feeling to x

and

(2a) There is an object x, such that x is a sense impression, x is red, x is square, and Paul stands in the relation of direct visual awareness to x,

respectively. What differentiates this approach from those already rejected (other than narrowness of scope) is that it *both* takes the relevant portion of our psychological talk to be true *and* (arguably) avoids mental events (within the sensory realm). In place of such events, there are various concrete sensory objects.

What reasons are there to adopt this theory? To begin with, it may be suggested that it is *just* obvious from inspection of our bodily and perceptual sensations that sense impressions (e.g., afterimages, appearances) and other sensory objects (e.g., pains, itches) exist. But it seems to me that this appeal has little force. Phenomenological inspection of a sensory experience will no more tell us whether there really is a pain or an afterimage than will inspection of a person's smiling face tell us whether there really is a smile, an event of smiling, or merely a person who smiles. What phenomenology tells us (at most) is that certain sentences of the sort 'I have a throbbing pain' or 'I have a yellow afterimage' are true. There remains unanswered the question of how to analyze these sentences so as to bring out their metaphysical commitments.

A second reason for postulating sense impressions – and historically a very important one – is the desire to account for the facts of hallucination and illusion: Since a person can have an image experience of a pink rat, say, even though there are no real pink rats, it is often inferred that the person must be related through the experience to a pink, ratshaped image or impression. This appeal again has little force, because, as I shall show later, the operator theory can also account for the relevant facts.

A third reason for adopting the sensory object theory is that its analyses accord well with the grammatical form of our talk about sensory experience. This argument falsely presupposes that the logical form of a sentence must coincide with its grammatical form. Still, some philosophers may want to defend the sensory object theory on the weaker grounds that grammatical form is a reasonable indicator of logical form, unless and until good reasons are given for adopting some *other*, less obvious logical form. An alternative defense of the sensory object theory rests on the grounds that the logical form it assigns to statements like (1) and (2) is ultimately the only one that gets the right results, that is, which preserves the validity and invalidity of all the appropriate inferences.[3] I claim, in opposition to the latter position, that the assignment provided by the operator theory yields the correct inferences. In response to the former position, I turn now to a summary of my reasons for choosing the operator view over an account that appeals to sensory objects.

It is well known that the thesis that there are concrete sensory objects generates all sorts of perplexing questions. For example, can sense impressions exist unsensed? Can two persons experience numerically identical sense impressions? Do sense impressions have "rear" surfaces that are not sensed? Are they located in private spaces? What is the connection between private sensory space and real space? If I blink my eyes while having a hallucinatory image, say, do I undergo two different images or only one interrupted one? If it appears to me that there is before me a speckled hen or a striped tiger without it appearing to me that the hen or tiger has a determinate number of speckles or stripes, does there really exist in my mind a sense impression that lacks a definite number of speckles or stripes? Are pains really located about the body as our ordinary pain talk suggests? If so, then presumably they are material objects. Why, then, are they never revealed by surgical examination of the appropriate limbs? Can pains exist in parts of the body without their being felt? Can two persons ever feel one and the same pain?[4] Historically, the desire to avoid questions like these was one reason for the development of the adverbial analysis of sensory experience, and it remains one of the underlying motivations for my operator theory.

3 E.g., Frank Jackson argues from considerations of logical form alone to the existence of sense data. See his *Perception* (Cambridge University Press, 1977).
4 Puzzling questions can also be raised about the supervenience and emergence of sensory objects. These questions will parallel those raised in Chapter 2 concerning the supervenience and emergence of nonphysical events.

It must be admitted that some (but not all) of the problems raised above dissolve if sensory objects are identified with neural entities. This identification, however, generates problems of its own. One problem is that of finding the "right" neural entity (or fusion of such) with which to identify a given sensory object. If sensory objects are held to be neural events, then the mental object theory is open to the very same objections as the token identity theory I repudiated earlier. Admittedly, the relatively short life of sensory objects makes it less likely that there will sometimes be multiple equally acceptable neural candidates for identification. But this difficulty, which is most acute for the token identity theory in connection with longer-lived mental states, still arises. Alternatively, if sensory objects are held not to be identifiable with neural events, it is hard to see what neural tokens are left available for the identification, since neural conditions, states, and processes all count as events under the present usage of 'event'. Furthermore, even if potentially appropriate neural tokens can be found, considerations of the sort presented in Chapter 1 will still generate difficulties for the claim that every sensory object is strictly identical with some neural token. This is because the relevant individuating criteria underlying specific claims of identity will surely have to remain causal.

There is another, rather different kind of difficulty for the claim that sensory objects are identical with neural tokens. This is the familiar objection that such identities violate Leibnitz's law. For example, pains are sometimes burning, stabbing, or dull; but it seems unintelligible to assert that anything in the brain is burning, stabbing, or dull. Similarly, afterimages are sometimes green; but there need be nothing in the brain, or the surrounding physical environment, of a person experiencing such an image that is itself green.

The usual response to this objection is that terms like 'green' and 'stabbing', in application to sensory objects, do not have the meanings they have in application to ordinary physical objects and phenomena. The task now becomes one of spelling out what these terms *do* mean in connection with sensory objects, and how their meanings relate to the meanings of the corresponding words in public contexts.

I shall take no position here on whether this task can be completed. The points I want to make are twofold. First, on my operator theory, questions about whether it makes sense to say that neural tokens are dull or stabbing or green do not arise. Hence, my theory has the advantage of not having to take such questions seriously. Second, once the sensory object theorist concedes that 'green', say, in application to an afterimage, has a special, peculiar meaning, the door is opened to *other* interpretations of 'green' that are incompatible with the sensory object theory. In particular one possibility that can now be taken seriously is my view that 'green' is not really functioning as a predicate at all but rather as the adverb 'greenly'.

A final objection I have to the sensory object theory is that it involves gratuitous metaphysical complexity. The sensory objects it posits are not needed, I maintain, in order to account for the truth of any psychological discourse. Hence, by Occam's razor, sensory objects, like mental events before them, should be excised from our ontology.

II

Consider again statement (2). According to the adverbial theory, (2) is logically on a par with a statement like

(3) Tom has a noticeable stutter

or

(4) Patrick dances a charming waltz,

rather than a statement like

(5) Jane strokes a ferocious dog.

Thus, just as (3) and (4) can be rewritten as

(3a) Tom stutters noticeably

and

(4a) Patrick waltzes charmingly,

so (2) can be recast as

(2b) Tom hurts (is pained) intensely.

In general, adverbialists maintain that statements of the sort

(6) Person x has an F sense impression

57

or

(7) x has an F sensation

can be reconstructed adverbially as

(8) x senses F-ly

or, as it is sometimes put,

(9) x senses in an F manner.

Thus, having a sensory experience, on the adverbial theory, is a matter of sensing in a certain way rather than sensing a peculiar sensory object.

It should be obvious that the adverbial view can account for the facts of hallucination and illusion. If, for example, I am correctly described as having a visual sensation of something blue, then 'blue' in this description is taken upon analysis to function as an adverb that expresses a mode of my sensing. Hence, my having the sensation does not require that there be a blue physical object (or anything else for that matter) in my general vicinity – it suffices that I sense bluely.

It should also be obvious that the adverbial theory sidesteps the many puzzling questions raised earlier in connection with the sensory object theory. Nonetheless, it should be equally obvious that the analyses presented above are in dire need of clarification. What exactly is the logical form of (2b) and other adverbially modified sensory statements? What are the metaphysical commitments of the adverbial theory? Is the theory committed to the existence of sensory events (sensings), for example, instead of sensory objects? If so, the theory is inconsistent with my earlier conclusion that there are no mental events. Can the adverbial theory be fully articulated so as to explain all the valid inferences involving sensory statements that must be explained? Can the adverbial approach be extended to statements about belief, desire, and other propositional attitudes?

Surprisingly, some of these questions have not been addressed at all by adverbial theorists, and others have received only the most cursory answers. I say "surprisingly" because the adverbial approach to sensory experience is very widely accepted.[5] In any event,

5 See, e.g., Bruce Aune, *Knowledge, Mind, and Nature* (New York: Random House, 1967), pp. 147–8; Chisholm, *Perceiving* and *Person and Object*; James Cornman, *Materialism and Sensations* (New Haven, Conn.: Yale University Press, 1971), pp.

my aim in the rest of the book is to work out in proper detail an entirely general adverbially based theory of mind that avoids both mental events and mental objects. I trust that it is clear by now that the attempt to construct such a theory can be well motivated (although I hasten to add that I shall introduce some further motivations later in connection with the propositional attitudes). All that remains is to show how the theory is to be developed!

To begin with, it should be noted that not all versions of the adverbial theory, as it applies to sensory statements, try to avoid mental events. James Cornman, for example, maintains that statements about how persons sense are to be analyzed as existential quantifications over particular concrete sensings or sensory events.[6] My arguments in Chapters 1 and 2 lead me to reject any such account. Furthermore, as I shall show later, there are special difficulties for adverbial theories of sensing that posit sensory events.

In my view, statements of the type

(8) x senses F-ly

are to be regimented as quantifier-free subject–predicate statements, the predicates of which are compound. The general idea here is that sensory adverbs are analyzable as predicate operators added to a standard predicate calculus. Syntactically, the primitive predicate operators are boldface capital letters in the following treatment.[7] These capital letters are concatenated with predicates by enclosing the letters within square brackets and placing them directly to the left of the predicates. Thereby they form more complicated predicates. Semantically, according to the proposal I made in earlier work, predicate operators can be viewed as signifying functions that take the properties expressed by the predicates they modify onto new properties.[8] On this approach, the open sentence

178, 185–90; C. J. Ducasse, "Moore's Refutation of Idealism," in *Philosophy of G. E. Moore*, ed. P. A. Schlipp (Evanston, Ill.: Northwestern University Press, 1942), pp. 225–51; Sellars, "Phenomenalism" and *Science and Metaphysics*.

6 See Cornman, *Materialism and Sensations*.

7 With the exception of 'N' and 'O', which I reserve for use as variables whose instances are primitive predicate operators.

8 See my "Adverbial Approach to Visual Experience," *Philosophical Review*, 93 (1984): 195–225; also my "Pain and the Adverbial Theory," *American Philosophical Quarterly*, 21 (1984): 319–28. See also Terence Parsons, "Some Problems Concerning the Logic of Grammatical Modifiers," in *Semantics of Natural Language*, ed. D. Davidson and G. Harman (Dordrecht: Reidel, 1972), pp. 127–41; also, for

(10) *x* senses redly

is regimented as

(10a) **[R]**Sx.

Sentence (10a) is made up of an operator '**R**' ('redly') concatenated with the formula 'Sx' ('x senses'). The function or operation that '**R**' expresses (the redly function) maps the property of sensing onto the property of sensing redly. It is worth stressing here that '**R**' cannot be thought of as expressing a second-order property. Properties are expressible by predicates, and predicates, even higher-order ones, attach to singular terms, not to predicates. Wisdom, for example, not wise, is a virtue. By contrast, 'redly' attaches to a predicate to yield a further predicate.

Metaphysically, the above operator theory is committed to more than just persons and other sentient creatures. Since the semantical statements proposed in connection with the interpretation of (10a) – statements like

(11) '**R**' expresses the redly function

and

(12) 'S' expresses the property of sensing –

use singular terms that designate properties or functions, the proposed theory is also committed to the existence of these abstract entities. There is, however, no commitment to the existence of concrete sensings or sensory events.

The version of the operator theory I now advocate has a semantics that eschews both properties and functions from properties to other properties. Such a semantics has the advantage of metaphysical simplicity. It also avoids the problem of having to frame satisfactory identity conditions for properties (or other intensional substitutes).

But just what is the interpretation I now favor, and why exactly in the first semantics are properties rather than sets introduced? To answer these questions, we must examine the aim of formal semantics. Some philosophers believe that there really are such entities as meanings and that the task of formal semantics is to explain rigorously how the meanings of semantically compound expres-

a closely related view, see Romane Clark, "Concerning the Logic of Grammatical Modifiers," *Nous*, 4 (1970): 311–55.

sions are determined by the meanings of their components.[9] Given this conception of formal semantics, it is possible to arrive at the semantics I proposed initially for complex predicates like 'senses redly' by the following reasoning. Consider the pair of complex predicates 'walks quickly' and 'thinks quickly'. The meanings of these predicates are evidently determined by the meanings of their components 'walks' or 'thinks', and 'quickly'. More generally, the meaning of 'quickly' is something that determines a meaning for the verb phrase '*V*s quickly' *given* the meaning of '*V*s'. Hence, the meaning of 'quickly' is really a function. Now this function cannot simply map sets onto sets, for if this were the case then the meaning of 'walks quickly' would automatically be the same as the meaning of 'thinks quickly', if it happened to be true that all walkers were thinkers and conversely. But obviously 'walks quickly' and 'thinks quickly' need not be even coextensive in the given circumstances. Hence, the function expressed by 'quickly' must map intensional entities, standardly properties, onto other entities of the same sort.

Properties having been introduced into the semantics of adverbs, it is now a simple matter to explain one very important kind of inference involving a range of adverbially modifed statements: that of adverb or operator detachment. For example,

(13) *x* walks quickly

logically entails

(14) *x* walks;

and there are parallel inferences for 'senses redly', 'thinks quickly', and many other modified phrases. We saw earlier that the validity of inferences like these is one of the factors that has been used to support the claim that there are events. However, within predicate-operator semantics, events are not needed. Instead, the explanation for the inferences is as follows. Properties themselves can be viewed as functions, functions that determine the extensions of the predicates expressing them in all possible situations. In other words, properties can be taken to be functions that go from each possible world to a set of things within that world. Thus, the property of sensing, for example, can be identified with a function that goes

9 See, e.g., David Lewis, "General Semantics," in *Semantics of Natural Language*, ed. Davidson and Harman, pp. 169–218.

from each possible world to the set of sensing creatures within that possible world. A standard adverbial operation is now taken to be a function that maps properties into other properties that they (the former properties) include, where a property expressed by 'F' is said to include a property expressed by 'G' if, and only if, for every possible world w each property goes from w to a set of things in w such that the set constituting the value of the property expressed by 'G' at w is a subset of the set forming the value of the property expressed by 'F' at w. This logically guarantees that the inference rule

(OD) $[O]Fx \rightarrow Fx$

is valid, assuming that 'O' is standard.[10]

For cases in which 'O' is nonstandard, I might add, the operator detachment rule (OD) does not apply. For example,

(15) Jones is almost done

does not entail

(16) Jones is done

but rather

(17) Jones is not done.

Nonetheless, these inferences are also unproblematic, once we have a semantics that utilizes properties, conceived of as functions from possible worlds to sets. Following Romane Clark, let us call operators that conform to the rule

(ON) $[O]Fx \rightarrow {\sim}Fx$

negators. The function a negator stands for is taken to map properties into other properties that they exclude, where a property expressed by 'F' is said to exclude a property expressed by 'G' if, and only if, for every possible world w, each property goes from w to a set

10 This justification for (OD) can be restated without the reductive assumption that properties are functions from possible worlds to sets of things within those worlds as follows. A standard adverbial operation is taken to be a function that maps properties onto other properties that they include, where one property is said to include another property if, and only if, for any possible world w, the set of entities having the latter property at w is a subset of the set of entities having the former at w. This suffices to guarantee that (OD) is valid for standard operators.

62

of things in w such that the set constituting the value of the property expressed by 'G' at w has no members in common with the set constituting the value of the property expressed by 'F' at w.[11] This ensures that the inferences that correspond to the pattern in (ON) are valid, given that the operators substituted for 'O' are negators.

It seems to me that the semantics sketched above has a certain elegance. But it pays a significant price (and one that, I believe, need not be paid) in its account of the metaphysical commitments of adverbially modified statements.[12] Let us therefore turn our attention to the alternative and much more austere predicate-operator semantics that I myself now advocate.

To begin with, I should say that I view formal semantics as a less ambitious enterprise than it is taken to be above. I grant that an adequate theory of meaning should in some sense be componential, that is, explain how the meanings of semantically compound expressions are determined by the meanings of their parts. But I deny that this meaning determination has to be expressly captured in formal semantics. In my view, the project of formal semantics in general is like the project of formal semantics for standard first-order quantification theory. Thus, I see it as concerned chiefly with giving a characterization of key logical/semantic notions like validity of sentences, consistency of sets of sentences, and the logical consequence relation. Of course, a preliminary task is to define such notions as interpretation and truth under an interpretation. But the goal is then to use these notions to characterize the key logical ones. Validity, for instance, is truth under every interpretation.

If we view formal semantics in this restricted manner, we can construct a semantical system that explains the validity of the inferences (OD) and (ON) in an appealing and natural way without recourse to any intensional entities.

---

11 Although this definition, like that of property inclusion, assumes that properties are functions from worlds to sets, it can be restated without such an assumption as follows. One property excludes another property if, and only if, for any possible world w, the set of entities having the latter property at w has no members in common with the set of entities having the former at w.

12 It might be argued that possible worlds are needed elsewhere in the semantics for modal discourse, so the price is not so high after all. I reject the premise of this argument. For a sketch of an approach to modality that avoids possible worlds, see Hartry Field, "Is Mathematical Knowledge Just Logical Knowledge?" *Philosophical Review*, 93 (1984): 509–52, esp. 549–52.

Suppose we have a standard first-order logic supplemented with predicate operators. We assign concrete individuals to the constants of our logic, and sets of individuals to the *core* predicates (i.e., the predicates that contain no predicate operators as parts).[13] We now require a further interpretation for the new predicates involving operators. If '**O**' is a predicate operator and '*F*' is a *core* predicate, then the set S assigned to the predicate '[**O**]*F*' will depend on the set S' assigned to '*F*' and on the kind of operator '**O**' is. This dependence is expressed as a condition that connects S and S' (the *satisfaction sets* of '[**O**]*F*' and '*F*', respectively). The condition for standard operators is $S \subseteq S'$. The condition for negators is $S \cap S' = \emptyset$.

We can now enlarge the standard truth definition to include the new complex predicates. For each individual constant '*c*', let i_c be the individual assigned to '*c*'. An atomic sentence of the type '[**O**]*Fc*' is *true* under our interpretation if, and only if, i_c is a member of S.[14]

Under this semantics, the inference rules (OD) and (ON) are clearly valid. By contrast, the inference from '*x* walks quickly' to '*x* thinks quickly' is invalid, even if all walkers are thinkers and conversely. This is because the sole requirement that the proposed semantics places on the sets assigned to 'walks quickly' and 'thinks quickly' is that they be subsets of the sets assigned to 'walks' and 'thinks'. Hence, even if the set of walkers is the same as the set of thinkers, the subset of quick walkers need not be the same as or include the subset of quick thinkers.

I should perhaps add that it is a straightforward matter to extend the semantics to sentences involving iterated predicate operators. If '**N**' is a predicate operator, then the set assigned to the predicate '[**N**][**O**]*F*' will depend on the set S assigned to '[**O**]*F*' and the nature of the operator '**N**' in the same manner as for the noniterated case. Thus, sentences containing iterated operators will be subject to the same rules of inference as before. In the case of sentences involving operators that form other operators, the situation is basically similar. Consider, for example,

---

13 The sets so assigned will not be *referred* to by the predicates. See here Chapter 2, p. 44 and note 21.

14 An alternative and more complex set-theoretic semantics is proposed by Terence Horgan in "The Case Against Events," *Philosophical Review*, 87 (1978): 28–47.

(18) Jefferson spoke impressively quickly.

Here 'impressively' operates on the predicate operator 'quickly' to form another predicate operator 'impressively quickly'. Formally, let us employ '$\mathcal{M}$' as a variable whose instances are operators that form predicate operators, and let us abbreviate individual such operators by capital script letters other than $\mathcal{M}$. Each of these operators (e.g., '$\mathcal{H}$') will directly precede the symbol on which it operates (e.g., the predicate operator '**R**'), thereby forming another predicate operator (e.g., '$\mathcal{H}$**R**').[15] The result of placing one of the latter operators inside square brackets before a predicate is the formation of a further complex predicate. The semantics for these predicates now proceeds as above with one addition: The set S^* assigned to a predicate of the type '$[\mathcal{M}\mathbf{O}]F$' will depend not only on the set S' assigned to 'F' and the kind of operator '$[\mathcal{M}\mathbf{O}]$' is, but also on the set S assigned to '$[\mathbf{O}]F$' and the kind of operator '$\mathbf{O}$' is. Assuming that '$\mathcal{M}$' and '$\mathbf{O}$' are standard, the dependence conditions are these: As before, $S^* \subseteq S'$; also $S^* \subseteq S$.

The standard truth definition can now be extended to include the relevant predicates in a straightforward manner: An atomic sentence of the type '$[\mathcal{M}\mathbf{O}]Fc$' is true under our interpretation if, and only if, i_c (i.e., the individual assigned to constant 'c') is a member S^*. Moreover, the condition that S^* be a subset of S justifies a new detachment rule for standard operators on predicate operators as follows:

(OPD) $[\mathcal{M}\mathbf{O}]Fx \rightarrow [\mathbf{O}]Fx$.

Thus, (18) logically entails

(19) Jefferson spoke quickly

on the proposed semantics. Later in this book we shall have cause to look at some very complicated constructions involving predicate operators. It will be seen that the semantics of these cases (discussion of which is best left until later) presents no difficulty for the general framework outlined above.

The formal semantics I have proposed involves no intensional entities. Rather, it invokes only sets of individuals. This approach

---

15 Typically such operators form predicate operators by operating on other predicate operators. However, they need not do so. In later chapters, we shall meet operators that form predicate operators by operating on singular terms and sentences, for example.

has two virtues. First, sets, unlike properties, have clear, agreed-upon identity conditions. Second, sets are utilized in formal semantics generally, and hence the appeal to sets in this context involves no *additional* ontic commitment.[16] It is also worth noting that the postulation of sets within my general metaphysics is not vulnerable to the standard objection that sets, being abstract, are incapable of standing in causal relations and hence are completely unknowable. This objection is inapplicable because, on my view, the term 'causes' does not express a relation at all. Rather, as we have seen, it is a sentential connective, and there is, on this approach, no obvious difficulty in claiming that, for example, *the fact that* Leonard belongs to the set of people who ate the poisoned fish *caused it to be the case that* Leonard belongs to the set of people who died.

Before I say something further about how I view the relationship of formal semantics to the theory of meaning within the view sketched above, I want to address a general objection I have encountered to the principle (OD), regardless of which semantics is adopted: (OD) is not universal; it holds for some predicate operators and not for others. Well, when does it hold? Apparently, it holds when it holds and does not when it does not. Operator detachment is valid in certain cases because those are these cases in which (OD) holds, that is, in which operator detachment is valid. One need not rack one's brains to find this unsatisfactory.

This objection is, I think, entirely unconvincing. The central claim is that no noncircular account can be given of why (OD) holds in certain cases and not in others. This is false, however. On the earlier semantics, (OD) holds when it does because, for a certain significant range of predicate operators, there are associated functions the very nature of which is to map the appropriate properties into other properties that they include. On the later semantics, (OD) holds when it does because, for a certain significant range of modified predicates, there are associated sets that by their very nature are subsets of the sets associated with the nonmodified predicates. There are, then, important metaphysical and semantic constraints

16 Perhaps the commitment to sets in formal semantics generally is merely apparent. If so, then the appeal to sets above will be eliminable. For an argument that purports to establish that sets can be dispensed with in formal semantics, see Terence Horgan, "A Nominalistic Theory of Truth," *International Logic Review*, forthcoming.

that govern the applicability of (OD). In those cases where (OD) fails to hold, the constraints specified above are lacking, and other constraints apply. For example, in cases where (ON) holds, the relevant constraints on the richer semantics involve functions that map the appropriate properties into other properties that they *exclude*. There is surely no *circularity* in any of this. Admittedly, *if* my approach required the use of a very large number of different formal principles like (OD) and (ON), each with its own special conditions of applicability, one might well object on the grounds of theoretical simplicity. But for such an objection to carry any real weight one would have to show first that the theoretical baggage of the operator theory is *unnecessary* – that there are alternative theoretical accounts involving less linguistic complexity. And, of course, one would also have to weigh the relative metaphysical complexity of the various accounts. It should also be said that my approach does not require a huge number of different principles anyway. Indeed, it requires very few. Finally, it is worth remembering that, however neat and simple we would like the linguistic facts about adverbs to be, adverbs cannot always be validly detached. For example,

(20) William almost sneezed

does not entail

(21) William sneezed

but rather

(22) William did not sneeze.

Those who accept the Davidsonian account of adverb detachment [and thereby avoid the introduction of (OD)] must accept this fact just as anyone else must. And since the Davidsonian view that adverbs are really predicates true of events is evidently not applicable to this case, some further principled account is necessary. It is extremely difficult to see what such an account would look like, unless it combined both events and predicate operators, together with a suitably modified version of (ON), in which case it would certainly be inferior to the proposed operator view.

I want now to make some more comments on how I currently view the relationship of formal semantics to the theory of meaning. Consider the following sentence:

(23) Mary sneezes loudly.

If we apply my favored formal semantics to this sentence, we get the following statement of truth conditions:

(23a) 'Mary sneezes loudly' is true if, and only if, there is an object x and a set S such that 'Mary' refers to x, S is the satisfaction set of 'sneezes loudly', and x belongs to S.

Statement (23a) on its own obviously does not give us much information about the meaning of 'Mary sneezes loudly'. After all, it does not even specify *which* object and *which* set are relevant. Still, once we are given *both* (23a) *and* this specification, we have enough information to differentiate the meaning of (23a) from that of, say, 'Tom writes illegibly'; for we now know that the truth values of these sentences are determined by different individuals and different sets. Let us say that the truth conditions in (23a), together with a specification of the relevant entities, give us the *truth-theoretic meaning* of (23).[17] And let us extend the use of the term 'truth-theoretic' so that singular terms and predicates can be said to have truth-theoretic meanings via their reference and satisfaction conditions.

Now, as far as truth-theoretic meaning is concerned, it should be clear that, on my proposal, (23) is no more complex than, for example,

(24) Mary sneezes;

for the latter sentence has an exactly parallel statement of truth conditions, namely

(24a) 'Mary sneezes' is true if, and only if, there is an object x and a set S such that 'Mary' refers to x, S is the satisfaction set of 'sneezes', and x belongs to S.

But 'sneezes' is syntactically unstructured, whereas 'sneezes loudly' is syntactically compound. Hence, we are led to the conclusion that, on my predicate-operator view, adverbially modified predicates have a syntactic complexity that is not mirrored in their satisfaction conditions.

This conclusion may be held to be problematic for two reasons. First, there are many philosophers who equate truth-theoretic meaning with meaning simpliciter. This equation entails that 'x sneezes loudly' has a meaning that is no more complex than the meaning of

17 Cf. Hartry Field, "Logic, Meaning and Conceptual Role," *Journal of Philosophy*, 74 (1977): 379–405.

'*x* sneezes'. But surely it is obvious that 'sneezes loudly' has a meaning that is determined in part by the meaning of 'sneezes' and in part by the meaning of 'loudly'. So 'sneezes' and 'sneezes loudly' cannot be on a par in terms of meaning complexity. Second (and relatedly), there is an influential argument due to Donald Davidson that a language containing predicate operators is unlearnable, given my semantics.[18] The argument, in brief, is as follows. On my account, no matter how many sentences involving predicate operators a would-be user of the language learns to construct and understand, there will still be others whose meanings are not given by the truth-conditional rules already mastered.[19] But if this is so, it seems to follow that there will always be parts of the language that cannot be learned (assuming, as Davidson notes, that would-be speakers "don't suddenly acquire the ability to intuit meanings without any rule; that each new item of vocabulary, or new grammatical rule takes some time to be learned; that man is mortal."[20]

One can answer the first of these objections by denying that a specification of truth-theoretic meaning must be a complete specification of meaning. To see this, suppose that the predicates '*F*' and '*G*' are coextensive. Then '*Fa*' will have the same truth-theoretic meaning as '*Ga*', since the truth values of the two sentences will be determined by the same individual and the same set. But evidently if '*F*' and '*G*' are accidentally coextensive, then '*Fa*' and '*Ga*' will *not* have the same overall meaning. In this case, then, there is more to meaning than truth-theoretic meaning.

Admittedly, one could escape this conclusion by arguing that the truth conditions for '*Fa*' and '*Ga*' should introduce nonlinguistic properties rather than sets, so that the truth values of the two sentences are determined by the same individual but different properties. My point, however, is not that the universal identification of meaning with truth-theoretic meaning cannot be defended, no matter what sorts of entities are introduced into the truth conditions. My point rather is that this identification can be resisted.

18 D. Davidson, "Theories of Meaning and Learnable Languages," in *Logic, Methodology and Philosophy of Science*, ed. Y. Bar-Hillel (Amsterdam: North Holland, 1966). I might add that Davidson's discussion does not *explicitly* address the case of predicate operators. However, his argument is obviously intended to apply to such a case.

19 Assuming that there is no upper bound on the number of predicate operators that can be attached to sentences such as (24).

20 Davidson, "Theories of Meaning," p. 388.

And indeed it must be resisted if nonlinguistic properties and other intensional entities are to be avoided.

In accordance with standard practice, I shall call the extra factor involved in meaning 'conceptual role'.[21] I should perhaps add here that I do not hold that *all* linguistic items must have a conceptual role. For example, I am inclined to think that ordinary proper names only have a truth-theoretic meaning. That is to say, I am inclined to suppose that the meaning of 'Hesperus', say, is fixed by the requirement that 'Hesperus' be assigned Hesperus as its referent.[22] Now the conceptual role of a term, as I view it, has to do with the network of laws, principles, or quasi-analytic generalizations in which the term is found. Where the term is an everyday experiential or propositional attitude predicate, the relevant network will consist of the principles of folk psychology in which the term figures; where the term is a predicate of some other common or garden-variety sort, the relevant network will consist of ordinary quasi-analytic generalizations that involve the term and that lie outside folk psychology; where the term is scientific, the network will consist of the theoretical laws and correspondence principles in which the term is embedded. Thus, if two terms differ in conceptual role, they will figure in different platitudes/laws/principles (and sometimes they will also figure in the same platitudes/laws/principles in different ways). For example, 'teapot' differs in conceptual role from 'barber', since *teapots* are vessels in which tea is brewed and from which it is served, whereas *barbers* are people whose business is cutting hair, trimming beards, and other related services. Collectively, platitudes such as these *implicitly define* the everyday terms that occur in them.[23] That is to say, under any proper as-

---

21 This proposal is, of course, not new. See Field, "Logic, Meaning, and Conceptual Role"; Brian Loar, *Mind and Meaning* (Cambridge University Press, 1981); idem, "Conceptual Role and Truth Conditions," *Notre Dame Journal of Formal Logic*, 23 (1982): 272–83; Colin McGinn, "The Structure of Content," in *Thought and Object*, ed. A. Woodfield (New York: Oxford University Press, 1982); Stephen Schiffer, "Indexicals and the Theory of Reference," *Synthese*, 49 (1981): 43–100.

22 Thus, unlike some advocates of the notion of conceptual role, I think that 'Hesperus is Hesperus' and 'Hesperus is Phosphorus' have the same meaning. I do not think, however, that anyone who believes that Hesperus is Hesperus must believe that Hesperus is Phosphorus. See my discussion of belief contexts in Chapter 7 esp. Sections II and III.

23 For ordinary experiential and propositional attitude predicates, there will be one relevant body of platitudes (those composing folk psychology); for everyday

signment of extensions to the terms, the platitudes must come out true or at least by and large true. Likewise, for theoretical scientific terms, under any proper assignment of extensions the relevant laws and correspondence principles must come out true or, again, by and large true (assuming that the pretheoretical terms occurring in the correspondence principles are assigned *their* proper extensions).[24]

Returning to the case of 'x sneezes loudly' and 'x sneezes', then, my proposal is that, although they do not differ in the complexity of their truth-theoretic meanings (or so I claim), they do nonetheless differ in the complexity of their conceptual roles. This is because the conceptual role of 'sneezes loudly' is determined in part by the conceptual role of 'sneezes' and in part by the conceptual role of 'loudly'. Since the last of these conceptual roles has special significance as far as Davidson's objection from learnability is concerned, I want next to present a brief account of how it can be elucidated. In my view, the conceptual role of 'loudly' (and, mutatis mutandis, of other syntactically unstructured adverbs) is given in a collection of platitudinous or quasi-analytic generalization *patterns*, each of which contains the sentence type 'x Vs loudly' and each of which yields a specific instance when the dummy letter '*V*' is replaced by an appropriate verb. Corresponding to each of these patterns are various inference schemata in which the sentence type 'x Vs loudly' figures. Three of the relevant patterns might be as follows:

(A) For any object x, if x Vs loudly then x Vs.
(B) For any objects x and y, if x Vs loudly and y Vs quietly, then x makes much more noise than y.
(C) For any object x, if x Vs and x can be heard to V from a great distance away then, ceteris paribus x Vs loudly.

The first of these patterns has a somewhat different status than (B) or (C) in that the inference schema corresponding to it (namely 'x Vs loudly'; so 'x Vs') is an instance of the operator detachment rule (OD), which itself governs a wide range of predicate operators. The third pattern (C) is, of course, a little rough and ready. It can

terms generally there will be another larger body – one that has the former body as a proper part.
24 In making these claims, I am not presupposing that there is only one assignment of extensions that will make the appropriate sentences come out true or by and large true. See here note 26 and the references therein. See also Chapter 5, Section IV.

be made more precise by the introduction of further qualifications that capture part of what is involved in the ceteris paribus clause. However, I do *not* wish to claim that the need for such a clause would inevitably be eliminated altogether with the addition of suitable complications. And what is true here for (C) is, I believe, true for many of the generalization patterns relevant to conceptual roles.

Now, the central shared feature of patterns or schemata such as (A)–(C) is that they yield platitudinous or quasi-analytic general truths upon replacement of 'V' by suitable verbs.[25] Knowledge of the conceptual role of 'loudly', in my view, consists essentially in the possession of a complex set of dispositions, specifically dispositions to assert various sentences of the type 'x Vs loudly' and to assent to them *only* when they are being used in a way that conforms with these platitudinous general truths. Thus, I do not presuppose that knowledge of the conceptual role of 'loudly' consists in the ability to state the generalization patterns, or the truths they generate, immediately upon request.

Turning now to the Davidsonian objection, it may be helpful if we focus on a very simple example. Suppose that I am given the meaning of (24) and that I am also given the meaning of

(25) Mary sings loudly.

Intuitively, the information I have here suffices for me to learn the meaning of (23). But if meaning is given by truth conditions as in (23a), together with a specification of which object and which set are relevant, then I cannot learn the meaning of (23); for although I have been given enough information to know that 'Mary' refers to Mary and that 'Mary sneezes loudly' is true if, and only if, Mary belongs to the satisfaction set of 'sneezes loudly', I do not yet know *which* set this satisfaction set is. That is the gist of Davidson's objection.

My response is first to reject (as before) the equation of meaning with truth-theoretic meaning and second to claim that once conceptual role becomes a part of meaning, I *can* understand the meaning of (23) in the given circumstances. Let me explain. If I am given the meaning of (25), I must already know not just its truth con-

---

25 A slightly weaker claim is that the generalizations generated by instantiation of meaning-giving schemata are *nearly all* platitudinous truths. The advantage of this weaker claim is that is does not matter if a small minority of the patterns we take to generate truths do not in fact do so.

ditions but also the conceptual role of 'sings loudly'. Knowing this conceptual role involves knowing the conceptual roles of 'sings' and 'loudly'. If I know the last of these roles, I further know the conceptual role of 'sneezes loudly', for, ex hypothesi, I have already been given the meaning of (24) and hence I must already know the conceptual role of 'sneezes'. Now I have the truth conditions for (24) in my possession, and I know *which* set satisfies 'sneezes'. It therefore seems reasonable to conclude that I also grasp the truth-theoretic meaning of (23). For I certainly know that (23) is well formed and hence I know that its truth conditions are those given in (23a). I know too that 'Mary' refers to Mary. And I know, or so it seems to me, which set is the satisfaction set for 'sneezes loudly'. This is because the conceptual role of 'sneezes loudly' places severe restraints on its extension. In particular, since 'x sneezes loudly' logically entails 'x sneezes' the satisfaction set assigned to 'sneezes loudly' must be a subset of the set of sneezers. Moreover, this subset cannot just be any old subset. Rather the choice of subset will be constrained by the requirement that under the correct extension assignment all (or nearly all) the generalizations produced by replacement of 'V' by 'sneeze' in the generalization patterns associated with the sentence type 'x Vs loudly' must come out true.[26] It appears, then, that I am able to understand (25).

---

26 Assuming, of course, that the other predicates in the generalizations have their proper extension assignments. As I indicated above, the overall assignment of extensions to common or garden-variety (modified and unmodified) predicates is constrained by the holistic requirement that the various ordinary platitudinous generalizations in which the predicates figure must come out (by and large) true. Could this requirement be met without there being a *unique* overall assignment of extensions for everyday modified and unmodified predicates? My answer is that, if it turns out that there is more than one initially acceptable interpretation, the rival candidates should be compared with respect to what David Lewis calls "naturalness" of the extension assignments. Since I also hold that greatest naturalness indicates correctness, other things being equal, and that there will very probably be just one way of assigning satisfaction sets to the various common or garden-variety predicates that is more natural than any other, I believe that there will ultimately be a single acceptable interpretation scheme. If I am wrong on this point, the conclusion I draw is that there is ineliminable indeterminacy of interpretation. For an account of naturalness and further discussion relevant to the above claims, see David Lewis, "New Work for a Theory of Universals," *Australasian Journal of Philosophy*, 61 (1983): 343–77; idem "Putnam's Paradox," *Australasian Journal of Philosophy*, 62 (1984): 221–36; also Terence Horgan, "Attitudinatives," *Linguistics and Philosophy*, forthcoming. See also my comments on naturalness and indeterminacy in Chapter 5, Section IV.

sentences involving predicate operators and indeed mutatis mutandis to sentences involving additional operator operators. Where Davidson goes wrong, from the present perspective, is in his assumption that any sentence that is semantically simple within Tarskian truth theory automatically has a simple overall meaning. There is, I claim, an important aspect to meaning that is not captured in truth-theoretic semantics, that of conceptual role. Furthermore, in cases where we have a syntactically complex predicate '[O]F', where 'F' has known satisfaction conditions and both 'O' and 'F' have known conceptual roles, I have argued that we thereby know enough to understand the overall meaning of the whole complex predicate. These cases contrast sharply, I suggest, with cases in which we are given an entirely new syntactically unstructured predicate (and nothing else). Here we clearly *cannot* draw upon our knowledge of satisfaction conditions or conceptual roles of other predicates in order to understand what the new predicate means.

I shall return to Davidson's objection from learnability in the context of my analysis of folk psychological propositional attitude sentences in Chapter 7. I hope that I have already said enough, however, to show that the objection rests on an assumption that can reasonably be denied.

My aim in this section has been to provide an introductory sketch of the metaphysical and semantic foundations of predicate operators.[27] These operators play a crucial role not only within my ver-

27 It has been suggested that there are adverbial contexts that cannot be satisfactorily analyzed on the predicate-operator view of adverbs. For example, in *Modes of Occurrence* (Oxford: Blackwell Publisher, 1985), Barry Taylor argues that the predicate-operator view encounters serious problems with respect to the ambiguous sentence

(a) Henry gracefully ate all the crisps.

This sentence can be read either as requiring that each and every crisp was eaten gracefully by Henry or as requiring that Henry's overall crisp-eating style was graceful (even though perhaps the odd crisp was devoured gracelessly). Davidson's event-proposal can handle the ambiguity by interpreting the sentence either as predicating gracefulness of each of Henry's individual crisp eatings or as predicating gracefulness of a further event formed by summing these crisp eatings, namely the event of Henry's eating all of the crisps. By contrast, according to Taylor, the predicate-operator approach can handle the second interpretation of the given sentence only by introducing the attribute abstraction operator λ, and this is not only "ugly" but also "engenders further problems" (p. 18).

Taylor's objection is unsound. There is no need for the predicate-operator

sion of the adverbial theory of sensing, but also within my general theory of mind. I turn in the next section to a brief preliminary account of how I intend to use predicate operators within my analyses of nonsensory psychological statements. This account, I should emphasize, is really no more than a skeleton exhibited in advance so that the reader will have *some* idea, however rough, of what the larger picture looks like on my view. Flesh for this skeleton will be supplied in the following chapters.

III

It is generally supposed that both folk psychological statements "about" propositional attitudes, for example,

(26) Smith has the belief that snow is white,
(27) Jones has the desire that people live in peace,

theorist to resort to the λ operator. On the contrary, an interpretation is available that is very natural and that runs parallel to the Davidsonian account. If (a) is taken to require merely that Henry's overall crisp-eating style was graceful, 'all the crisps' in (a) should be taken as a singular term designating the aggregate of crisps present. On this account, (a) is a relational statement in which the operator 'gracefully' modifies the two-place dyadic predicate 'x ate y'. Admittedly, in the earlier formalizations in this chapter, predicate operators always operated on monadic predicates. But the introduction of operators on dyadic predicates creates no special semantic difficulty. On the richer semantics, such operators will stand for functions that map two-place relations into other two-place relations. On the semantics I am advocating, a two-place relational predicate 'F' will be assigned a set of ordered pairs, as will the same predicate modified by an operator. For standard operators, such as 'gracefully', the latter set will be a subset of the former. Whether or not the operator is standard, if individuals i_c and $i_{c'}$ are assigned to individual constants 'c' and 'c'', an atomic sentence of the type '$[O]Fcc'$' will be true if, and only if, $\langle i_c, i_{c'} \rangle$ is a member of the set assigned to '$[O]F$'.

Other adverbial contexts have been alleged to present difficulty for the predicate-operator view. See Sally McConnell-Ginet, "Adverbs and Logical Form," *Language*, 58 (1982): 144–84; also Terence Parsons, "Modifiers and Quantifiers in Natural Language," *Canadian Journal of Philosophy*, supp., 6 (1980): 29–60; idem, "Underlying Events in the Logical Analysis of English," in *Actions and Events*, ed. E. Le Pore and B. McLaughlin (Oxford: Blackwell Publisher, 1985). I will not take up the contexts discussed by McConnell-Ginet, since Romane Clark has argued persuasively that contexts of the sort she deems problematic are amenable to a predicate-operator treatment. See Clark, "Predication: The Copula," a presentation to the Guelph–McMaster Conference on Ontology and Language, which honored the memory of N. L. Wilson, May 1985. For a reply to Parsons's arguments, see my "Events and Logical Form" (with Terence Horgan), forthcoming.

75

and statements made by cognitive psychologists "about" mental representations, for example,

(28) Jones has a (mental) quasi-pictorial representation of a boat,
(29) Smith retrieves a (mental) quasi-linguistic representation of a car,

are fundamentally *relational*. In the case of belief and desire statements, there is no general agreement as to the objects to which persons are said to be related. Sometimes these objects are taken to be abstract propositions. On other occasions, they are taken to be mental sentence tokens that themselves express abstract propositions or, in some other way, have meaning. On still other occasions, it is said that the objects of belief and desire are concrete mental events or state tokens that are nonlinguistic and that have the relevant propositional content. In the case of the representational statements of cognitive psychology, there is no corresponding disagreement. On the standard construal, these statements require for their truth that persons be related to concrete mental representations. Thus, (28), if true, is taken to relate Jones to a concrete mental quasi-picture, and (29), if true, is taken to relate Smith to a concrete mental quasi-linguistic item.

I reject all these positions. In my view, statements like (26)–(29) are no more relational than are statements "about" bodily and perceptual sensations. Admittedly these statements have a relational "look" about them; but then so do sensory statements. And just as sensory statements about persons and other sentient creatures are, I claim, really subject–predicate statements, the predicates of which involve operators, so too are propositional attitude and cognitive representation statements. In the case of (26) and (27), I have two alternative proposals. On one account, as analogs for the predicate 'senses', we have (upon analysis) the predicates 'believes' and 'desires'; and as analogs for operators like 'redly' we have the predicate operators 'that-(snow is white)-ly' and 'that-(people live in peace)-ly'. Within these predicate operators, 'that' is a further operator operating on the sentence in parentheses it precedes. On the other account, 'has the belief that' and 'has the desire that' become 'believes that' and 'desires that', where these expressions are taken to be operators operating on the sentences they precede to form predicates. I spell out these two accounts in detail in Chapter 7. All I want to note now is that, on the line I am proposing, (26) and (27) involve *no* commitment either to mental tokens, linguistic or

76

otherwise, or to abstract propositions. Metaphysically they are on a par with my earlier adverbialized sensing statements and indeed with predicate-operator statements of a subject–predicate sort generally.

Consider next (28). Here the approach is just like that taken for sensory statements. As an analog for 'senses', we have (upon analysis) 'represents'; and as analogs for operators like 'redly', we have 'a-boat-ly' and 'quasi-pictorially'. Thus, (28) as a whole is recast as

(28a) Jones represents a-boat-ly quasi-pictorially.

Less succinctly, what (28) is saying, according to (28a), is that Jones is representing in a certain way, a-boat-ly, and that he is doing that quasi-pictorially. This talk is in need of further explanation, of course, and in Chapter 8 I shall discuss how it is to be elucidated. I want to stress, however, that terms like 'quasi-pictorial' in contexts like (28) are themselves in need of further explanation. Hence, the usual approach, which has it that 'quasi-pictorial' is really functioning as a predicate, is, I suggest, no easier to comprehend at least initially than my predicate-operator approach. In any event, (28), on my view, is really a subject–predicate statement rather than a relational statement, and it involves iterated predicate operators.

Turning finally to (29), it is obvious that (29) entails that Smith has a quasi-linguistic representation of a car. What (29) asserts, then, can be put this way:

(29a) Smith has a (mental) representation that he retrieves (is retrieving) and that is of a car and quasi-linguistic.

Once we have (29) in this form we can convert 'representation' to 'represents', and we can introduce associated predicate operators. Thus, (29a) becomes

(29b) Smith represents a-car-ly quasi-linguistically retrievingly.

In (29b) the three operators iterate. Again I readily grant that the meanings of these operators need clarification. The point to grasp now is that on the above analysis (29), like (28), is not really a relational statement. Hence, it is not committed to the existence in Smith's head of a concrete quasi-linguistic representational item.

That, then, is the barest outline of my general operator theory of the metaphysics of mind. As I remarked earlier, this operator theory is really an extension of the adverbial theory of sensing. I prefer to call my view an *operator* theory rather than an adverbial theory for three reasons. First, the central logicolinguistic category I utilize in my analyses is that of the operator. Typically the operators I introduce operate on predicates, but sometimes they operate on predicate operators or sentences or singular terms. Since not all these operators can be classified as adverbial, it seems too restrictive to classify my theory as adverbial. Second, the adverbial theory, in many philosophers' minds, is nothing more than a theory of sensory experience. Since my view has much wider scope I prefer to use a title that immediately distances it from any such restrictive associations. Finally, there are in the literature versions of the adverbial theory (e.g., Cornman's account mentioned earlier) with which my position has really nothing significant in common other than an eschewal of sense data. In another sense, then, the title "adverbial theory" is a little too general to be apt.

4

Bodily sensation

We certainly speak as if pains are felt objects that are located in sundry parts of our bodies. We say, 'There is a pain in my foot', 'The pain I feel in my right arm is more intense than the one in my left ankle', and so on. In this respect we group pains with itches and tickles, for example. We saw earlier that talk of bodily sensations, such as these, if taken literally, generates a variety of problems. I want now to take a detailed look at how the operator theory can be applied here. I shall focus my discussion on the case of pain, but what I say can be extended mutatis mutandis to other bodily sensations.

The chapter is divided into three sections. In Section I, I lay out a formal analysis of pain statements and defend it against possible objections. In Section II, I show how a version of the functionalist view of pain meshes with my formal analysis. In Section III, I address certain issues having to do with my proposed account of pain location.

I

On the operator theory, adjectives that modify the noun 'pain' become operators that modify the predicate 'is pained' or 'hurts'. For example,

(1) Jones has a searing pain

becomes

(1a) Jones is pained searingly.

This analysis has several potential difficulties. Consider first the question of revealing the connection between Jones's having a

79

throbbing pain and Jones's having a nagging pain. On the operator theory, the former is represented by

(2) [T]Pj

and the latter by

(3) [N]Pj,

where 'T' and 'N' are the operators 'throbbingly' and 'naggingly' and 'j' is a name for Jones. Both (2) and (3) logically entail

(4) Pj,

via the operator detachment rule

(OD) [O]Fx → Fx.

Hence, the connection between the one case and the other is successfully revealed.

Consider next the problem of explaining the entailment from

(5) Jones has a burning throbbing pain

to

(6) Jones has a burning pain,

without collapsing the distinction between

(7) Jones has both a burning throbbing pain and a dull nagging pain

and

(8) Jones has both a dull throbbing pain and a burning nagging pain.

This problem, which is called the "many-property problem," was first raised by Frank Jackson[1] in the context of the adverbial analysis of visual sensations. Jackson has claimed that it cannot be solved by the adverbial theory. We shall see later that for visual sensations there is a way out of Jackson's problem.[2] I shall argue now that for the case of pain there is also a successful strategy.

Speaking commonsensically, we can say that (5) is true if, and only if, Jones has a sensation of burning pain in the very same place

---

1 See Frank Jackson, "On the Adverbial Analysis of Visual Experience," *Metaphilosophy*, 6 (1975): 127–35.
2 See also my "Adverbial Theory: A Defense of Sellars against Jackson," *Metaphilosophy*, 6 (1975): 135–43; and my "Adverbial Approach to Visual Experience," *Philosophical Review*, 93 (1984): 195–225.

that he has a sensation of throbbing pain. This leads to the idea that (5) is to count as true if, and only if, there is a space–time region s such that Jones hurts burningly at s and Jones hurts throbbingly at s.

Formally we can now analyze (5) as

(5a) $(\exists x)(Sx \ \& \ [\mathscr{A}x][\mathbf{B}]Pj \ \& \ [\mathscr{A}x][\mathbf{T}]Pj)$.

In (5a), 'S' is a predicate meaning 'is a spatiotemporal region', '$\mathbf{B}$' is the adverbial operator 'burningly', '$\mathbf{T}$', 'P', and 'j' are as before, and '$\mathscr{A}$' is the operator 'at'. Both '$\mathbf{B}$' and '$\mathbf{T}$' are to be thought of as modifying the predicate 'P'. However, '$\mathscr{A}x$' is to be thought of as modifying the entire complex predicate it precedes. Thus, in the second conjunct of (5a), '$\mathscr{A}x$' modifies '$[\mathbf{B}]P$', and in the third conjunct '$[\mathbf{T}]P$'.

The operator '$\mathscr{A}$' requires some explanation. In general, as I stipulated in Chapter 3, capital script letters are operators that operate on the symbols they directly precede, thereby forming predicate operators. The result of placing the latter operators inside square brackets before predicates is the formation of further complex predicates. Thus, although '$\mathscr{A}$' is not itself a predicate operator it forms such an operator when it precedes an individual term for a spatiotemporal region, say 's', as in '$\mathscr{A}s$'. Semantically, '$\mathscr{A}$' can be viewed in two ways. On the property-function semantics, we can take '$\mathscr{A}$' in '$\mathscr{A}s$' to express a function that maps the space–time region named by 's' onto another function expressed by '$\mathscr{A}s$'. The latter function maps the property expressed by the entire predicate it precedes (e.g., being pained burningly) onto a new property (e.g., being pained burningly at s). On the favored semantics that eschews properties, the set assigned to a predicate of the form '$[\mathscr{A}s]Fx$' will depend on (i) the set assigned to 'F'; (ii) the kind of operator '$\mathscr{A}s$' is; and (iii) the referent of the singular term 's'. Consider, for example, '$[\mathscr{A}s]Px$'. Since '$\mathscr{A}s$' is standard, we may say immediately that the set S assigned to '$[\mathscr{A}s]Px$' is a subset of the set assigned to 'Px'. But how we do capture the dependence of S on the referent of 's'? I suggest we impose the further condition that for every member m of S there is an ordered pair consisting of m and s such that each of these ordered pairs belongs to the satisfaction set of the *binary* structured predicate '$[\mathscr{A}y]Px$'. This condition is not intended to suggest that the extension of '$[\mathscr{A}s]Px$' depends on a *prior* extension assignment to the binary predicate '$[\mathscr{A}y]Px$'. So perhaps

81

this formulation is less misleading: For any objects o and o' (in the domain of our interpretation for the formal language), if 's' designates o then o' belongs to the set assigned to '$[\mathcal{A}s]Px$' if, and only if, the ordered pair $\langle o, o' \rangle$ belongs to the set assigned to '$[\mathcal{A}y]Px$'.[3]

The two conditions imposed above seem intuitively reasonable, and together they suffice to justify both inferences in which operators of the type '$\mathcal{A}x$' are detached and inferences that existentially generalize on the singular terms embedded in such operators as, for example, in '$[\mathcal{A}s]Px$'; therefore, '$(\exists y)[\mathcal{A}y]Px$'. Of course, the set-theoretic semantics sketched above does not give us the full meaning of sentences of the type '$[\mathcal{A}s]Px$'. But as I emphasized in Chapter 3, it was never intended to. The meaning of such sentences is not just a matter of truth conditions; conceptual role is also crucial. I shall make some comments pertinent to understanding the meaning *qua* conceptual role of the operator '$\mathcal{A}$' below.

Returning now to (5a), it should be noted that there are iterated predicate operators in the second and third conjuncts. Nevertheless, there is no restriction on the permutation of the operators within these conjuncts on either semantics. This is because it is necessarily true that one belongs to the set of individuals who hurt G-ly at region s if, and only if, one belongs to the set of individuals who hurt at region s G-ly. And what is true here for sets is true for ownership of the properties, hurting G-ly at s and hurting at s G-ly. Hence, given '$[\mathcal{A}x][\mathbf{B}]Pj$', for example, it is safe to infer '$[\mathbf{B}][\mathcal{A}x]Pj$' and vice versa. Equivalences of this sort, I might add, hold generally for cases involving pairs of iterated predicate operators, one of which contains the spatiotemporal operator 'at'. For example,

(9) Jones sings off-key at the beach

is equivalent to

(10) Jones sings at the beach off-key.[4]

On the proposed formalization, the inference from (5) to (6) is easy to explain, since the formalized counterpart of (6), namely

3 The introduction of ordered pairs poses no threat to the metaphysical framework of my preferred semantics; for by the Kuratowski procedure, ordered pairs can be analyzed as sets of sets (specifically, $\langle o, o' \rangle = ((o), (o, o))$).

4 For more on the permutation of adverbs in iterated constructions, see Chapter 5, Section III.

(6a) $[\mathbf{B}]Pj$,

is entailed by (5a) via applications of existential instantiation, conjunctive simplification, and the operator detachment rule (OD).[5]

Turning to (7) and (8), a similar strategy applies. Thus, (7) is rewritten as

(7a) Jones has a burning pain at the same space–time region as a throbbing pain and a dull pain at the same space–time region as a nagging pain,

and (7a) is analyzed as

(7b) $(\exists x)\{Sx$ & $[\mathcal{A}x][\mathbf{B}]Pj$ & $[\mathcal{A}x][\mathbf{T}]Pj\}$ & $(\exists x)\{Sx$ & $[\mathcal{A}x][\mathbf{D}]Pj$ & $[\mathcal{A}x][\mathbf{N}]Pj\}$.[6]

The same approach is taken to (8). Thus, (8) becomes

(8a) $(\exists x)\{Sx$ & $[\mathcal{A}x][\mathbf{D}]Pj$ & $[\mathcal{A}x][\mathbf{T}]Pj\}$ & $(\exists x)\{Sx$ & $[\mathcal{A}x][\mathbf{B}]Pj$ & $[\mathcal{A}x][\mathbf{N}]Pj\}$.

Since (7b) and (8a) are not equivalent, the difference between (7) and (8) is preserved.[7]

The metaphysical cost of the above solution to the many-property problem, as it applies to pains, is the introduction of spatiotemporal regions. In my view, this cost is minimal. For one thing, we saw in Chapter 2 that once events are repudiated it becomes natural to introduce spatiotemporal regions to handle certain inferences among statements involving putatively event-denoting definite descriptions that have nothing to do with sensations. For another, it can be argued that spatiotemporal regions are needed in our metaphysics anyway for still other purposes.[8] There is a sig-

---

5 In this case (OD) is used to detach an iterated predicate operator.

6 Here '**D**' abbreviates 'dully'; the other symbols are as before.

7 The position I have taken here has another consequence worth noting. On my analysis, the truth of (7) [or (8)] entails that there are spatiotemporal regions where Jones hurts. Hence, from the truth of a statement attributing more than one pain to Jones, Jones may deduce the existence of an external world, albeit in its most exiguous form. This conclusion is inconsistent with and, in my view, refutes those skeptics who assert that common or garden-variety sensory statements like (7) or (8) can be known to be true even if nothing external exists. I owe this point to José Bernadette. To the objection that ordinary pain locutions never entail anything at all about physical space, since everyone's completely and permanently disembodied existence is a metaphysical possibility, I respond by denying the premise. See my "On the Possibility of Disembodied Existence," *Australasian Journal of Philosophy*, 61 (1983): 275–82.

8 See, e.g., David Lewis and Stephanie Lewis, "Holes," *Australasian Journal of Philosophy*: 48 (1970): 206–12. It is also worth noting that identity conditions for material objects standardly involve quantification over spatial or spatiotemporal regions.

nificant objection, however, to the proposal I have made. According to my analysis, (5) logically entails

(11) Jones hurts (is pained) at some spatiotemporal region.

Now if (5) is true and Jones is pained in a leg, say (and nowhere else), then the space–time region at which Jones hurts is occupied by some part of his leg. Since (11) is regimented as

(11a) $(\exists x)(Sx \ \& \ [\mathcal{A}x]Pj)$,

(11) in this case does not commit us to the *existence* of a pain located inside Jones's leg. Still, if, as is widely supposed, the property of hurting (or being pained) is a functional property of individuals,[9] then it will be realized in Jones on the above occasion by one or more of his neural properties, and it seems clearly false that those neural properties will be exemplified by Jones at a space–time region occupied by some part of his painful limb (i.e., his leg).

One could try to escape this objection by rejecting the view that being pained is a functional property. But obviously the same argument could be made if instead being pained were identified with a physicochemical property. Admittedly, if being pained were held to be an irreducible nonphysical property, the objection would lose its force (assuming it is intelligible to speak of individuals exemplifying such properties at space–time regions). But my earlier arguments concerning the supervenience and emergence of nonphysical properties lead me to reject this response.[10] What, then, can be said?

My response has two parts. First, I deny that there is any such property as the property of being pained. This view is, of course, a direct consequence of the semantics I now advocate for statements like (11). Thus, the objection, as stated, has a false presupposition. Second, I maintain that the operator 'at', as I have used it in the context of the analysis of pain statements, has a specialized conceptual role.[11] This conceptual role is given in various generalizations, central among which are the following:

9 For a discussion of the functionalist view, see Section II.
10 See Chapter 2, Section I.
11 It retains this conceptual role in the analysis of bodily sensation statements generally. In taking this view, I diverge from the position I presented in my "Pain and the Adverbial Theory," *American Philosophical Quarterly*, 21 (1984): 319–29. The theory elaborated in that article is vulnerable to the objection I am now considering.

(12) For any creature x, and for any space–time region y, if there is a part z of x's body occupying y and z is damaged and *the fact that* z is damaged *causes it to be the case that* x hurts then, ceteris paribus, x hurts at y.

(13) For any creature x, and for any space–time region y, if x hurts at y then, ceteris paribus, there is a part z of x's body occupying y and z is damaged.[12]

Given the specialized role of 'at' in the analysis of pain statements, it may be wondered why I use the term 'at' at all. Other than ease of exposition there is one real reason. In ordinary everyday contexts we sometimes use the term 'in' to specify where people hurt; we say, for example,

(14) Smith has a pain in his left big toe.

In these contexts, there is good reason to suppose that 'in' has a special conceptual role. My use of 'at' may be thought of as finding a counterpart in the established use of 'in' in statements like (14). I should add that the conceptual role of 'at' in statements of the type

(15) Individual x hurts at space–time region y

is specialized, on my account, in the same way as the meaning of 'in'; for as we shall see shortly, 'in', as it occurs in statements locating pains in bodily limbs, has a partly causal meaning.[13] This connection between the conceptual roles of 'at' and 'in' is not fortuitous; after all, it is intuitively reasonable to suppose that (14) is equivalent to

(16) Smith is pained at a space–time region occupied by some part of his big left toe,

however the latter statement is to be *further* analyzed.

I want now to show how my operator theory can deal with a

---

12 Corresponding to these generalizations are others in which, in place of the verb 'hurt', there is a different verb of bodily sensation, e.g., 'itch'. Strictly speaking, the conceptual role of 'at' is given in the generalization patterns to which these various generalizations conform. For a discussion of conceptual roles, see Chapter 3, pp. 70–1.

I might add here that philosophers who prefer the property-function semantics for statements such as (11) need not grant that their view is refuted by the above objection; for they can maintain that 'at' has a specialized *explicit* definition in the relevant contexts.

13 In my "Pain and the Adverbial Theory," I rejected this claim. Later, in Section III, I answer the objections that led me to this rejection.

number of perplexing problems having to do with the location of pains. To begin with, let us consider the well-known phantom-limb phenomenon. Take the statement

(17) Jones has a pain in a phantom limb.

How are we to understand it? Clearly, it is not the case here that Jones's pain is located in one of his actual limbs. Nor surely is it the case that there exists *outside* of Jones's body a pain that Jones is somehow feeling. In my view, what (17) asserts is

(17a) Jones hurts at a space–time region that is not occupied by any part of any of his limbs but that would have been occupied by part of one of his limbs had it not been amputated and had no other physical object been in the way

or, formally,

(17b) $(\exists x)(Sx \ \& \ [\mathcal{A}x]Pj \ \& \ Lx \ \& \ \sim Ox),$

where 'Ox' means 'Some part of some limb of Jones occupies x', 'Lx' means 'x would have been occupied by part of one of Jones's limbs had it not been amputated and had no other physical object been in the way', and the other symbols are as before. The reason for the second conjunct in the counterfactual in (17a) can be brought out by consideration of the following case. Suppose Jones's stump is placed flush against a large block of concrete at a time at which he has a pain in his phantom leg. What is true here is that Jones hurts at a space–time region that his leg would have occupied had it not been amputated *and* had the block of concrete not been present.

The advantages of this analysis are threefold. First, it allows us to take the natural view that the term 'in', as it occurs in (17) and (17a), has at least in part a spatiotemporal connotation. Second, (17b) does not commit us to the existence of any pains located outside the body (nor even to any pains located inside the body). Third, the entailment from (17) to

(18) Jones has a pain

is given a simple natural explanation on the proposed analysis, since

(18a) Pj

follows from (17b) by standard rules plus modifier detachment.

Another familiar problem for understanding the location of pain is presented by the following three statements:

(19) Jones has a pain in his foot.
(20) Jones's foot is in his shoe.
(21) Jones has a pain in his shoe.

It appears that (21) is not entailed by (19) and (20), but it also appears that it *ought* to be, given the transitivity of 'x is in y'. This problem is, I think, best solved by denying that 'in' in (19) and (21) has the same conceptual role as it does in (20). In (20) 'in' is a relational term, whereas in (19) and (21) 'in' is an operator. This operator, in the context of pain statements, means 'at a space–time region occupied by some part of' (or else some minor variation on this);[14] and 'at', as it is used here, has a specialized conceptual role. We saw earlier two generalizations central to this role. The following, it seems to me, is another:

(22) For any creature x, and for any part y of x's body, if x hurts at a space–time region occupied by y and y is inside some physical object z not a part of x's body then, ceteris paribus, it is not the case that x hurts at a space–time region occupied by z.

The upshot is that (19) and (20) do not entail (21). Rather, given (22), they entail the negation of (21).

A third problem connected with the location of pain derives from the fact that it is sometimes possible to mislocate one's pains. Kurt Baier explains this fact as follows:

Under certain conditions of observation, as when he is not allowed to see the relevant parts of his body, a person may make claims about where on his body he was pricked and where he felt the pain, claims concerning which he later accepts corrections. When told by the experimenter or when allowed to explore the area with his own finger or to watch as he is being pricked again in the same place, he admits that the pains (and the pricks) were not in the place where he first said they were.[15]

This possibility of error creates a problem for behaviorist analyses of pain location, according to which (19), for example, is equivalent to

(19a) Jones has a pain that disposes him to nurse his foot, call attention to his foot. . . .

Since Jones could conceivably have a pain in his foot and yet direct attention to some other part of his leg, (19) and (19a) might differ in

14 As, e.g., in the context of (17).
15 Kurt Baier, "The Place of a Pain," *Philosophical Quarterly*, 14 (1964): 142–3.

truth value. But, it seems to me, there is no real difficulty here for the analysis I am proposing. On my account, error occurs if a person misidentifies the space–time region at which he hurts. I may, for example, think that the region at which I am hurting is occupied by the second toe on my right foot. Subsequently, I may discover that this region is really occupied by my first toe. There is no special mystery.

I shall have more to say on the topic of pain location in Section III. I want now to consider two further objections, each of which may appear to present serious difficulties for my proposal.

The first objection has to do with the fact that we sometimes employ definite descriptions in our identification of pains. For example, I may say

(23) The pain in my right leg is intense.

How on the adverbial approach are we to analyze this sort of statement?

The approach I favor is as follows. What is it to have exactly one pain in my right leg? The adverbial theorist can say that it is to hurt at exactly one (continuous) space–time region that is occupied by some part of my right leg. This proposal leads to the following regimentation for (23):

(23a) $(\exists x)\{Sx \ \& \ Rx \ \& \ [\mathcal{A}x]Pa \ \& \ (y)((Sy \ \& \ Ry \ \& \ [\mathcal{A}y]Pa) \supset y = x) \ \& \ [\mathcal{A}x][\mathbf{I}]Pa\}.$

In (23a), 'a' names me, '$\mathbf{I}$' is the operator 'intensely', 'Rx' means 'x is occupied by some part of my right leg', and the other symbols are as before. Sentence (23a) is, I maintain, equivalent to (23). For example, (23) entails

(24) I have an intense pain in my right leg

and

(25) I have exactly one pain in my right leg.

Sentence (23a) does likewise via standard rules. Hence, the objection is answered.

The final objection I wish to discuss arises with respect to the analysis of comparative judgments about pains. Suppose I say

(26) I have not only a pain in my right leg but also a pain in my neck, and the former is more intense than the latter.

How, on an operator theory, is (26) to be understood? The analysis

I suggest here can be stated informally as

(26a) I hurt in my right leg and I hurt in my neck, and I hurt more intensely in the former place than in the latter

or formally as

(26b) $(\exists x)(\exists y)\{Sx$ & Sy & Rx & Ny & $[\mathcal{A}x]Pa$ & $[\mathcal{A}y]Pa$ & $[(\mathcal{A}x)\mathcal{I}(\mathcal{A}y)]Pa\}$.

In (26b), 'Ny' means 'y is occupied by my neck' and '$(\mathcal{A}x)\mathcal{I}(\mathcal{A}y)$' is a compound predicate operator meaning 'more intensely at x than at y'.[16] This compound operator consists of the predicate operators '$\mathcal{A}x$' and '$\mathcal{A}y$' modified by the two-place comparative operator 'more intensely than' or '$\mathcal{I}$'. The inferential role that (26) plays is preserved by this sort of analysis. Hence, my operator theory of pain is still unscathed.

Before I close this section, I want to say something more about two-place operators such as '$\mathcal{I}$'. In Chapter 3, '$\mathcal{M}$' was introduced as a variable whose instances are operators that form predicate operators. Individual such operators (capital script letters other than '$\mathcal{M}$') have been taken to precede directly the symbols on which they operate. It is convenient now to modify this earlier usage so that it covers operators that operate on two predicate operators to form further predicate operators. Let us therefore permit capital script letters to be flanked by predicate operators on both sides, thereby creating more complicated operators. And let us enclose in curved parentheses the predicate operators that are operated on whenever those predicate operators are structurally complex [as in (26b)].

Semantically, there are again two alternative views. On one account, operators such as '$\mathcal{I}$' express functions that map the functions expressed by the predicate operators flanking them onto the functions expressed by the compound predicate operators they form. So, for example, in '$(\mathcal{A}s)\mathcal{I}(\mathcal{A}t)$', the function that '$\mathcal{I}$' expresses maps the functions expressed by '$\mathcal{A}s$' and '$\mathcal{A}t$' onto the function expressed by the whole compound operator. Let us say that a two-place operator '$\mathcal{M}$' is a *standard* operator if, and only if, for any two predicate operators '**O**' and '**N**' the functions expressed by '**O**' and '**N**' include the function expressed by '**O**$\mathcal{M}$**N**', where one function on a property is said to include another just in case for any predicate 'F' the property the former function maps the property expressed

16 The other symbols retain their earlier meanings.

by 'F' onto *includes* the property onto which the latter function maps the property expressed by 'F'. Understanding property inclusion as we did in Chapter 3[17] now logically guarantees that the operator simplification inferences

(OS₁) [O$\mathcal{M}$N]Fx → [O]Fx,
(OS₂) [O$\mathcal{M}$N]Fx → [N]Fx

are valid, assuming that '$\mathcal{M}$' is standard.

On the second semantics (the one I now advocate), a compound predicate '[O$\mathcal{M}$N]F' will be assigned a set S^*, which depends on the set S, assigned to '[O]F', and the set S', assigned to '[N]F'. If '$\mathcal{M}$' is standard, the dependence conditions are as follows: $S^* \subseteq S$; $S^* \subseteq S'$. These conditions suffice to underwrite the validity of (OS₁) and (OS₂).[18]

Given either semantics, I might add, the conjuncts '[$\mathcal{A}x$]Pa' and '[$\mathcal{A}y$]Pa' in (26b) are really redundant, since they are entailed by the final conjunct, *if* '$\mathcal{I}$' is classified as a standard two-place operator. Intuitively, this classification seems reasonable enough; for if I hurt more intensely at one region than another, it seems to follow that I hurt to some degree at both regions. And what is true in this one instance seems true generally for 'more intensely than'. Still, some may want to contest these claims. Hence, we might as well leave open the question as to whether '$\mathcal{I}$' is best taken as standard. If we do this, we will need to retain '[$\mathcal{A}x$]Pa' and '[$\mathcal{A}y$]Pa' as conjuncts in our analysis of (26).

It is time, I think, to draw some general conclusions. The operator theory I have sketched is able to handle a variety of powerful objections. Furthermore, as we saw earlier, the logic it uses can be applied to the understanding of inferences in action theory and elsewhere that present problems for standard predicate logic (inferences like 'Jones is almost done'; therefore, 'Jones is not done'). It is also worth pointing out that, on the more austere semantics, the metaphysics associated with the operator theory is much simpler than any other theory of bodily sensations with which I am acquainted. Even on the less austere semantics, the operator theory

---

17 See Chapter 3, note 10 and relevant text.
18 The standard truth definition can be extended to include predicates of the type '[O$\mathcal{M}$N]F as follows: where i_c is the individual assigned to individual constant 'c', an atomic sentence of the type '[O$\mathcal{M}$N]Fc' is true if, and only if, i_c is a member of S^*.

remains relatively simple in terms of its metaphysical commitments. The operator theory, therefore, has a variety of virtues.

II

In this section, I sketch out the functionalist view of pain and show how a version of this view goes hand in hand with my operator theory. Initially, for ease of exposition, I use 'event' and 'state' talk. Later, in the presentation of my own position, I dispense with this talk.

Functionalists have been quick to point out that pain is not a state the essence of which can be defined in phenomenal terms. Pains vary enormously in how they feel. Consider, for example, the pain of a burn, a headache, a very loud noise close to the ear, a pinprick, a bee sting. Nonetheless, such pains do at least typically elicit the same mental reaction, namely dislike. This leads to the thought that the characteristic of typically eliciting a reaction of dislike is *part* of the essence of pain.[19] I say "part" here because there are other effects (and causes) that seem to many philosophers no less important to the classification of a given state as pain. Consider, for example, such typical causal relationships as these: resulting from bodily damage or trauma; giving rise to worry and distress; causing attempts to move the body away from the damaging stimulus; causing nursing of the relevant part of the body.

Functionalists have asserted that causal relationships like these themselves exhaust the essence of pain. According to functionalism, any sensory state type (and indeed any mental state type) can be defined via its causal connections with certain standard stimuli, certain other types of mental states, and certain standard behavioral responses. This view is reminiscent of behaviorism. But there is an important difference. Behaviorists tried to define each given mental state type exclusively in terms of the appropriate sensory stimuli and behavioral responses. Functionalists, by contrast, insist that behavioral responses are typically dependent on whole *groups* of mental states. For example, my desiring a glass of champagne causes me to reach for the champagne bottle, but only if I recognize

19 In some cases of prefrontal lobotomy, patients report having pains even though they are indifferent to how their sensations feel. These cases present a problem for the claim that necessarily pain always elicits a reaction of dislike but not for the claim that necessarily pain typically elicits such a reaction.

it as a champagne bottle, and only if I do not have some other desire that outweighs the first. So from the functionalist's perspective, any satisfactory definition of a given mental state type *must* take account of its causal connections to other mental state types, and hence the behaviorist's definitions are doomed to failure.

The most precise statement of the functionalist's view has been given by David Lewis. Given the basic conception of a mental state as a state that has certain typical causes and effects (including other mental states), Lewis has described a procedure for defining any mental state term using sensory input and behavioral output terms, as well as quantification over mental states, but no mental language.[20] This procedure is very briefly as follows. Let T be our common-sense psychological 'theory'. This 'theory' consists of a variety of platitudes concerning the causal relations of mental states, sensory stimuli, and behavioral responses and also platitudes to the effect that one mental state falls under another – for example, 'Toothache is a kind of pain'. Theory T is first reformulated as one long conjunctive sentence having all mental state terms as singular terms. The next step is to replace each of these terms with a variable and to prefix existential quantifiers to the sentence to form the Ramsey sentence of the theory. Let the Ramsey sentence be written as

$$(\exists y_1)(\exists y_2) \ldots (\exists y_n) T(y_1, y_2, \ldots, y_n).$$

If y_i is the variable replacing 'pain', we can now state an explicit definition for 'pain' as follows:

x has pain if, and only if, $(\exists y_1) (\exists y_2) \ldots (\exists y_n) [T(y_1, y_2, \ldots, y_n)$ & x has $y_i]$.

Some functionalists have urged that, if we are to arrive at an accurate account of the essence of pain and other mental states by a procedure of the sort Lewis describes, we should begin not just with our everyday folk psychological theory, but also with what is known to us through scientific psychology. The suggestion, in other words, is that the causal relationships by reference to which pain is to be analyzed should include theoretically discovered relationships in addition to those familiar to us in ordinary, everyday

20 See his "Psycho-physical and Theoretical Identification," *Australasian Journal of Philosophy*, 50 (1972): 249–58; idem, "How to Define Theoretical Terms," *Journal of Philosophy*, 67 (1970): 427–44.

contexts. On this issue, it seems to me that Lewis is correct. Surely if we were to discover creatures who satisfied the common-sense functional criteria for the presence of pain but who failed to satisfy the relevant theoretical criteria (because their "deeper" psychological organization was very different from ours), we would still say that these creatures experienced pain.[21] Scientifically discovered causal relationships, then, form no part of the essence of pain. I might add that the relevant common-sense relationships, on Lewis's view, are formulated by *a priori* reflection on our ordinary use of 'pain' and its applicability in a range of actual and counterfactual cases. According to Lewis, then, 'pain' has an *a priori* definition that specifies its meaning.[22]

If we take this functionalist view for 'pain', what are we to say about such adjectival modifiers as 'intense', 'burning', and 'throbbing'? One view we might take is that modifiers like these cannot be defined. In each case, the role of the modifier is simply to express a single phenomenal quality present in all instances of the relevant kind of pain. This view does not sit well with the functionalist perspective on 'pain' however. Furthermore, it does not seem very plausible. Consider two different burning pains. These pains will likely feel similar, but I doubt that they *have* to do so. What seems to me (and other functionalists) to be crucial if these pains are to count as burning is that they be of a sort typically brought about in the relevant creatures by burning some part of the body. Thus, on this account, if Martians underwent pains that felt just like my most recent burning pain, they would *not* themselves thereby be subject to burning pains unless those pains were of a sort typically caused in Martians by bodily burns (and typically causing beliefs and reports likening them to pains produced in such manner).

The functionalist holds, then, that ordinary, everyday adjectival modifiers of the term 'pain' have functionally specifiable meanings just as 'pain' itself does. So, for example, to say that a pain is intense is (roughly) to say that it tends to elicit a very strong and immediate

---

21 Cf. Ned Block, "Troubles with Functionalism," *Minnesota Studies in the Philosophy of Science,* Vol. 9, ed. C. Savage (Minneapolis: University of Minnesota Press, 1978).

22 This view is also held by D. M. Armstrong and Sydney Shoemaker. See D. M. Armstrong, *Consciousness and Causality* (with Norman Malcolm) (Oxford: Blackwell Publisher, 1984), pp. 140–3; Sydney Shoemaker, "Some Varieties of Functionalism," *Philosophical Topics,* 12 (1981): 93–119.

reaction of dislike. Relatedly, to say that a pain is throbbing is (roughly) to say that its intensity increases and diminishes in a regularly alternating way through time.

One standard objection to functionalism, as I have characterized it above, is that it ignores or overlooks the felt character of pain. For a token state to be a token of pain it must do more than stand in the appropriate causal relationships to other states, inputs, and outputs – it must also feel like a pain. This objection is indecisive. If the objector means that a (token) state cannot feel like a pain unless it has *the* phenomenal quality common to all pains, then no state can feel like a pain; for as I indicated earlier, there is no such quality. If the objector means that a (token) state of pain must have some felt quality, then there is no reason for the functionalist to dispute the claim; for as I noted in my account of the composition of the platitudes composing folk psychology, some of these platitudes will be to the effect that one mental state falls under another. So the sentence 'Pain is a kind of feeling' will be a part of the theory relative to which 'pain' is defined. There are also other relevant platitudes, for example, 'Pain typically causes introspective awareness of its presence' and 'Pain enables one to recognize it when it comes again'. The functionalist, then, can reasonably argue that he has not left out of his account the felt character of pain.

Still, the objector may not be satisfied. Surely, she may say, particular pains have very definite phenomenal qualities even though these qualities are not shared by all pains. These qualities *themselves* are not functionally definable. It seems to me that the philosopher who holds that pain is a functional state should grant that names introduced to designate specific phenomenal qualities have no *a priori* functional definitions. This admission in no way threatens his general position. For such names form no part of our everyday psychological vocabulary and it is the terms of this vocabulary that, according to Lewis, Armstrong, and others, have *a priori* functional definitions. What, then, are such phenomenal qualities, or qualia (assuming for the moment that there are psychological properties generally)?

One reasonable view is that they are physicochemical properties. Another not implausible view is that qualia are internal functional properties, the essences of which are discoverable only by scientific investigation. These functional properties will have inputs and outputs that are specified by neural impulse descriptions. Both views impose restrictions on the possible instantiation of qualia, with the former being the more restrictive of the two. Still, the former view is not as restrictive as it is sometimes supposed. For it no more entails that creatures whose neurophysiology is very different from ours cannot share our qualia than does the claim that temperature is a molecular property entail that humans and electromechanical robots cannot share the same temperature.[23]

The above views have various advantages over the claim that qualia are entirely nonphysical entities. For example, they avoid the problems I raised in Chapter 2 in connection with the emergence and supervenience of nonphysical properties. Admittedly, there are powerful arguments against both accounts of qualia. But as I shall show in Chapter 6, these arguments are not compelling.

It remains to be shown just what comes of the functionalist account of pain within the context of the semantic and metaphysical confines of the operator theory. I shall assume, in what follows, that the relevant semantics is the austere one.[24]

To begin with, it should be recalled that according to the position adopted in Chapter 3, there is (typically) more to meaning than truth conditions or satisfaction conditions. Syntactically structured predicates such as 'is pained burningly' have satisfaction conditions no more complex than unstructured predicates such as 'is pained'. Complexity relevant to meaning arises in conceptual role. The predicate 'is pained burningly' has a conceptual role fixed in part by the predicate 'is pained' and in part by the operator 'burningly'. These conceptual roles, in turn, are given in various platitudinous generalizations. In the case of the predicate 'is pained', some of the relevant generalizations are (very roughly) these:

(27) For any creature x, if x is pained then, ceteris paribus, *the fact that x is pained causes it to be the case that x* is distressed.

(28) For any creature x, and for any stimulus y, if x is pained *because x's*

---

23 Cf. Jaegwon Kim, "Phenomenal Properties, Psycho-physical Laws, and the Identity Theory," *Monist*, 56 (1972): 177–92.

24 In the case of the richer property-function semantics, little need be said: Since mental properties of individuals, such as being pained, are available to serve in place of mental states, such as pain, the reconstruction of functionalism is entirely straightforward. As far as the phenomenal properties of token mental states are concerned, these are replaced by phenomenal properties of individuals. As before, one reasonable view of such properties is that they are physicochemical. Another possibility is that they are internal scientific functional properties of individuals.

body is damaged by y then, ceteris paribus, x moves x's body away from y.

(29) For any creature x, if x's body is damaged then, ceteris paribus, *the fact that x's body is damaged causes it to be the case that x is pained.*[25]

In the case of the operator 'burningly', obvious relevant generalizations are

(30) For any creature x, if some part of x's body is burned then, ceteris paribus, *the fact that x's body is burned causes it to be the case that x is pained burningly*

and

(31) For any person x, if x is pained burningly then, ceteris paribus, *the fact that x is pained burningly causes it to be the case that x believes that some part of x's body is burned.*[26]

My general suggestion, then, is that psychological predicates and operators have their conceptual roles given in the platitudinous generalizations and generalization schemata composing folk psychology.[27] Now, this view of the conceptual roles of psychological predicates and operators obviously fits rather well with the functionalist view of psychological terms proposed by David Lewis. Where I differ from Lewis on the issue of functional definition is with respect to the need to construct the Ramsey sentence of our folk psychological theory. If one believes, as Lewis does, that there are everyday psychological states (such as pain) and psychological

25 The "ceteris paribus" clauses in these and other such generalizations can be elaborated to some extent by introducing specific qualifications. However, I am inclined to think that the resulting, more complicated generalizations will still require "ceteris paribus" clauses. This view is in keeping with my earlier comments in Chapter 3, p. 72.

26 'Burningly', as it applies to 'is pained', has a conceptual role that is fixed by generalizations such as (30) and (31) rather than by generalization *patterns*. This makes it unlike most everyday adverbs, e.g., 'loudly'. See Chapter 3, pp. 71–2. The reason for this difference is simply that 'burningly', in its present sense, is restricted to the modification of the predicate 'is pained' (and also occasionally to the more general predicate 'senses'). Thus, generalization *patterns* are not called for.

27 We shall see later, in Chapter 7, that generalization schemata play a crucial role in giving the meanings of propositional attitude predicates and operators. Very briefly, this is because if we hold that psychological predicates are implicitly defined *only* by platitudinous generalizations then the fact that there are infinitely many belief predicates, for example, will require us to admit infinitely many *meaning-giving* platitudinous generalizations. Once generalization schemata are introduced, however, no such admission is necessary, since a finite number of schemata can have an infinite number of instances.

properties (such as being in pain), one must face the question as to their nature. Thus, if one is a functionalist, one will hold that such states and properties are functional entities and, by necessity, one will also hold that explicit functional definitions of the corresponding psychological terms are possible. If one's functionalism is *a priori*, like that of Lewis, one will take these definitions to give the meaning of the psychological terms. Now, what Lewis has shown is that, once one constructs the Ramsey sentence of a psychological theory, it is a trivial matter to state explicit definitions for mental state (or property) terms. If, however, one denies that there are any real, nonlinguistic psychological states or properties, as I do, then no question arises as to their nature. And there is no motivation to try to construct explicit definitions. Instead, one can rest content with *implicit* definitions. The only question one faces, then, on an approach of the sort I advocate is the question of how psychological predicates, be they adverbially modified or not, are assigned extensions. The answer, I suggest, is that the extension assignments are constrained by the holistic requirement that all (or nearly all) the various folk psychological generalizations must come out true.[28]

It may perhaps be objected that the generalizations of folk psychology, taken as a group, form such a complex net that it is entirely implausible to suppose that they give the meanings of psychological predicates. After all, each of us knows the meaning of common or garden-variety psychological terms; but few of us can produce the relevant underlying meaning-giving generalizations off the cuff. This objection is unsound. On my view, knowing the meaning, *qua* conceptual role, of a psychological predicate, for example, 'is in pain', is essentially a matter of being able to use the predicate correctly. One has the ability to use 'is in pain' correctly insofar as one has a complex set of dispositions to assert and assent to sentences of the type '*x* is in pain' *only* when those sentences are being used in a way that conforms with the appropriate folk psychological generalizations. Possession of such dispositions clearly does not

28 Might there not remain ineliminable indeterminacy with respect to extension assignments? I concede that it is a possibility. But as I noted in Chapter 3, I think it unlikely that there will be two or more interpretation schemes that meet the stated requirement and that are also equally *natural* (in David Lewis's sense of the term 'natural'). Since I hold that naturalness makes for truth, other things being equal, I doubt that there is ineliminable indeterminacy. See note 26, Chapter 3, and the references therein. See also my discussion of naturalness in Chapter 5, note 36 and the relevant text.

require one to be able to state the underlying generalizations upon request.[29]

As to the objection that my proposal leaves out the felt character of pain, my reply runs parallel to that given earlier. One of the platitudes forming part of the theory relative to which 'pain' is defined is 'Pain is a feeling'. This platitude can be reconstructed, on my view, as the following generalization:

(32) Any creature who is pained thereby feels.

And (32) can itself be restated as

(32a) For any creature x, if x is pained then (x is pained *and thereby* x feels).

The other platitudes cited earlier, which connect pain with the desire that it cease, with the introspective awareness of pain, and with the recognition of pain when it comes again, will also be relevant (in reconstructed form) to the conceptual role of the predicate 'is pained'. Hence, I maintain, nothing is left out by my position.

If I am now asked, "But just what are the phenomenal properties of particular pains, on your view?" I reject the question. It presupposes that there are phenomenal properties of particular pains, and not only do I deny that there are any pains, I also deny that there are any psychological properties, phenomenal or otherwise. Does this mean that I am denying that ordinary talk of knowing what it is like to feel pain is unintelligible? No it does not. What I deny is that this talk requires the existence of phenomenal properties for its intelligibility. The predicate 'knows what it is like to feel pain' will be true of any given creature c, it seems to me, just in case either c is pained and c is introspectively aware that c is pained or c is able to remember having been pained. This account preserves our basic intuition that one cannot know what it is like to feel pain unless one has actually been in pain. But it does not depend on there being any such entities as phenomenal properties.[30]

29 This point parallels the one made earlier in Chapter 3, p. 72.
30 In Chapter 6, I present and defend an analysis of knowing what it is like to be in a state having a phenomenal quality Q. This analysis, which obviously presupposes the existence of phenomenal qualities, is offered in an attempt to show that, even if one countenances such qualities, one is not compelled to concede that they are irreducibly nonphysical. The present suggestion with respect to the predicate 'knows what it is like to feel pain' derives from the discussion in Chapter 6, note 11 and the relevant text.

I want, in concluding this section, to say something about the issue of multiple physical realizability. Functionalists generally have been prepared to grant that pain and other psychological states may be realized by any number of different physicochemical states. This is because what is crucial, according to functionalism, to the application of the term 'pain' to any given state is its functional role. Thus, there is no *a priori* reason to deny that there could be creatures who feel pain but who are subject to physicochemical states quite unlike ours. On my view, there is no state of pain and there are no physicochemical states. So what happens to the issue of multiple realizability? Well, nothing in the conceptual role of the predicate 'is pained' prevents its satisfaction set from including creatures whose physiology is radically different from ours. So there is no *a priori* reason to insist that 'is pained' cannot apply to such creatures.

III

In this final section, I take up certain residual objections to my earlier account of pain location. The objections I am concerned with are those I myself raised in an earlier article[31] to standard causal accounts of pain location. I now wish to show that these objections create no insuperable difficulties for my present view.

A consequence of my claims in Section I is that generalizations of the following sort are true:

(33) For any person x, and for any limb y, if y belongs to x and y is damaged and x is pained *because* y is damaged then, ceteris paribus, x is pained in y.

(34) For any person x and for any (real) limb y, if x is pained in y then, ceteris paribus, some part of y is damaged.

The objections I shall consider are all directed against (33) and/or (34).

Consider first this objection. Suppose Jones's right leg was amputated in early childhood and that since that time Jones has regularly suffered from pains in his phantom right leg. Here the pains that Jones experiences are normally caused by disturbances in his stump. Hence, given (33), it seems to follow that, on the occasions

31 See my 'Pain and the Adverbial Theory,' p. 324.

of such disturbance, Jones is pained in his right stump. This surely is false.

This objection overlooks the fact that the predicate 'is damaged' is used in (33) and not the predicate 'is disturbed'. Furthermore, even if the objection is revised to accommodate this fact, it remains ineffective. Statement (33) utilizes a "ceteris paribus" clause. Hence, what follows from (33) in the given case is not that on the relevant occasions of disturbance Jones is pained in his right stump, but rather that on those occasions, ceteris paribus, Jones is pained in his right stump. Now part of what is involved in the "ceteris paribus" of (33), in my view, is the requirement that x be a typical fully embodied person. Since Jones is not a typical fully embodied person, the fact that certain pains are caused in him by disturbances in his stump is therefore irrelevant to my proposal.

Another apparent problem case is provided by certain disturbances in the heart. These disturbances typically cause pains in the left arm and neck and *not* pains in the heart. This objection, like the last one, presents no direct threat to (33), since (33) speaks of damage and not of disturbance. Moreover, although it may be true that certain specific sorts of damage to the heart typically cause pains in the arm and neck, it is not true that heart damage of *any* sort typically causes such pains. Thus, it seems reasonable to say that the "ceteris paribus" clause in (33) should be taken to include the general qualification 'it is usually the case that' rather than the qualification 'when there is a certain sort of disturbance (or damage), it is usually the case that', as the objection seems to presuppose. And what goes here for (33) goes also for (34).

A third problem case can be brought out by imagining a futuristic community of masochists whose pains are typically brought about by their owners' directly stimulating the appropriate neural centers. Here the masochists will feel pains about their bodies without those pains being typically caused by damage to the relevant bodily limbs.

This case clearly does not undermine the claim that (33) is true, for what (33) requires is (roughly) that people who feel pain *as a result of* damage to their right leg usually are pained in their right leg. In the case of (34), the issue again hinges on how the "ceteris paribus" clause is to be understood. It seems to me that the requirement that x be a typical person should be interpreted as having a context-dependent sense better captured by the requirement that

x be a typical person within the relevant population group.[32] Once we adopt this interpretation, we should take the relevant population group to be one relative to which the community of masochists is either atypical or excluded altogether. For example, we could take the relevant group to be made up of *all* persons in the futuristic world whether or not they belong to the community of masochists. Alternatively, we could require that the relevant group be made up of persons whose pains are not artificially induced. Given either of these background groups with which to restrict the range of the variable 'x' in 'x is a typical person', the imagined community of masochists no longer furnishes counterexamples to (34).

This completes my account of the operator theory for the case of pain. The theory can be extended to other bodily sensations without difficulty and also, farther afield, to moods and emotions. In the case of perceptual sensations, however, new problems arise. The application of the operator theory in this context will occupy us in the next chapter.

32 Cf. David Lewis, "Mad Pain and Martian Pain," in *Readings in the Philosophy of Psychology*, Vol. 1, ed. Ned Block (Cambridge, Mass: Harvard University Press, 1980).

5

Perceptual sensation

Traditionally, the most popular analysis of perceptual experience has been the sense-datum theory. According to this theory, having a perceptual experience amounts to standing in a relation of direct perceptual awareness to a special immaterial entity. In particular visual cases (those most frequently addressed), this entity is called an afterimage or a mirage or an appearance and, in the general case, a sense impression or a sense datum. We saw in Chapter 3 not only that the arguments for this theory are uncompelling, but also that it encounters a host of puzzles and problems. Historically, the adverbial theory of perceptual sensations grew out of a dissatisfaction with the sense-datum theory. Usually, adverbial theorists arrived at their view by reflecting on the fact that, on standard views, appearances, afterimages, and so on cannot exist when not sensed by some person. The explanation adverbial theorists offered for this fact is that statements purporting to be about appearances, afterimages, and so on are in reality statements about the way or mode in which some person is sensing.

Although the adverbial approach to perceptual experience has a broad following, the versions of it that are to be found in the literature are typically either superficial or open to serious objections. My primary aim in this chapter is to show how the adverbially based operator theory can be applied to the task of understanding perceptual experience. A secondary aim is to offer a critical examination of two other theories, each of which has some right to be classified as adverbial, and to argue that the operator theory is the most promising of the three. At the end of the chapter, I shall make some remarks from a functionalist perspective on how I view perceptual experience. I should add that throughout the chapter I shall focus on the case of visual experience (as is usual in philosophical discussions of perceptual sensations). But I intend what I say to apply mutatis mutandis to other kinds of perceptual experience.

I

The first adverbial theory I wish to examine, the unstructured predicate theory, has it that statements about how persons sense, that is, statements of the type

(1) Person x senses F-ly,

are to be analyzed as quantifier-free subject–predicate statements, the predicates of which are semantically simple. This approach can be extended to cover statements about specific types of sensing, for example,

(2) Jones hallucinates a red circular object.[1]

Since a sensing is a hallucination only if it has been caused in a certain way, (2) is regimented, on the unstructured predicate view, as

(2a) Rj because Hj,

where 'R' abbreviates the predicate 'senses-in-a-red-circular-manner', 'j' names Jones, and 'H' expresses the causal factors in hallucinations.[2]

Metaphysically, the general suggestion here is that for a person to have a visual experience it suffices that there be a person who satisfies the appropriate unstructured sensory predicate. Thus, on this theory, there is no sensory object that is required for the experience to take place: There is merely the person who is sensing.

The unstructured predicate view faces a number of difficulties. Consider, for example, the following statements:

---

1 It is perhaps worth noting that, to my knowledge, no adverbial theorist holds that statements of the type 'Person x sees an object that is F' can be true even if there is no real F object that x sees. The adverbial approach is offered for statements of the type 'x has a sensation of an F object', 'x hallucinates an F object', 'x seems to see an F object', i.e., sensory statements that can be true even if there is no real appropriate object in the offing. This simple point is sometimes missed by critics of the adverbial theory. See, e.g., Jon Barwise, "Scenes and Other Situations," *Journal of Philosophy*, 78 (1981): 388–9. For more on the analysis of seeing, see my "Causal Analysis of Seeing," *Philosophy and Phenomenological Research*, 42 (1982): 311–25.
2 'Because' in (2a) is a sentential connective.

103

(3) Jones has a sensation of a circle.
(4) Jones has a sensation of a triangle.

One important feature that (3) and (4) share is that both entail

(5) Jones has a sensation.

It can be argued that the unstructured predicate theory fails to explain this shared feature, since (3)–(5) are analyzed, respectively, as

(3a) Cj,
(4a) Tj,

and

(5a) Sj,

where 'C', 'T', and 'S' are three entirely distinct monadic predicates.[3]

The unstructured predicate view also leaves mysterious the entailment from (2) to

(6) Jones hallucinates a red object.

This difficulty, of course, is well known. It is part of a more general problem called the many-property problem, to which I shall return in Sections II and III.[4]

Another problem worth noting is posed by the following statements:

(7) The red afterimage Jones has is the same as the circular afterimage Jones has.
(8) Jones has a red and circular afterimage.

Statement (7) entails (8). On the sense-datum theory of visual experience this inference is explained easily enough. But on adverbial approaches the inference seems to present a problem (let us call it the "identity problem");[5] for there are no sensory objects, no afterimages, in terms of which the inference can be understood.

I suppose someone sympathetic to the adverbial position might

---

3 A criticism along these lines is found in Robert Kraut, "Sensory States and Sensory Objects," *Nous*, 16 (1982): 277–95.

4 See Frank Jackson, "On the Adverbial Analysis of Visual Experience," *Metaphilosophy*, 6 (1975): 127–35.

5 This problem was first raised by Wilfrid Sellars. See his "On the Objects of the Adverbial Theory of Sensation," *Metaphilosophy*, 6 (1975): 144–60, esp. 155–60.

be tempted to argue that since there neither are nor could be any such entities as sense data, be they afterimages or appearances, (7) is necessarily false. The inference from (7) to (8), therefore, is trivially valid, since anything follows from a necessary falsehood.

It seems to me that this is confused, for at least two reasons. First, we can well imagine occasions on which ordinary speakers would accept that (7) is true. Consider, for example, the following case. Jones takes part in an experiment, during the course of which some bright lights are shone into his eyes. Upon looking away, Jones reports that he has two afterimages, which are red, blue, circular, and square. Jones is then asked whether the red afterimage is the same as the circular one. He replies "yes." In these circumstances, Jones has assented to (7), and unless there were some reason to doubt Jones's veracity, any nonphilosopher hearing the question and reply would surely accept that (7) is true. It is therefore entirely counterintuitive for the adverbial theorist to try to undercut the identity problem by maintaining that (7) is necessarily false.

Second, the claim that there neither are nor could be any afterimages does not entail that (7) is necessarily false, any more than the claim that there neither is nor could be any such entity as a sake entails that

(9) Smith fought for the sake of his country

is necessarily false. Grammar is sometimes misleading. As far as the identity problem is concerned, therefore, the first task for the adverbial theorist is to produce an analysis of the logical form of (7) that explains how (7) can be true. This accomplished, the remaining task is to show how, given this analysis, (7) entails (8).

It is, I think, quite obvious that the unstructured predicate view lacks sufficient resources to do justice to (7). Consequently, the identity problem cannot be solved by our first adverbial theory.

There appear to be two ways to try to overcome the difficulties faced by the unstructured predicate view without giving up the basic adverbial approach. One strategy is to accept that statements about how persons sense are quantifier-free subject–predicate statements while denying that the predicates in these statements are semantically simple. Another strategy is to reject the assumption that the sensing statements of the adverbial theory are quantifier-free. In the next section, I shall address what seems to me to be the only worthwhile version of the latter strategy.

The basic idea of this approach is that statements about how persons sense are to be analyzed as existential quantifications over particular, concrete sensings or sensory events.[6]

Perhaps the simplest way for me to motivate this event version of the adverbial theory is to try to draw a parallel between (7) and

(10) The seductive smile Mary is smiling is the same as the smile Mary is directing at Paul.

At first glance, (10) seems to identify a certain object, namely a seductive smile, which Mary is related to through the 'smiling' relation with another such object. But arguably (10) is somewhat misleading; for it seems reasonable to maintain that there are no smiles that are objects of smiling – there are only the smilings themselves. Statement (10), then, really identifies events, and what it says is

(10a) The event of Mary's smiling seductively = the event of Mary's smiling at Paul.

The adverbial theorist can maintain that (7) is like (10). Hence, on this view (7) is really concerned with events (i.e., afterimagings or sensings, not afterimages), and what it says, given an adverbial analysis of sensory adjectives, is

(7a) The event of Jones's sensing redly = the event of Jones's sensing circularly.

It seems to me that the parallel drawn here between (7) and (10) is plausible. One reason for appealing to events, therefore, in the analysis of visual experience is the belief that, if the basic adverbial approach is correct, statements like (7) are to be understood along the lines sketched above for statements like (10). Let us now see how the event theory solves the earlier puzzles, beginning with the identity problem.

Given an adverbial event analysis, the earlier statement (8) becomes

---

6 James Cornman adopts an event view in the adverbial analysis he presents in *Materialism and Sensations* (New Haven, Conn.: Yale University Press, 1971), pp. 178, 185–90. However, Cornman's discussion is very sketchy indeed, and none of the semantical issues is fully addressed.

(8a) $(\exists x)(x =$ the event of Jones's sensing redly and circularly).[7]

Statement (8a), in turn, can be analyzed further as

(8b) $(\exists x)($Jones is the subject of x & x is a sensing-redly & x is a sensing-circularly).[8]

Similarly, (7a) can be regimented as

(7b) $(\exists x)(\exists y)\{$Jones is the subject of x and x is a sensing-redly & Jones is the subject of y & y is a sensing-circularly & $(z)[($Jones is the subject of z & z is a sensing-redly$) \supset z = x]$ & $(w)[($Jones is the subject of w & w is a sensing-circularly$) \supset w = y]$ & $x = y\}$.

The inference from (7b) to (8b) is valid in virtue of its logical form. Hence, the entailment from (7) to (8) is now explained.

This response to the identity problem naturally raises at least three questions. First, what account is to be given of the nature of the events quantified over in (7b) and (8b)? Are we, for example, committed to holding that events are Davidsonian particulars without any constitutive properties? Second, what explanation can be offered of the meanings of the event-characterizing sortal predicates 'is a sensing-redly' and 'is a sensing-circularly'? This question is a pressing one, since the terms 'redly' and 'circularly' as they occur in these contrived predicates are certainly not functioning as adverbs that modify in a straightforward way 'is a sensing'. After all, redly and circularly are ways of sensing, not ways of being a sensing. Third, what principle of counting underlies the formalization of (8) by (8a) [and (8b)] rather than by

(8c) $(\exists x)(\exists y)(x =$ the event of Jones's sensing redly & $y =$ the event of Jones's sensing circularly)?

This question, I might add, is of crucial importance to the many-property problem, as we shall shortly see.

With respect to the first question, it seems to me that (7b) and (8b) certainly do not *entail* that events are particulars lacking constitutive properties. All that these analyses require is that the constitu-

---

7 This is to oversimplify a little. Statement (8a), unlike (8), will be true if, for example, Jones has a visual sensation of a red circular object as a result of looking at a red circular disk in standard circumstances. This shortcoming is easily rectified, however, by the addition of a clause that specifies the causal ancestry appropriate to having an afterimage. I have ignored this qualification in (8a) [and (7a) as well as the following analyses] for ease of exposition.

8 I assume in (8b) (and all other event analyses in this section) that the variables are restricted to events.

tive properties of sensory events not be sensory properties like sensing redly. One might hold, for example, that events are complexes of objects exemplifying properties at times, where the relevant constitutive properties are nomologically congruous microphysical properties. Then sensory properties exemplified by persons, for example, sensing redly, can be taken to be identical with such properties as being the subject of an event that is a sensing-redly, where being a sensing-redly is an event-characterizing property that supervenes on the appropriate microphysical properties.[9]

If sensory events are conceived of as complexes of sentient creatures exemplifying properties at times, these events lose their independent metaphysical status. Sensory events are now entities that, by their very nature, could not exist without sentient creatures, entities that have the creatures undergoing them as literal constituents. These entities, I might add, have every right to be viewed as concrete particulars; for they exist only in those possible worlds in which their subjects exist. Furthermore, they can be spatially located wherever their subjects are so located.[10]

With these brief comments I hope I have said enough to provide a fairly clear sketch of one possible approach to the nature of sensory events. I turn now to the question of explicating the meaning of the event-characterizing sortal predicates such as 'is a sensing-redly'.

Here one reasonable account (in first approximation) is as follows. An event e is a sensing-F-ly if, and only if, e is a sensing of a type that is usually brought about in normal perceivers by their viewing F objects in standard circumstances and that usually causes those perceivers to believe that there is an F object present.[11] On

---

9 There are theories of events in the literature that spell out this line in some detail. See, e.g., Terence Horgan, "Humean Causation and Kim's Theory of Events," *Canadian Journal of Philosophy*, 10 (1980): 663–79.

10 For more on this approach to the location of events, see Jaegwon Kim, "Events as Property Exemplifications," in *Action Theory*, ed. Myles Brand and Douglas Walton (Dordrecht: Reidel, 1976), pp. 159–77.

11 Since this account of what it is for an event to be a sensing-F-ly involves no adverbs, it may be questioned whether the event theory is really an adverbial view. It seems to me that this issue is largely terminological. If we define an adverbial theory of sensation rather narrowly as one that retains irreducible adverbs in its final regimentations of sensation statements, then the proposed event theory is not adverbial (nor, I might add, is the unstructured predicate view). However, if we define an adverbial theory of sensation more loosely as a theory that is initially arrived at through the use of adverbial transformations, whether or not it then goes on to give any further reductive analysis of sensory

this view, the predicate 'is a sensing-redly', for example, really means 'is a red sensing', where 'red' is a concealed description with a comparative normal cause connotation. There is, I think, one main advantage to this approach: It explains how there can be a conceptual connection between the redness of an afterimage and the redness of a physical object without violating the intuitive claim that when we say that an afterimage is red we are not attributing to it the very property we attribute to a physical object when we say that it is red.

Turning finally to the question of counting, the general thinking underlying the regimentation of (8) by (8a) and (8b) is simple enough: Statements seemingly about afterimages or appearances are reconstructed, on the event version of the adverbial theory, as statements about sensory events, just as statements seemingly about smiles can be reconstructed as statements about smilings. Hence, the analyses offered by the advocate of the event theory should contain existential quantifiers over as many sensory events as there seem to be sensory objects existentially quantified over in the ordinary, everyday statements about visual experience that are being analyzed. In the case of (8), for example, the obvious sensory object analysis is

(8d) $(\exists x)(x$ is an afterimage & x is red & x is circular & Jones has $x)$.

Hence, in the event analysis of (8), there should be an existential quantifier over an event that is both a sensing-redly and a sensing-circularly, as in (8b).

There are some difficult questions lurking here for the event theory, which I shall put aside for the moment in order to see how the theory handles the remaining problems raised in Section I. Let us examine first the many-property problem. This problem, in brief, is to explain how

(2) Jones hallucinates a red circular object

can entail

(6) Jones hallucinates a red object

without collapsing the distinction between

adverbs, then the event theory is adverbial. In this chapter, for purposes of classification I am assuming that the latter definition is operative.

(11) Jones hallucinates a red circular object and a blue triangular object

and

(12) Jones hallucinates a blue circular object and a red triangular object.

Consider, to begin with, statement (11). This seems to involve existential quantifiers over two distinct hallucinated objects. Hence, on the event theory, the regimentation of (11) requires existential quantifiers over two distinct events as follows:

(11a) $(\exists x)(\exists y)$(Jones is the subject of x & x is a sensing-redly & x is a sensing-circularly & Jones is the subject of y & y is a sensing-bluely & y is a sensing-triangularly & $x \neq y$).[12]

Similarly, (12) is regimented as

(12a) $(\exists x)(\exists y)$(Jones is the subject of x & x is a sensing-bluely & x is a sensing-circularly & Jones is the subject of y & y is a sensing-redly and y is a sensing-triangularly & $x \neq y$).

Statements (12a) and (11a) are not equivalent. Hence, the difference between (11) and (12) is preserved. Furthermore, it is patently clear that the inference from (2) to (6) is revealed as valid on the event theory. Hence, the many-property problem is solved.

It may be objected that the proposed regimentations of (11) and (12) are incorrect, since they require that one and the same person be the subject of two simultaneous (visual) sensings – which is impossible. But it seems to me no less possible for a person to undergo two simultaneous (visual) sensings than it is for a person to be on the receiving end of two simultaneous punches or stabbings. After all, having a visual sensation is normally something that happens to one, given the appropriate stimuli (rather than something one consciously does). Why, then, shouldn't one be caused to undergo two simultaneous visual sensings (by, e.g., looking at two bright lights and turning away) just as one can be caused to undergo simultaneous tactual and visual sensations (by, e.g., touching an object in one's line of sight)?

I come next to the problem of explaining the entailment from

(3) Jones has a sensation of a circle

---

12 Of course, a sensing cannot be a hallucination unless it is caused in an appropriate way. Hence, (11a) [and (12a)] should really include appropriate causal clauses. I take these clauses to be understood.

and

(4) Jones has a sensation of a triangle

to

(5) Jones has a sensation.

The event theory formalizes (3) by

(3b) $(\exists x)$(Jones is the subject of x & x is a sensing-circularly)

and (4) by

(4b) $(\exists x)$(Jones is the subject of x & x is a sensing-triangularly).

Since being a sensing is part and parcel of being a sensing-F-ly, for any given F, both (3b) and (4b) entail

(5b) $(\exists x)$(Jones is the subject of x & x is a sensing).

Hence, the problem is solved.

I want now to take up the questions about individuation that I put aside earlier. Consider first the question of identity through time for sensing-events. Suppose I blink my eyes while viewing a white patch on a wall. Are there then two (or more) sensings, on the event theory, or only one interrupted one? Alternatively, suppose I view a patch that continuously changes its color. Is there a single sensing-event that constantly changes its 'color' qualitative character, or are there many different successive sensing-events? These questions cannot be answered in the way I suggested a few pages earlier by counting sensory objects, for as we saw in Chapter 2, exactly the same questions arise with respect to sensory objects.[13]

What I suggest the event theorist should say here is that sensory events are always momentary (even if they appear to persist through time without changing). This position, which directly follows from the view that sensory events are complexes of creatures exemplifying properties at times, requires us to modify the general principle of counting that we use for sensings. The revised principle can be stated as follows. (i) At any given time t a person undergoes as many sensory events at t as there appear to be sensory objects existentially quantified over in the true statements describing the

---

13 W. H. F. Barnes, "The Myth of Sense-Data," in *Perceiving, Sensing, and Knowing*, ed. R. J. Swartz (Garden City, N.Y.: Doubleday/Anchor, 1965), p. 150.

person's visual experience at t; (ii) no sensory event exists at more than one time.

Unfortunately, problems of individuation still arise even for this modified principle. Suppose, for example, I have a visual field, half of which is red and half blue. Should we say here, on the event theory, that I am subject to one sensing-event or two? Counting sensory objects at a time does not seem to help answer this question, since we can equally well say that there is one sensory object, half red and half blue, or two sensory objects, one red and one blue.[14]

Another problem case that is no less puzzling raises the issue of determinacy for sensings. Suppose I see a tiger in the distance, and it appears to me to have numerous stripes (though no definite number). How many sensings do I undergo? One for each apparent stripe? But as far as I am aware, there is no definite number of apparent stripes. Once again, then, counting sensory objects, even at a single time, is of little help to the event theory.

It seems to me that these last two problem cases bring out a serious weakness in the present version of the adverbial theory. Any sound motivation for adopting an adverbial approach to visual experience must surely include the desire to avoid the sorts of puzzles that plague the sense-datum theory. Unfortunately, it now appears that questions exactly like some of those that historically led many philosophers to reject the sense-datum theory must be taken seriously by the advocate of the event view. Furthermore, if events are individuated in much the same way as sensory objects or sensa, then with respect to some important issues, the event theory stands or falls with the sense-datum theory. Of course, the event theorist may yet be able to construct an alternative principle of individuation that not only avoids any appeal to the number of sensa, but also settles the above problem cases. It is not easy to see what this alternative principle would look like, however. There is also the point that without any link between the apparent number of sensa and the actual number of sensing-events, the earlier parallel between the case of smiling and the case of sensing collapses. This means that there is no reason to adopt the earlier formalizations (7) and (8) and the subsequent solution to the identity problem.[15]

14 Ibid., p. 151.
15 It should be noted too that the proposed solution to the many-property problem requires a numerical link between sensa and sensings.

I conclude that the event version of the adverbial theory of perceptual sensations is not entirely satisfactory, *even if* my earlier arguments against the existence of mental events are put to one side. I turn in the next section to what is, I believe, the best approach to perceptual experience.

III

The general semantic and metaphysical framework of the operator theory has already been explained. My aim now is to show that the application of the theory to perceptual experience is without any obvious difficulties. To this end, I propose to investigate how the operator theory fares with the problems distinguished in Section I.

Consider, for example, the earlier question of explaining the entailments from statements (3) and (4) to (5). On the operator view, (3) is regimented as

(3c) $[\mathbf{C}]Sj$

and (4) as

(4c) $[\mathbf{T}]Sj,$

where '$\mathbf{C}$' and '$\mathbf{T}$' are the operators 'circularly' and 'triangularly' and 'S' is as before. Both (3c) and (4c) entail

(5c) Sj

via the operator detachment rule

(OD) $[\mathbf{O}]Fx \rightarrow Fx.$[16]

Hence, the inferences from (3) and (4) to (5) are successfully validated.

Turning next to the problem of explaining the entailment from

(2) Jones hallucinates a red circular object

to

(6) Jones hallucinates a red object,

---

16 For a discussion of (OD), see Chapter 3, Section II.

our initial question is how to analyze (2) on the operator theory. It seems reasonable to assume initially that (2) is equivalent to

(2b) Jones senses redly and circularly.[17]

However, we cannot rewrite (2b) as

(2c) [**R**]Sj & [**C**]Sj,

since (2c) says the same as

(2d) Jones senses redly and Jones senses circularly.

And (2d), unlike (2), will be true if, for example, Jones hallucinates two objects, one red and square, the other blue and circular.

Suppose, then, we formalize (2b) as

(2e) [**R𝒻C**]Sj.

Here '**R𝒻C**' is a compound operator in which the two-place conjuctive operator '𝒻' operates on the predicate operators '**R**' and '**C**'. This operator is subject to the standard operator detachment rule (OD). It is also subject to the standard operator simplification rules

(OS_1) [**O𝓜N**]$Fx \rightarrow$ [**O**]Fx,
(OS_2) [**O𝓜N**]$Fx \rightarrow$ [**N**]Fx.

The inference from (2) to (6) now goes through, since the formalized counterpart of (6), namely

(6a) [**R**]Sj,

is entailed by (2e).

The trouble with this maneuver is that it is not clear how (2e) and (2c) differ. It does not help to say that '**R𝒻C**' expresses an operation that maps the property of sensing onto the property of sensing redly and circularly, since a question still arises as to how the latter property differs from the conjuctive property of sensing

---

17 Strictly speaking, a causal clause should be added to the end of (2b). As with the unstructured predicate view, this clause will take the form 'because . . .', where the ellipsis points are filled by a sentence describing the causal factors in hallucinations and 'because' is a sentential connective. The adverb 'visually' should also be appended to the verb 'senses'. I shall take such additions as understood in all the analyses of statements about hallucinations hereafter. I shall do likewise mutatis mutandis for analyses of statements about afterimages.

redly and sensing circularly.[18] It appears, then, that we have merely assumed a difference between (2e) and (2c) without explaining it.

One way of supporting the claim that (2e) and (2c) are not equivalent is to find some uncontroversial examples in ordinary English of parallel nonequivalences. But this is no easy task. One possible example, suggested by Terence Parsons,[19] is provided by the following two statements:

(13) John wrote painstakingly and illegibly.
(14) John wrote painstakingly and John wrote illegibly.

According to Parsons, (13) and (14) are not equivalent (even assuming a single time of writing), since John may have written painstakingly with one hand and illegibly with the other.

Frank Jackson has argued persuasively against Parsons here.[20] In brief, Jackson's response is that if 'John wrote F-ly' is to count as true if any part of John's writing was F, then not only (14) but also (13) is true in the case Parsons describes, whereas if 'John wrote F-ly' is to count as true only if most of John's writing was F, then 'John wrote F-ly with one hand' does not entail 'John wrote F-ly', and hence the given case fails to establish that (14) may be true without (13) being true.

Even if this argument is not successful, as Jackson notes, the case of (13) and (14) is of no real help; for any attempt to distinguish the meanings of these sentences (assuming a single time of writing) must rely heavily on the fact that there is in addition to Jones another concrete entity, namely his hand, whereas in the case of (2c) and (2e) there is, according to the operator theory, no concrete entity other than Jones.

I am not aware of any other examples from ordinary English that could be used to support the view that (2c) and (2e) are not

18 Nor does it help much to say that (2c) permits different times of sensing while (2e) requires a single time. It is a simple enough matter to introduce explicit temporal operators into (2c) that guarantee one shared time of sensing. Still, there supposedly remains a difference between (2c), so revised, and (2e) with respect to the case where Jones hallucinates two objects simultaneously, one red and the other circular. This difference is the crucial one, and it is yet to be explained. Hereafter, my references to (2c) take it for granted that (2c) is temporally restricted in the above way.

19 Terence Parsons, "Some Problems Concerning the Logic of Grammatical Modifiers," in *Semantics of Natural Language*, ed. D. Davidson and G. Harman (Dordrecht: Reidel, 1972), p. 131.

20 See Frank Jackson, *Perception* (Cambridge University Press, 1977), pp. 69–71.

equivalent. In the absence of such examples, it may appear that the operator view of perceptual experience rests on very shaky ground indeed.

There is a way out, however, even if (2c) and (2e) do not significantly differ. What must be rejected is the initial assumption that (2) is equivalent to (2b). I want next to consider three alternative analyses of (2), each of which is consistent with the general operator theory.

One possible approach is to analyze (2) as

(2f) Jones senses redly and he does that circularly

or formally as

(2g) $[\mathbf{C}][\mathbf{R}]Sj$.

Since the modifier detachment rule (OD) can be extended to iterated adverbial constructions, the inference from (2) to (7) is explained on this analysis via detachment of the operator '$\mathbf{C}$'.

Although this proposal appears quite promising, it is, I believe, ultimately unsatisfactory. Let me explain. In many cases, the order of adverbs in an iterated construction alters its meaning. Suppose, for example, that Jones spoke carefully but without any intention of speaking tediously. Suppose also that as it happened Jones's speech was tedious. Then

(15) Jones spoke tediously and he did that carefully

or

(15a) Jones carefully spoke tediously

is false. But

(16) Jones spoke carefully and he did that tediously

or

(16a) Jones tediously spoke carefully

is true. To appreciate the relevance of this point, it should be noted that the order of the predicates 'red' and 'circular' in (2) makes no difference at all to its meaning. Thus, on the above proposal, (2g) ought to mean the same as

(2h) $[\mathbf{R}][\mathbf{C}]Sj$.

116

A question arises, therefore, as to why there should be an equivalence in this case when there is not in a case like that of (15) and (16). One possible explanation is that the permutation of adverbs of manner in iterated constructions is permissible if, and only if, none of the adverbs has an intentional connotation. This seems to fit the cases at hand and, so far as I can tell, it also works elsewhere. Consider, for example, the following two statements:

(17) The bomb destructively exploded loudly.
(18) The bomb loudly exploded destructively.

It seems to me that (17) and (18), unlike (15a) and (16a), are equivalent.

The problem that lies hidden here for the operator theory is that in those cases where permutation of adverbs of manner is permissible it is, I believe, always possible to rewrite the adverbs conjunctively. In the case of (17) and (18), for example, I can think of no situations in which either of these statements has a different truth value from

(19) The bomb exploded destructively and loudly.[21]

Consequently, if (2g) is equivalent to (2h), as it must be if it is to serve as an analysis of (2), then (2g) says no more than (2e). Hence, the operator theorist has failed to come up with a genuine alternative to the first proposal.[22]

Another possible approach to (2) is to try to model its analysis on a statement like

21 I suppose it might be objected that if the destructiveness of the bomb's explosion was responsible for its loudness but not conversely, then (18) is true but (17) false. I find this objection unconvincing. It seems to me that what (17) says is merely that the bomb exploded loudly and it did that destructively, not that the bomb exploded loudly and it thereby in virtue of the loudness exploded destructively. Hence, according to my intuitions, (17) is true in the above situation. Still even if there is disagreement here, what is directly threatened is not the general principle that where permutation of adverbs of manner is permissible it is always possible to rewrite the adverbs conjunctively, but rather the claim that permutation of adverbs of manner in iterated constructions is permissible if, and only if, none of the adverbs has an intentional connotation; for clearly if (17) *is* false in the above situation, then by similar reasoning (18) is true and the permutation of the adverbs in (17) must be disallowed.

22 It is perhaps worth adding here that any philosopher who takes the extreme view that adverbs of manner in iterated constructions are never permutable is in no position to analyze (2) as (2g). This is because, as I have already indicated, (2g) can serve as an analysis of (2) only if it is equivalent to (2h).

(20) Jones speaks excessively angrily.

What distinguishes (22) from the above iterated constructions is that 'excessively' modifies 'angrily' (rather than 'speaks' or 'speaks angrily'), thereby forming the compound adverb 'excessively angrily'. Applying this approach to (2), we get

(2i) Jones senses redly circularly.

This proposal faces two difficulties. First, there seems to be no nonarbitrary way of deciding which adverb modifies which in (2i). Should we say 'redly' modifies 'circularly', or vice versa? Suppose that somehow this question is settled and the former option is chosen. Then a second problem arises. In the earlier statement

(6) Jones hallucinates a red object,

'red', according to the operator theory, is a predicate operator, but in (2) 'red' is now held not to be a *predicate* operator at all. This has the counterintuitive consequence that 'red' has a different role in (2) and (6). It also makes the entailment from (2) to (6) entirely mysterious.

It seems to me that these objections, taken together, are compelling.[23] I shall therefore pass on to the third alternative analysis of (2). This analysis, which I accept, requires some preliminary stage setting.

If Jones hallucinates a red circular object, then he senses redly and he senses circularly. But the total way in which he senses is different from the total way in which he senses when he hallucinates both a red object and a circular object. What, I suggest, the operator theory needs, therefore, in its analysis of (2) is some nonconjunctive combinatory operator that operates on 'redly' and 'circularly' to form another predicate operator. Let us introduce, then, a new two-place operator 'coincidental with', or 'W'.[24] On the property-function semantics, this operator expresses a function that, in the above case, maps redly and circularly onto the compound function redly-coincidental with-circularly. We can explain the latter function, which, in turn, maps the property of sensing onto the property

23 For a more detailed presentation of these objections, see Jackson, *Perception*, pp. 65–6.
24 I oversimplify here in my classification of 'coincidental with' as a two-place operator. Strictly speaking, it is best taken to be multigrade. I discuss this complication later.

118

of sensing redly-coincidental with-circularly, by saying that it is the function that is typically operative in cases of sensation involving normal perceivers as a result of those perceivers viewing, in standard circumstances, a real physical object that is both red and circular. The operation of coincidence itself, therefore, can be thought of as mapping any two given sensory modes or functions F-ly and G-ly onto a function that, in turn, maps the property of sensing onto a further sensing property that is usually instantiated in normal perceivers by virtue of their viewing a physical object, which is both F and G, in standard circumstances.

It may be objected that this specification of coincidence is too indirect to carry any real explanatory force. But, it seems to me, this is not so. It is commonly held that what makes a given sensation a sensation of red is the presence within that sensation of a feature that is normally brought about by perceiving red physical objects in standard circumstances. This sort of view provides us with an indirect or extrinsic characterization of sensory redness. But it can hardly be said to be vacuous or unilluminating. My comments on coincidence are to be taken in the same vein.

Formally, we may now analyze (2) as

(2j) $[\mathbf{R}\mathcal{W}\mathbf{C}]Sj$.

In (2j), the compound predicate operator '$\mathbf{R}\mathcal{W}\mathbf{C}$' is subject to the operator detachment rule (OD) and the same sort of simplification rules as '$\mathbf{R}\mathcal{C}\mathbf{C}$'.

On the more austere semantics, since "$\mathcal{W}$" is a standard operator, the set assigned to '$[\mathbf{R}\mathcal{W}\mathbf{C}]S$' is a subset of the sets assigned to '$[\mathbf{R}]S$' and '$[\mathbf{C}]S$'. The specific sets assigned here are determined by the conceptual roles of the relevant predicates. I shall make some comments on the central features of these conceptual roles in Section IV. For the moment, it suffices to note that the inference from (2) to (6) is unproblematic given either of the above semantics.

Let us see next how the above proposal handles the many-property problem. This problem, it will be recalled, is to explain how (2) can entail (6) without collapsing the distinction between (11) and (12). We have already seen how the entailment from (2) to (6) is preserved. In the case of (11) and (12) a similar strategy applies. Thus, (11) is rewritten as

(11b) Jones senses (redly-coincidental with-circularly)-ly and (bluely-coincidental with-triangularly)-ly,

119

and (11b) is formalized as

(11c) $[\mathbf{R}\mathcal{W}\mathbf{C}]Sj$ & $[\mathbf{B}\mathcal{W}\mathbf{T}]Sj$.[25]

The same approach is taken to (12). Thus, (12) becomes

(12b) $[\mathbf{B}\mathcal{W}\mathbf{C}]Sj$ & $[\mathbf{R}\mathcal{W}\mathbf{T}]Sj$.

Since (11c) and (12b) are not equivalent, the difference between (11) and (12) is preserved.

The identity problem is more troublesome. How, on the operator theory, are we to represent the logical form of statement (7)?

(7) The red afterimage Jones has is the same as the circular afterimage Jones has.

It will not do to argue that (7), in the final analysis, is to be regimented, not as an identity statement, but rather as

(7c) $[\mathbf{R}\mathcal{W}\mathbf{C}]Sj$;

for (7) has now become equivalent to

(8) Jones has a red and circular afterimage.

And this is clearly wrong. If, for example, Jones has two red afterimages, one circular and one square, (8) will be true but (7) false.

At this stage, it might be suggested that perhaps what the adverbial theorist must do is supplement the operator approach with another system of terminology, one that speaks of sensory objects. This maneuver, due to Wilfrid Sellars,[26] can succeed only if talk of sensory or phenomenal objects is viewed as a *façon de parler*. This clearly is Sellars's position. Thus, according to Sellars, the only ontologically perspicuous representations of sensory experience are those formulated in the adverbial language. Those formulations that use sensory object vocabulary supposedly avoid any ultimate commitment to sensory objects in virtue of their links with the adverbial language through introduction and elimination rules.

---

25 Here '**B**' is the operator 'bluely'; the other symbols are as before.
26 See Sellars, "On the Objects of the Adverbial Theory of Sensation." For an informal discussion of the Sellarsian solution to the many-property problem, see my "Adverbial Theory: A Defense of Sellars against Jackson," *Metaphilosophy*, 6 (1975): 136–43.

This strategy explains the inference from (7) to (8) as follows.[27] Using the sensory object vocabulary, (7) is reconstructed as

(7d) $(\exists x)(\exists y)\{Rx \,\&\, Sjx \,\&\, Cy \,\&\, Sjy \,\&\, (z)[(Rz \,\&\, Sjz) \supset z = x] \,\&\, (w)[(Cw \,\&\, Sjw) \supset w = y] \,\&\, x = y\}$,

where the variables are restricted to sensory objects, and 'Rx', 'Cx', 'Sxy', and 'j' abbreviate 'x is red', 'x is circular', 'x senses y', and 'Jones', respectively. Statement (7d) entails

(8e) $(\exists x)(Rx \,\&\, Cx \,\&\, Sjx)$,

and (8e), in turn, entails the ontologically perspicuous adverbial statement

(8f) $[\mathbf{R}\mathcal{W}\mathbf{C}]Sj$

via the elimination rule

(ER) $(\exists x)(Syx \,\&\, Fx \,\&\, Gx) \rightarrow [\mathbf{F}\mathcal{W}\mathbf{G}]Sy$.[28]

Since (8f) is the operator theorist's analysis of (8) the problem presented by the inference from (7) to (8) supposedly dissolves.

The difficulty with this strategy is that it still gives us no way of formalizing (7) in adverbial terms. If the existential quantification over sensory objects in (7d) is not to be taken at face value, there must be some further way of analyzing the logical form of (7) that avoids that quantification. Obviously, the elimination rule (ER) is not going to help us to formulate this perspicuous adverbial analysis of (7). Nor, it seems clear, is the introduction rule

(IR) $[\mathbf{F}\mathcal{W}\mathbf{G}]Sy \equiv (\exists x)(Syx \,\&\, Fx \,\&\, Gx)$[29]

of any assistance either. Hence, the claim that the sensory object system of terminology is really a *façon de parler* seems entirely unfounded.

---

27 The formal analyses and rules presented below are based on Sellars's formalizations.
28 Here 'Fx' and 'Gx' express noncompound sensory properties of sensory objects. For the case where, instead of '$Fx \,\&\, Gx$', we have merely 'Fx', (ER) takes the following form:

$(\exists x)(Syx \,\&\, Fx) \rightarrow [\mathbf{F}]Sy$.

29 For the simpler case where '$\mathbf{F}$' replaces '$\mathbf{F}\mathcal{W}\mathbf{G}$', the right hand side of (IR) loses its final conjunct.

At this juncture it is tempting to conclude that the operator theory cannot solve the identity problem. This would be too hasty, however, for there remains one further strategy. Consider the statement

(21) Jones has exactly one red afterimage.

Speaking commonsensically, we may say that (21) is true if, and only if, exactly one distinct portion of Jones's visual field is red. This leads to the idea that (21) is to count as true if, and only if, (i) Jones has a sensation of a red expanse; (ii) Jones does not have a sensation of a red expanse spatially separated within his field from another such expanse. On an adverbial analysis, this amounts to equating (21) with

(21a) Jones senses redly but it is not the case that Jones senses (redly-spatially separated from-redly)-ly.

Formally, the suggestion here is that (21) is to be analyzed as

(21b) $[\mathbf{R}]Sj$ & $\sim[\mathbf{R}\mathcal{P}\mathbf{R}]Sj$.

In (21b), '$[\mathbf{R}\mathcal{P}\mathbf{R}]$' is a compound predicate operator that consists of two occurrences of the predicate operator '$\mathbf{R}$' modified by the spatial separation operator '$\mathcal{P}$'. The latter operator is a standard two-place operator.[30] On the property-function semantics it expresses a function whose character we can explain by saying that it maps sensory modes or functions, such as redly, onto further functions that are included in those sensory modes or functions[31] and that themselves map the property of sensing onto sensing properties of a kind typically instantiated in normal perceivers as a result of their viewing, in standard circumstances, real physical objects that are spatially separated from one another.

On the set-theoretic semantics, the set assigned to '$[\mathbf{R}\mathcal{P}\mathbf{R}]S$' is a subset of the set assigned to '$[\mathbf{R}]S$'. The choice of subset is constrained by the conceptual role of '$[\mathbf{R}\mathcal{P}\mathbf{R}]S$'. I shall make some remarks on this conceptual role in Section IV.

Returning now to (7) my suggestion is that we adopt the following regimentation:

---

30 'Spatially separated from' should really be classified as a multigrade operator rather than a two-place operator. I ignore this complication here for ease of exposition in the preliminary presentation of my position. For further discussion, see pp. 123–5.

31 Function inclusion is to be understood as in Chapter 4, pp. 89–90.

(7e) $[\mathbf{R}]Sj$ & $\sim[\mathbf{R}\mathcal{P}\mathbf{R}]Sj$ & $[\mathbf{C}]Sj$ & $\sim[\mathbf{C}\mathcal{P}\mathbf{C}]Sj$ & $[\mathbf{R}\mathcal{W}\mathbf{C}]Sj$.

Since (7e) logically implies the earlier statement (8d), which is the formal equivalent of (8), the identity problem is solved.

I suppose some philosophers will reject this proposal on the grounds that it is obvious from inspection of our visual experiences that our visual images sometimes stand in genuine spatial relations with one another. It seems to me that this response has little force. As I noted in Chapter 3, phenomenological inspection of a visual experience will no more tell us whether there really are (spatially separated) images than will inspection of a person's smile tell us whether there really is a smile, a smiling, or merely a person who smiles. Furthermore, the fact that we sometimes use spatial expressions in our talk of images is perfectly well explained by our saying that we are thereby likening our experiences to those we undergo when we view physical objects in various spatial relationships. To insist that, on the contrary, these spatial expressions denote spatial relations among private objects is to be faced with the problem of explaining the nature of private sensory space and its connection with physical object space. Surely an approach that sidesteps this problem is to be preferred.

Still, there are certain complications surrounding the spatial separation operator. These complications do not threaten the solution I have given to the identity problem. However, they must be addressed, if my discussion is to be complete. 'Spatially separated from' is best formalized as a multigrade operator (one whose polyadicity is unfixed) rather than a two-place operator, as I asserted above. As far as syntax goes, I propose that the variable '$\mathcal{M}$' now be permitted to take as its instances *any* operator that operates on one or more other symbols, thereby forming a predicate operator. Hereafter, then, multigrade operators on predicate operators as well as the previous two-place and one-place operators may substitute for '$\mathcal{M}$'. As before, the instances of '$\mathcal{M}$' will be other capital script letters. I also propose that each multigrade operator of polyadicity n operates on n predicate operators any one of which is placed to its left while the rest are placed to its right. The operator formed by this entire operation is itself a further predicate operator.

Semantically, once more there are two possible views. On one account, a multigrade operator expresses a function that maps the functions expressed by the predicate operators flanking it onto the

123

function expressed by the compound predicate operator it forms. Let us say that such an operator 'M' is standard if, and only if, (i) for any n predicate operators 'O_1', 'O_2', . . . , 'O_n', the functions expressed by 'O_1', 'O_2', . . . , 'O_n' each include the function expressed by '$O_1MO_2 \ldots O_n$' and (ii) where $n \geq 3$, the function expressed by '$O_1MO_2 \ldots O_{n-1}$' *includes* the function expressed by '$O_1MO_2 \ldots O_n$'. In the case that $n = 2$, the only condition is the first one, so that what results is the same definition as that given earlier for a standard fixed two-place operator on predicate operators. Taking function inclusion as in Chapter 4 now logically guarantees that an extended version of operator simplification

(OS_E) $[O_1MO_2 \ldots O_n]Fx \rightarrow [O_1]Fx, [O_2]Fx, \ldots, [O_n]Fx$

will be valid, assuming that 'M' is standard. A further rule of inference is also validated for standard multigrade operators. This rule, which we call "partial simplification" (PS), can be stated as follows:

(PS) $n \geq 3$: $[O_1MO_2 \ldots O_n]Fx \rightarrow [O_1MO_2 \ldots O_{n-1}]Fx$.

On the other semantics, if 'M' is standard, a compound predicate '$[O_1MO_2 \ldots O_n]F$' will be assigned a set S^*, which depends on the sets S_1, . . . , S_n assigned to '$[O_1]F$', . . . , '$[O_n]F$', and, where $n \geq 3$, on the set S' assigned to '$[O_1MO_2 \ldots O_{n-1}]F$'. The dependence conditions are $S^* \subseteq S_1, S^* \subseteq S_2, \ldots, S^* \subseteq S_n; S^* \subseteq S'$. These conditions again guarantee the validity of (OS_E) and (PS) for standard multigrade operators.

Let us go back now to the operator 'spatially separated from', or '$\mathcal{P}$'. Partly for ease of exposition and partly to avoid unnecessary repetition, in what follows I shall assume the property-function semantics. But what I say applies mutatis mutandis to the other semantics too. In (21b), '$\mathcal{P}$' has two places, and the function it expresses, Sep_1, should really be elucidated by reference to the viewing (by normal perceivers) of pairs of spatially separated physical objects. In the case of

(22) Jones has exactly two red afterimages,

the regimentation will be

(22a) $[R\mathcal{P}R]Sj$ & $\sim[R\mathcal{P}RR]Sj$.

Here '$\mathcal{P}$' has two places in the first conjunct and three in the second. Thus, in the former conjunct, '$\mathcal{P}$' expresses Sep_1 and, in the latter, another function, Sep_2, which is like Sep_1 except that it is to be elucidated by reference to triples of spatially separated objects. Similar functions with additional places will be introduced for cases involving a greater number of afterimages.

I maintain that '$\mathcal{P}$' is a *standard* multigrade operator. Hence, it is subject to (OS_E) and (PS). Given (PS), valid inferences involving statements putatively about many afterimages can now be justified. Consider, for example, the inference from

(23) Jones has at least three red afterimages

to

(24) Jones does not have exactly one red afterimage.

The former statement is regimented as

(23a) $[\mathbf{R}\mathcal{P}\mathbf{RR}]Sj$,

and the latter becomes

(24a) $\sim([\mathbf{R}]Sj \mathrel{\&} \sim[\mathbf{R}\mathcal{P}\mathbf{R}]Sj)$.

By (PS), (23a) entails

(25) $[\mathbf{R}\mathcal{P}\mathbf{R}]Sj$.

And by disjunction addition, (25) entails

(26) $\sim[\mathbf{R}]Sj \lor [\mathbf{R}\mathcal{P}\mathbf{R}]Sj$.

Since (26) is logically equivalent to (24a), the original inference is validated.

Just as 'spatially separated from' is really a multigrade operator, so too is the earlier operator 'coincidental with'. I ignored this fact earlier in order to simplify the initial discussion. But we are now in a position to understand the new complication. Consider the statement

(27) Jones has a dim, yellow, round afterimage.

How is this statement to be analyzed? If we have at our disposal the two-place operator '$\mathcal{W}$' and the predicate operators '$\mathbf{D}$', '$\mathbf{Y}$', and '$\mathbf{R}$' (abbreviating 'dimly', 'yellowly', and 'roundly', respectively), then the obvious analysis is

(27a) $[\mathbf{D}\mathcal{W}\mathbf{Y}]Sj \mathrel{\&} [\mathbf{D}\mathcal{W}\mathbf{R}]Sj \mathrel{\&} [\mathbf{Y}\mathcal{W}\mathbf{R}]Sj$.

Unfortunately, (27a) is not equivalent to (27). If, for example, Jones has a dim yellow afterimage (which is not round) *and* a dim round afterimage (which is not yellow) *and* a yellow round afterimage (which is not dim), (27a) will be true but (27) will be false. The way out of this problem is to take 'coincidental with', or '$\mathcal{W}$', to be a multigrade operator rather than a two-place operator. Now (27) is analyzed as

(27b) [**D**$\mathcal{W}$**YR**]Sj.

In (27b), '$\mathcal{W}$' takes on three places, and the function it expresses (assuming a property-function semantics) will be elucidated by reference to the viewing (by normal perceivers) of real dimly lit, yellow, round physical objects. By contrast, in the final analysis of the statement (2), '$\mathcal{W}$' takes on two places. Of course, '$\mathcal{W}$', like '$\mathcal{P}$', will be subject to the inference rules (OS$_E$) and (PS). Hence, none of the earlier inferences will present any problems.

It appears, then, that the operator theory is generally defensible. In the next section, I make some further comments on the nature of perceptual experience.

IV

Standard functionalist views on the essences of common or garden-variety perceptual experiences run parallel to those presented at the end of Chapter 4 for pain. Consider, for example, the state of having a sensation of red. There is, functionalists maintain, no one phenomenal quality common to all sensations of red. Such sensations range widely through many shades and hues. (Think, for example, of extremes close to brown and pink.) What unites these sensations into a single class is their functional role. Having a sensation of red is (very roughly) being in a state that is usually caused in normal perceivers under standard conditions by their viewing red objects and that usually causes (in those perceivers under those conditions) the belief that there is a (real) red object present. Of course, having a sensation of red is also in part having a phenomenal experience. But on any *full* functional specification of having a sensation of red, this condition will already be included according to functionalists.

I shall assume that the general points made above can be reconstructed within the operator theory, just as the parallel points for pain were reconstructed earlier. There are, however, certain issues on which I want to make some further comments. To begin with, I want to stress that my explanations in the preceding section of

126

the meanings of such operators as 'coincidental with' and 'spatially separated from' were intended to be no more than partial sketches. Any full account of the meanings of these and other operators will require not only clauses listing standard causes, but also clauses listing standard effects. Assuming the austere set-theoretic semantics, the conceptual roles of the above operators will be given in various quasi-analytic generalization schemata, for example,

(28) For any person x, if x senses in the F-ly-coincidental with-G-ly manner, then x senses F-ly.

(29) For any person x, if x is a normal perceiver in standard conditions and x senses in the F-ly-coincidental with-G-ly manner then, ceteris paribus, *the fact that x senses in this manner causes it to be the case that x* believes that there is a (real) F, G object present.

(30) For any person x, if x views a (real) F, G object and x is a normal perceiver in standard conditions then, ceteris paribus, x senses in the F-ly-coincidental with-G-ly manner *because* there is a (real) F, G object present.

(31) For any person x, if x is a normal perceiver in standard conditions and x senses in the F-ly-spatially separated from-G-ly manner then, ceteris paribus, *the fact that x senses in this manner causes it to be the case that x* believes that there is an F object and also another G object present.

Statements (28)–(31) yield *a priori* necessary truths, I maintain, once the dummy terms 'F' and 'G' are replaced by appropriate predicates, for example 'red' or 'square'. Thus, any assignment of satisfaction sets to sensory predicates that makes any of (28)–(31) yield a falsehood must be incorrect.

It may be wondered whether the above proposal generates sufficient semantic complexity in the relevant sensory predicates. On my earlier view, the semantic complexity of predicates such as 'walks quickly' or 'is pained intensely' is a matter of these predicates having conceptual roles that are determined by the conceptual roles of their components. Is this also true for a predicate such as 'senses (redly-coincidental with-squarely)-ly'? The answer, I think, is yes. The conceptual role of 'redly' (or 'squarely') is given in the generalizations generated by substituting 'redly' (or 'squarely') for 'F-ly' in the appropriate schemata. Two examples of these schemata are

(32) For any creature x, if x senses F-ly then x senses

and

(33) For any person x, if x is a normal perceiver in standard conditions and x senses F-ly then, ceteris paribus, *the fact that x senses F-ly causes it to be the case that* x believes that there is an F object present.

The conceptual role of 'senses' is given in the above *schemata* themselves (and others of their ilk). In saying this, what I mean is that one who knows this role must have dispositions to assert and to assent to a variety of sentences with the underlying form 'x senses F-ly' *only* when those sentences are being used in a way that conforms with the generalizations generated via instantiation of schemata such as (32) and (33). The conceptual role of 'coincidental with' is given in like manner in (29)–(31) and other schemata containing the predicate type 'senses (F-ly-coincidental with-G-ly)-ly'. In my view, one who knows all of these conceptual roles thereby knows the conceptual role of 'senses (redly-coincidental with-squarely)-ly'. As far as the general determination of conceptual role goes, then, there is no important difference between this predicate and my earlier examples.

The second point I want to make concerns my overall view that psychological predicates are implicitly defined by the principles of folk psychology. I hope it is clear by now that this view is really part and parcel of a much broader view that gives everyday platitudes or quasi-analytic generalizations an important semantic role both inside and outside psychological contexts. Functionalism, then, as I advocate it, is far from being an isolated view that treats psychological vocabulary as being radically different, meaning-wise, from the rest of our ordinary, everyday language.

I should emphasize that, in claiming that psychological predicates are implicitly defined by folk psychology, I am *not* claiming that there is inevitably only one assignment of satisfaction sets to predicates under which the generalizations of folk psychology come out true (or, less strongly, by and large true).[32] What I believe is rather that there is very probably only one assignment that makes folk psychology come out true and that is more *natural* than any of the competing assignments. I commented on the appeal to naturalness earlier.[33] Let me now add one further point that makes it quite clear

32 The suggestion that under a correct extension assignment the generalizations of folk psychology need come out only by and large true is one that David Lewis endorses. See his "Psychophysical and Theoretical Identifications."
33 See Chapter 3, note 26 and Chapter 4, note 28. The term 'naturalness' is due to David Lewis.

that this appeal is not ad hoc. The possibility of multiple equally good extension assignments for psychological predicates is really only a special case of another possibility – that of multiple equally good interpretations for singular terms and predicates generally. This possibility has been stressed by Hilary Putnam in his model-theoretic argument against realism.[34] What is needed to overcome Putnam's argument is, I suggest, a global constraint on reference and interpretation. And this is just what the appeal to naturalness provides, as David Lewis has argued in a reply to Putnam.[35] Thus, the suggestion that naturalness be used to provide an additional constraint on acceptable extension assignments for psychological predicates can be seen as part of a more general suggestion about how to solve the problem of the determinacy of reference.[36]

The next issue I shall address, albeit very briefly, is whether the use of schemata such as (33) presupposes the doctrine that there are real mind-independent colors, for example, physical object redness. This issue deserves comment, since some philosophers maintain that the given doctrine is scientifically implausible. Since I deny that the use of predicates (or abstract singular terms for that matter) carries with it an ontic commitment to nonlinguistic properties, I deny that the instances of (33) require the existence of colors in order to be true, and I reject the question "Which scientific properties are individual colors to be identified with?" This quick response is not available, I might add, if one accepts the version of the operator theory that utilizes a property-function semantics. On this view, one has two options: Either one argues that the individual colors *can* be identified with physical properties (including perhaps disjunctive physical properties) or one rejects the assumption that if color words express properties then colors are nonfunctional

34 Hilary Putnam, *Reason, Truth, and History* (Cambridge University Press, 1981); idem, *Realism and Reason: Philosophical Papers*, Vol. 3 (Cambridge University Press, 1983).

35 David Lewis, "Putnam's Paradox," *Australasian Journal of Philosophy*, 62 (1984): 221–36.

36 Two further comments: (i) If an appeal to naturalness is needed to choose between alternative extension assignments for psychological predicates, it is a mistake to claim that psychological predicates have explicit definitions constructible from the Ramsey sentence of folk psychology; (ii) if, contrary to my view, it turns out that there is no unique assignment of satisfaction sets to psychological predicates that meets all the semantic constraints, if, that is, there are two or more equally natural assignments, then there will be indeterminacy that *cannot be eliminated.*

properties found within physics or chemistry. In the latter case, one might then go on to claim that colors are functional properties, each of which supervenes on a number of different underlying physical properties. Further questions will then arise about whether the functional characterization of colors should be completed *a priori* or *a posteriori*.[37] One advantage of the version of the operator theory that eschews properties is that it avoids these complications.

Another issue on which I want to comment is whether, as some philosophers have supposed,[38] visual sensations have beliefs or other conscious interpretative acts as components. This issue, like the one above, rests on presuppositions that I repudiate, namely that there are visual sensations and beliefs. Still, it may be wondered whether, on my view, it is possible for a person to sense *F*-ly without thereby responding cognitively. First, we should note that it is certainly possible to sense *F*-ly without believing that there is an *F* object present. Consider, for example, the case of the person who *knows* that he is hallucinating. Similarly, a person can sense *F*-ly without seeing that there is an *F* object present since the latter, unlike the former, requires that there really be an object that is *F*. Furthermore, I can surely see an *F* object without seeing that it is an *F* object or indeed noticing its presence at all, as, for example, when I walk down a road covered with leaves while deep in thought.

Suppose it is now suggested that one must be introspectively aware that one is sensing *F*-ly whenever one senses *F*-ly. This, it seems to me, is also false. Suppose I am viewing a scene with many different components. If my attention is wandering or if I view the scene only very briefly, it is natural to assume that there are things I see that I do not consciously notice. And if this is true, I must sense in ways of which I am not introspectively aware. The general conclusion I am led to is that persons can sense visually *without* thereby conceptualizing.

I want now to address two possible problems for my position

---

37 David Lewis is one philosopher who seems to think that both the state of having a sensation of red and real-world redness have *a priori* functional analyses. Lewis maintains that the combination of these views generates no vicious circularity. See his "Psychophysical and Theoretical Identification," note 15.

38 See, e.g., D. M. Armstrong, *A Materialist Theory of Mind* (London: Routledge & Kegan Paul, 1968); George Pitcher, *A Theory of Perception* (Princeton, N.J.: Princeton University Press, 1971); J. W. Roxbee Cox, "An Analysis of Perceiving in Terms of the Causation of Beliefs I," in *Perception: A Philosophical Symposium*, ed. F. N. Sibley (London: Methuen, 1971), pp. 23–64.

on sensing and conceptualization. This problem can be brought out as follows. Suppose, for the moment, that there are visual sensations and that I have a hallucinatory experience of an elephant. If, as is asserted above, persons can sense without thereby conceptualizing, it may seem that the only way my experience can represent or be of an elephant is via its having a phenomenal character that is brought about in normal perceivers under standard conditions by their viewing elephants. The trouble with this account is that, when generalized, it entails that, if there had been, in addition to elephants, other creatures ('celephants', as I shall call them) that looked just like elephants even though they really belonged to another species, then my experience would have represented both an elephant and a celephant; for it would have been phenomenally like experiences produced by viewing either real elephants or real celephants. This seems wrong, however. After all, I might never have seen or heard of celephants. Moreover, even if I had, I might have insisted that on this occasion I was hallucinating an elephant. It appears, then, that interpretation is somehow bound up with the fact that my experience is of an elephant. The problem is to say *how* this can be so, if sensing need not be accompanied by belief.

At the beginning of this section, I suggested that, according to functionalism, for a state to be a sensation of red it must, in part, typically cause the belief that there is a red object present. This proposal was intended to be merely a rough sketch. I want now to be a little more precise. In the elephant case, it seems to me that what the (metaphysically liberal) functionalist should say is something like this: My experience is of an elephant in part because of its phenomenal qualities and the causal connection with real elephants and in part because *were* I to introspect that experience and *were* I also to believe that I am a normal perceiver in standard perceptual conditions, then I *would* be caused to believe that there is an elephant before me. This *a priori* analysis gets the right result in the elephant–celephant case, and it is compatible both with the claim that visual experiences need not give rise to conceptualization and with the claim that interpretation is a factor in determining sensory content.

Now if one denies that there are any visual sensations, as I do, there can be no answer to the question "What makes my visual sensation a sensation of an elephant?" So the problem, as stated, is a pseudoproblem. However, if one adopts the property-function

131

6

Physicalism and the phenomenal qualities of experience

It has frequently been urged that there are facts about our sensory experiences, both perceptual and bodily, that no amount of physical information can capture. These facts, we are told, are familiar to all of us in our everyday conscious lives: They pertain to the subjective phenomenal qualities, or qualia, that characterize our pains, our itches, our sensations of color. In Chapter 4, I suggested that, if there are such entities as qualia, they are best identified either with physicochemical properties or with scientifically discovered functional properties the inputs and outputs for which are specified by neural impulse descriptions. For the purpose of the present chapter, I shall classify not only the former but also the latter view as physicalistic, and I shall call any philosopher who accepts either view a 'physicalist'. I believe that the arguments adduced for the view that qualia lie outside the physicalist's net are unsound. I also believe, however, that at least one of the arguments, which I call the "argument from knowledge," deserves a great deal more careful attention than it has received heretofore. This argument in one form or another has exerted a powerful influence on many philosophers, and it has been a thorn in the side of physicalism for a number of years. In what follows, my primary concern is to present a conclusive refutation of this argument.

Throughout this chapter, I speak as if there are facts, sensory tokens, phenomenal qualities of sensory tokens, and so on. This, of course, is not really my view. Given my adherence to the operator theory, I am not prepared to countenance any of these entities. Indeed, I am not prepared to countenance phenomenal properties at all, be they properties of events, individuals, or any-

133

thing else.[1] My aim in this chapter, however, is not to wield my metaphysical scheme against the presuppositions of the argument from knowledge and the other arguments I shall discuss but rather to show that *no* philosopher who denies that there are any non-physical mental entities has anything to fear from these arguments. As far as the present chapter is concerned, therefore, talk of facts, phenomenal properties, and so on may be taken at face value.

The structure of the chapter is as follows. In Section I, I distinguish one main strand of argument for the claim that there are subjective experiential facts that physical information cannot capture. I call this the "argument from possibility." I briefly take up two variants of this argument and I suggest that they have little force. In Section II, I turn to a detailed examination of my primary topic, the argument from knowledge, versions of which constitute the second main strand of argument from qualia against physicalism. I here give clear analyses of knowing what it is like to undergo such and such a type of subjective experience and knowing what a given token experience is like. I maintain that once these concepts are properly understood the physicalist has nothing to fear from the argument from knowledge. I also show that the physicalist can accept the thesis, dear to the hearts of empiricists, that there are (or can be) terms for the subjective qualities of experience whose meanings cannot be fully understood by persons who have not experienced the relevant qualities. Finally, in Section III, I briefly address certain objections that may appear to threaten the central claim in my defense of physicalism.

I

The argument from possibility is any argument of the following general form. Let 'Q' be a rigid designator for a given phenomenal quality. Let 'N' be a rigid designator for a given physical property with which the physicalist wishes to identify Q. Then if Q is identical with N, it is metaphysically necessary that Q be identical with N. But it is not metaphysically necessary that Q be identical with N. Hence, Q is different from N.

---

1 On the alternative, richer semantics for the operator theory, talk putatively about phenomenal properties of sensory tokens will be reconstructed as talk of phenomenal properties of persons and other sentient creatures. So on this semantics, there will be phenomenal properties.

134

The crucial claim in this argument is the second one. Why should we accept that it is metaphysically possible that Q is not identical with N? Different answers to this question result in different versions of the argument from possibility.

Consider first what has come to be called the "absent qualia argument."[2] According to this argument, it is metaphysically possible that Q is not identical with N, since it is metaphysically possible for N to be instantiated without *any* phenomenal quality. Why is this possible? Well, supposedly it is imaginable. Simply imagine having attached to your skull a cerebroscope that registers the fact that N is tokened in your brain while you yourself lack any sensation or feeling.

Another form of the argument from possibility is the "multiple realizability argument."[3] This argument rests on the claim that qualia can be multiply realized, that the physical state or property N that realizes a given quale Q in me might be different from the physical state or property M that realizes that quale in you or in creatures of other possible species.[4] It is then metaphysically possible that Q is not identical with N, since it is metaphysically possible that Q is instantiated without N. This claim, like the earlier claim in the absent qualia argument, is itself supported by an appeal to imaginability. Sitting in our armchairs, we can easily imagine Q instantiated without N, since we can imagine feeling the characteristic feeling 'Q' designates while viewing an autocerebroscope that indicates the presence of some physical property other than N.

These two versions of the argument from possibility have received extensive analysis in the recent literature,[5] and I cannot pos-

---

2 See, e.g., Keith Campbell, *Body and Mind* (Garden City, N.Y.: Double-day/Anchor, 1970), pp. 100–4; Robert Kirk, "Sentience and Behavior," *Mind*, 83 (1974): 43–60; Ned Block, "Troubles with Functionalism," *Minnesota Studies in the Philosophy of Science*, Vol. 9, ed. C. W. Savage (Minneapolis: University of Minnesota Press, 1978), pp. 261–325; Colin McGinn, *The Character of Mind* (New York: Oxford University Press, 1982), pp. 35–6.

3 See, e.g., Saul Kripke, "Naming and Necessity," in *Semantics of Natural Language*, ed. D. Davidson and G. Harman (Dordrecht: Reidel, 1972) pp. 253–355; also Colin McGinn, "Anomalous Monism and Kripke's Cartesian Intuitions," *Analysis*, 37 (1977): 78–80.

4 In some extreme versions of the multiple realizability argument, it is held that Q could be instantiated without *any* physical property, as, e.g., in a disembodied soul.

5 See, e.g., Sydney Shoemaker, "Functionalism and Qualia," *Philosophical Studies*, 27 (1975): 291–315; idem "Absent Qualia are Impossible – A Reply to Block,"

sibly discuss them fully in the present section. Still I hope to say enough to show that they are flawed.

Consider again the general assertion that it is metaphysically possible that Q is not identical with N, where N is a physical property. We are urged to accept this assertion *either* on the grounds that we can imagine a possible world w_1 in which Q is coinstantiated with some other neural property M instead of N (as in the multiple realizability argument) *or* on the grounds that we can imagine a possible world w_2 in which N is instantiated without Q or any other phenomenal quality (as in the absent qualia argument). Obviously these appeals to what we can imagine will be successful *only if* imaginability entails possibility. This presupposition is widely accepted, and it strikes me as entirely reasonable. However, it might be questioned. On one possible view of imaginability, if a person believes that something is the case, he or she can imagine that it is. For example, if Smith, when young, believed that he would some day successfully square the circle, then *a fortiori* he could have imagined that he would. Evidently, on this view, imaginability entails mere *epistemic* possibility. On another view, now widely held, where a person claims to be imagining something that is (unknown to him) impossible, he does not really imagine what he claims. If, for example, a man without scientific knowledge claims to be imagining that gold has atomic number 80 (rather than its actual 79), what he *really* imagines is that some substance with the manifest observable qualities of gold has atomic number 80 (rather than 79), and *that* is something quite different. Of the two views, my linguistic intuitions fit the latter much better. In any event, it is the latter view that must be presupposed if the appeal to imaginability is to get off the ground. The question we have to address, then, is whether w_1 and w_2 are genuinely imaginable.

The imaginability of w_2 is more contentious than the imaginability of world w_1, since many philosophers hold that phenomenal properties supervene upon neural properties in the way that aesthetic or moral properties are sometimes held to supervene on naturalistic properties. For these philosophers, it will not be possible (and so not imaginable) that N is instantiated without Q. These

Philosophical Review, 90 (1981): 581–99; Ned Block, "Are Absent Qualia Impossible?" *Philosophical Review*, 89 (1980): 257–74; William Lycan, "Form, Function, and Feel," *Journal of Philosophy*, 78 (1981): 24–50.

complications are best avoided in the present context. Let us therefore concentrate on w_1.

It seems to me that what we really imagine when we claim to imagine w_1 is this: We imagine ourselves undergoing experiences that instantiate the felt quality Q, and we imagine ourselves (or others) viewing our brains through cerebroscopes that we (or they) take to indicate the presence of physical property M rather than N. But does this suffice to imagine w_1? I think not, for the cerebroscopes we imagine may be malfunctioning or N may have the appearance in w_1 that we associate in the actual world with M.[6]

It may now be replied that we can imagine what we imagine above while also imagining (i) that the cerebroscopes are functioning normally without outside interference and (ii) that N and M appear in w_1 exactly as they would in the actual world. The major problem with this reply can be brought out in the following way. Suppose I claim to be able to imagine that Goldbach's conjecture is false. When pressed for details, I say that I can imagine famous mathematicians excitedly reading the printout tape from an appropriately programmed computer and exclaiming "So there are even numbers that are not the sum of two primes!" Does this make it plausible to say that I have succeeded in imagining that Goldbach's conjecture is false? Obviously not. The computer I imagine may be malfunctioning, or the scientists in their excitement may have misread the tape.

Suppose I reply to this point by insisting that the computer I imagine is functioning normally and that the scientists make no mistakes in reading the printout tape. Have I now imagined that Goldbach's conjecture is false? If so, then my thought experiment entitles me to believe that Goldbach's conjecture is possibly false and hence that the conjecture is in fact false.[7] But on the basis of my thought experiment, it is evidently wrongheaded for me to say that I may rationally deny Goldbach's conjecture. Surely I have no logical right to an opinion on the matter (assuming that I have no other relevant information).

It seems to me that there is a parallel between the above case and the one involving Q and M. Our grounds for thinking that we can

---

6 Cf. Ned Block, "Troubles with Functionalism," p. 287.
7 I assume that mathematical hypotheses always have truth values and that their truth values are the same in all possible worlds.

imagine Q coinstantiated with M rather than with N are no stronger than our grounds for thinking that we can imagine the property of being an even number coinstantiated with the property of being a number that is not the sum of two primes. And just as the latter grounds are insufficient unless we already have independent evidence that the properties can be coinstantiated, so too are the former. Where I suggest we go wrong in our thought experiments is in the belief that, if it seems to us that we have imagined things, A, B, C, ... occurring together in some possible world w_n, it automatically follows that we have really done so. In some cases we may have failed to imagine one of A, B, C, ..., instead imagining something different but with the same appearance. In other cases we may have succeeded in imagining all of A, B, C, ... but not together in a single possible world.

I conclude that variants of the argument from possibility do not demonstrate that there are experiential facts that are nonphysical. I turn next to the argument from knowledge.

II

Suppose that Jones is an extraordinarily brilliant scientist of the twenty-third century who has acquired exhaustive knowledge of what goes on in us physically when we see colors and use color words. Suppose also that Jones is congenitally blind and that, although he has recently agreed to take off enough time from his scientific studies to undergo a corneal transplant, he has not as yet been operated on. Is there anything Jones does not know that his fellows with normal color vision do? The natural obvious response to this question is "He doesn't know what red, green, blue, and so on look like." But ex hypothesi he has all the knowledge there is to have about what is going on in the optic nerves, the brain, the central nervous system, and the vocal chords of his fellows when light of various wavelengths strikes their eyes and they respond by saying, "This is red," "That is green," "That is blue." It follows that there is knowledge of experiential facts that lies beyond the reaches of any physicalist theory.

This, in brief, is what I am calling the "argument from knowledge." It has, I think, substantial intuitive force, since it is very hard to deny that the blind Jones does not know what red, green, blue, and so on look like. After all, when Jones has recovered from the operation and acquired normal sight, he will surely *learn* something new about visual experience, about how the colors appear.

The argument I have sketched has a long history. Versions of it are to be found in the early Russell,[8] where they are associated with the famous doctrine of knowledge by acquaintance and the thesis that phenomenal color words have meanings that cannot be grasped by persons who have not experienced the relevant subjective qualities. In the more recent past, the argument, or something very like it, is to be found in the writings of numerous philosophers.[9] In some versions of the argument, the primary concept is that of understanding. Thomas Nagel, for example, in his much discussed article "What Is It Like to Be a Bat?"[10] presents a version of the argument that can be reconstructed as follows. To undergo an experience is for there to be something it is like for the subject of that experience. Now what it is like to have a given set of experiences can be understood only from a single (type) of point of view, that conferred by being oneself the subject of a similar set of experiences. For example, what it is like to have the sorts of experiences a bat has can be understood only from a bat's point of view, which certainly is not our point of view. But physical facts can be understood from *any* point of view, irrespective of the phenomenology of the experiences of the creatures occupying the points of view. Hence, there are facts about experience that are not physical.

It is obvious that this argument is very closely related to the one I stated earlier. Indeed, Nagel's version can be restated (without loss of content) as an argument from knowledge in the following manner. We cannot (even in principle) know what it is like to undergo the experiences a bat undergoes since we ourselves, given our neurophysiology, cannot be visited by similar experiences. But

8 See, e.g., "The Philosophy of Logical Atomism," in *Logic and Knowledge*, ed. R. C. March (London: Allen & Unwin, 1956), p. 194.
9 See, e.g., B. A. Farrell, "Experience," in *The Philosophy of Mind*, ed. Vere Chappell (Englewood Cliffs, N.J.: Prentice-Hall, 1962); Paul Meehl, "The Compleat Autocerebroscopist," in *Mind, Matter and Method*, ed. Paul Feyerabend and Grover Maxwell (Minneapolis: University of Minnesota Press, 1966), pp. 151–60; M. T. Thornton, "Ostensive Terms and Materialism," *Monist*, 56 (1972): 193; Thomas Nagel, "What Is It Like to Be a Bat?" *Philosophical Review*, 83 (1974): 435–50; Colin McGinn, "Philosophical Materialism," *Synthese*, 44 (1980): 182–3; Frank Jackson, "Epiphenomenal Qualia," *Philosophical Quarterly*, 32 (1982): 127–32.
10 Nagel, "What Is It Like to Be a Bat?"

we can (in principle) know all the physical facts about bat brains, bat bodies, and bat sonar. Physicalism, therefore, is incomplete.

Stated in this manner, it appears that there is no significant difference between Nagel's argument and the version that makes reference to Jones; for instead of saying that the blind Jones does not know what the various colors look like, it appears that we could equally well say that the blind Jones does not know what it is like to undergo the experiences involved in seeing the various colors. Let us, then, return to the original argument, which has the benefit of restricting itself to familiar experiences of a possible member of our own species, and let us begin our response by trying to say what it is to know what a given sort of experience is like.

It might be proposed that the only salient thing Jones lacks is the capacity to undergo the visual sensations or experiences that normal perceivers undergo when they see objects of given colors. This leads to the thought that statements of the type

(1) Person x knows what it is like to have an experience with a certain phenomenal quality Q

can be analyzed as

(1a) x has the capacity to undergo experiences with Q.

There is an immediate difficulty, however, with this very straightforward analysis. As I argued in Chapter 4, visual sensations are nonconceptual episodes that can and do occur whether or not they are introspected by their subjects. Thus, a person who satisfies (1) must have *more* than just the capacity to undergo the relevant experiences. Intuitively, the person must also stand in the appropriate cognitive relationship to those experiences either via present introspective awareness or via memory.

These reflections suggest the following as a replacement for (1a):

(1b) Either x is presently undergoing an experience with Q and x is introspectively aware that his experience has Q, or x can remember having an experience with Q.

Unfortunately, (1b) is still not quite right; for (1b) requires x to have correctly identified, either presently or in the past, some experience of his as having Q on the basis of introspection (since x surely cannot remember having had an experience with Q unless he was at some past time introspectively aware that an experience of his had Q). Yet (1) requires no such thing. If Q is a complex phenomenal quality, x may know what it is like to undergo an experience with Q by imagining such an experience on the basis of what he remembers of past experiences having (separately) Q's components. Alternatively, if Q is phenomenally simple – for example, a phenomenal color shade quality – x may perhaps know what it is like to undergo an experience with Q by imaginatively extrapolating from his memories of very similar color experiences.

These objections can be answered by adding a further disjunct to (1b) as follows:

(1c) *Either* x is presently undergoing an experience with Q and x is introspectively aware that his experience has Q, *or* x can remember having an experience with Q, *or* x can remember having experiences with qualities either phenomenally similar to Q or phenomenally constitutive of Q and x, on the basis of what he is here able to remember, can imagine having an experience with Q.

On this analysis, correct identification via introspective awareness remains a central requirement in knowing what it is like to have an experience with a given phenomenal quality. Since such identification yields knowledge *that* (i.e., knowledge of fact), it is clear that knowing what it is like, according to (1c), is grounded on factual knowledge that is obtained in the appropriate manner, namely by introspection. It is also worth noting that (1c) draws a conceptual link between knowing what it is like and the possession of certain abilities. The analysis we have reached, therefore, is really a *hybrid* one, and it has, I suggest, considerable intuitive plausibility.[11] We are now ready to pursue further the case of Jones.

11 If one denies that there really are any phenomenal qualities, as I do, one need not also repudiate all talk of knowing what it is like. After all, it is one thing to fill in the blank in the schema 'Person x knows what it is like to _____' with the phrase 'undergo an experience having Q' where 'Q' is a name for a phenomenal quality. It is something quite different to fill in the blank with such phrases as 'feel pain' and 'have an itch'. These everyday phrases do not involve *names* for phenomenal qualities and hence the intelligibility of talk involving such phrases does not rest on the existence of phenomenal qualities. As to how talk of knowing what it is like to feel pain (or have an itch) is to be elucidated, my view is that (1c) can form the basis for an appropriate account, given certain minor modifications. Specifically, it seems to me that knowing what it is like to feel pain is at root a matter of either presently being pained and being introspectively aware that one is pained or being able to remember having been pained. I suppose that a third disjunct might be added to this proposal, namely being able to imagine being pained. After all, a disjunct of this sort does seem appropriate in some everyday cases of knowing what it is like. In the case of pain, if such a disjunct is added, we will either have to grant that someone could know what is like to feel pain without ever being pained or require that the appropriate imaginative act involves the person's drawing on his memories of

141

The problem Jones presents for physicalism is supposedly that Jones does not know what it is like to undergo the experience involved in seeing red (or blue or green, etc.). But the primary reason that Jones does not know this is that he has never undergone the appropriate experiences. When he *does* undergo these experiences and he identifies them as the experiences they are via introspective awareness, *then* he will know what it is like to have the experience of seeing red, blue, green, and so on. So after the operation he will indeed *learn* something. But in learning something he will not come to know facts of a new sort different in kind from those he knew before, or so the physicalist can insist. Rather he will come to undergo experiences of a sort *he* has not undergone before, and by introspectively responding to those experiences, he will come to know facts of an old sort, facts just like those he already knew about the experiences of his sighted fellows, but in a new way.[12] Before the operation, he knew facts of that sort only by external physical observation of his fellows' bodies and brains; after the operation, he knows them by introspective awareness. The point here is a subtle one and it requires further defense. I propose to support it by considering a new version of the argument from knowledge that appears still harder for the physicalist to answer.

Suppose that Smith is a normal perceiver in the twenty-third century who, as it happens, is facing a red object in good light. Suppose also that Smith is introspectively aware of the visual experience (call it 'e') that he is presently undergoing and that he

past pain. In the latter case, the extra disjunct becomes superfluous. In the former, we take a position that seems counterintuitive. In any event, if a third disjunct is added, we will certainly need to assume that, if a person claims to be imagining being pained and describes himself, in the imagined situation, as satisfying various predicates that are not typically associated with pain, he is not *really* imagining being pained.

12 Sydney Shoemaker makes this point in "The Inverted Spectrum," *Journal of Philosophy*, 79 (1982): 357–81. However, his comments, which appear in a footnote, are extremely brief. They are also associated with an analysis of knowing what it is like to which counterexamples can be constructed. Moreover, there are difficulties brought out below for the stated response to the argument from knowledge that Shoemaker does not discuss. Terence Horgan takes a similar line in his "Jackson on Physical Information and Qualia," *Philosophical Quarterly*, 34 (1984): 147–51. Horgan's comments are not quite as brief as Shoemaker's, but they are still too terse to do full justice to the argument from knowledge. Furthermore, there is a significant difficulty for Horgan's discussion. In this connection, see note 14 below.

142

believes truly of e that it has a certain phenomenal color content that he rigidly names 'R'. Then clearly Smith knows of e that it has R. The knowledge Smith has here is knowledge *of* one particular experience. It is not identical with knowledge of what it is like to undergo *an* experience with content R, since the latter knowledge, unlike the former, can be possessed by persons who hold no beliefs at all about the particular experience e.

Jones, it may be suggested, cannot know of e that it has R, no matter how much he knows of Smith's body, brain, and behavior. This is not to say, of course, that had Jones not been blind he could never have known that fact. If, for example, Jones had not needed a corneal transplant and if he had been located next to Smith, facing the very same red object, he would have known of his own experience that it had content R on the basis of introspection, and hence he would also have known of the experience Smith was undergoing that it had that content too (unless he had some reason to think that his color vision was unlike that of his fellows). The point is that there is something Smith knows that Jones, given his blindness, does not, *despite* his exhaustive knowledge of the physical world. That this is so, it may be argued, is clearly shown by the fact that after the operation Jones will surely *learn* or *discover* something about e in particular and its phenomenal content. Indeed, how can this be denied? By finding out what he himself experiences facing the same red object in the same good light and by checking that he and Smith are alike physically, Jones will come to know of e that it had a certain phenomenal content – the one that Smith called 'R' and that he now, like Smith, is experiencing in the presence of the appropriate red object. This is new knowledge, knowledge he did not have before. It is knowledge of what e was like, how e appeared, knowledge of e that it had specific phenomenal content R. The conclusion we reach, then, is that *there are* facts that physicalism leaves out.

It seems to me that this is a powerful argument, and great care must be taken in disarming it. It is also important to notice that this version of the argument, if sound, entails not just that after the operation Jones will discover a *new* fact about one particular experience of Smith's but also that he'll discover *new* facts of a more general sort, for if Jones before the operation does not know of e that it has R, then by similar reasoning Jones for that period does not know of *any* experience that takes place that it has R. It must be true, then, that Jones, after the operation, *also* comes to learn various general facts, like the fact that there are experiences having phenomenal content R and the fact that persons physically like Smith and Jones undergo experiences having R in the presence of physical objects of the appropriate shade of red. Hence, Jones *does* discover facts of a new sort, both general and particular, when he gains his sight. Hence, my earlier claim that Jones merely comes to know facts of an old sort in a new way is now completely undermined.

I believe that the way the physicalist should answer this argument is by claiming that the blind Jones *does* know of Smith's experience e that it has phenomenal content R. This claim is, on the face of it, counterintuitive. Let us see, then, what the physicalist can say to make it plausible.

Suppose it is said that Jones and Smith, in knowing of e that it has R, both know of e that it is a token of such and such a physicochemical type. Smith knows this fact about e via introspection; Jones knows it via information transmitted to him from a cerebroscope. Is *this* claim at all plausible? I think not. For Smith need not have the foggiest idea of what is going on in his brain.

Suppose the physicalist now suggests that, although R is indeed a physicochemical property instantiated within the brain, no reductive analysis is possible of what Smith and Jones both know. In knowing of e that it has R, Smith and Jones know just that. On this proposal, the crucial difference between Smith and Jones with respect to e is merely that Jones alone knows the nature of the physicochemical property that is identical with R.

It may be instructive here to consider a possible parallel. Suppose Brown is an ordinary man who does not know that salt is NaCl but who reliably discriminates salt from other substances. Clearly there will be occasions on which it is true to say that Brown knows of the stuff in a given container that it is salt. But Brown will not know of the stuff in the container that it is NaCl. Since 'salt' is, let us agree, a rigid name for NaCl, just as 'R' is a rigid name for a property that is, according to the physicalist above, physicochemical, the two situations seem parallel. And just as Brown's ignorance in the latter situation presents no problem for physicalism so, it may be suggested, neither does Smith's ignorance in the former.

I conclude that Smith can know of e that it has R without knowing of e that it has such and such a physicochemical property, even if R is a physicochemical property.[13] But are there any positive grounds for saying that *Jones* knows of e that it has R in these circumstances? I believe that there are.

To see this point, consider the following parallel case. Suppose that someone we will call 'Johnson' knows of a given beaker of liquid, b, that it contains the colorless, tasteless liquid that comes out of taps. Suppose further that 'water' is a rigid name with which Johnson is acquainted and that he knows a description that fixes its referent, namely 'the colorless, tasteless liquid that comes out of taps'. Then Johnson knows that water itself is the colorless, tasteless liquid that comes out of taps. This knowledge together with the knowledge above of b clearly suffices for Johnson to know of b that it contains water.

Jones is in the same epistemic situation with respect to e and R as Johnson is with respect to b and water. One of the things Jones knows of e is that it has the phenomenal content (whatever it actually is) that is typically caused in Smith by his viewing red objects. Jones is also aware of Smith's rigid name, 'R', and he knows a description that fixes its referent, namely 'the phenomenal content that is typically caused in Smith by his viewing red objects'. Hence, Jones knows that R is the phenomenal content that . . . and so on. Hence, Jones, like Smith, must surely know of e that it has R.[14]

---

13 A parallel argument establishes that Smith can know of e that it has R without knowing of e that it has such and such a scientifically discovered functional property having inputs and outputs that are specified by so and so neural impulse descriptions, even if R is a property of that sort.

14 It is convenient, at this time, to make some comments on the position Terence Horgan adopts in his "Jackson on Physical Information and Qualia." Horgan agrees with Jackson that a person who, for the first time, is introspectively aware of the characteristic experience of seeing red gains new knowledge about, for example, what it is (phenomenally) like to see ripe tomatoes. But this new knowledge, according to Horgan, is expressible in the sentence

(S) Seeing ripe tomatoes has this property,

where 'this property' is used to designate the color-quale instantiated in the person's present experience. And the knowledge expressible in (S), so Horgan argues, presents no problem for physicalism. This response to the argument from knowledge is unsatisfactory. The knowledge expressible in (S) is equally well expressible in

(S*) Seeing ripe tomatoes has R,

if the given person is presently experiencing R. Since our man Jones, before gaining his sight, *already* knows that seeing ripe tomatoes has R, it follows that

145

This conclusion will, no doubt, still strike some philosophers as unsatisfactory, since it appears to be inconsistent with the obvious fact that after the operation Jones will *find out* something about *e* in particular and its phenomenal content. But there is no inconsistency. Jones will certainly learn something about *e* when he gains his sight. He will learn or discover what *e* was (phenomenally) like. This is new knowledge, knowledge of one particular experience, but it is *not* knowledge of any new facts. This requires a little explanation.

Intuitively, knowing what *e* is like is a matter of knowing what it is like to undergo experiences of *e*'s phenomenal type, that is, *R*, and knowing of *e* in particular that it has *R*. The latter knowledge links the former to *e* and thereby ties down general knowledge of what experiences with content *R* are like to the token event *e*. The analysis, I propose, then, of knowing what a token event *y* is (phenomenally) like is as follows:

(2) *x* knows what *y* is like = df. There is a phenomenal content *C* such that (i) *x* knows what it is like to undergo experiences with *C*, and (ii) *x* knows of *y* that it has *C*.

Given this analysis, the blind Jones does not know what Smith's color experience *e* is like, since for reasons given earlier he fails to

knowledge of what it is (phenomenally) like to see ripe tomatoes is not the same as the knowledge expressible in (S).

Note that I am not claiming here that (S) and (S*) have the same meaning. Obviously, there could be occasions when (S) expressed a truth and (S*) did not, as, e.g., when a person with inverted color vision saw ripe tomatoes for the first time and uttered (S). My point is that, if 'this property' is used to designate *R*, then (S) and (S*) convey exactly the same factual information, information that is already in the blind Jones's possession.

Horgan insists that a hearer of (S) cannot obtain the information that the speaker expresses by (S), unless she, the hearer, experiences *R* herself and knows that 'this property' designates the same property that she experiences. I concede that the hearer must know that 'this property' designates *R* but I deny that she must experience *R* herself. A requirement of the latter sort is not needed in other indexical contexts (e.g., I can know what you are saying when you utter the sentence, 'This book is interesting,' even if I do not perceive, and have never perceived, the book you are referring to, if, say, I already know, on other grounds, that it is Iris Murdoch's latest novel). Why, then, should such a requirement be imposed here? What, I suggest, Horgan should have said is the following. A speaker cannot express her knowledge that seeing ripe tomatoes has *R*, by uttering (S), unless she knows the fact that 'this property' designates *R in a certain way*, namely via introspective awareness of the presence of *R* in his experience and the application of 'this property' to *R*. Still, the fact she knows can be known in *other* ways by persons who have not experienced *R*.

satisfy condition (i). But he *does* satisfy condition (ii) – the condition that imposes *de re* knowledge of *e* – and hence he knows just as many facts about *e* as Smith. After the operation, Jones comes to know what it is like to undergo experiences with content *R* by undergoing the appropriate experiences and introspectively identifying them. He, then, satisfies both (i) and (ii) in the *analysans* of (2). Hence, he discovers or comes to know what *e* in particular was like. I conclude that the case of Smith and Jones presents no difficulty for the physicalist.

There is one further complication left to consider. Suppose that there is a congenitally blind person who, like Jones, has exhaustive knowledge of what is going on physically in his fellows when they see colors and use color words, but who knows much more than Jones. In particular, this person – Super-Jones, as I shall call him – knows every physical fact there is to know about his own past, present, and future. Now if *R* is a physical property, then Super-Jones, before the operation that gives him sight, already knows of every future color experience of his that has *R* that it has *R*. For he has complete knowledge of what will go on in his brain after the operation, and he will therefore already know of various future states of his brain that they have the appropriate physical property. Super-Jones, then, when he recovers from the operation cannot *come to know* of any of his own new color experiences that they have *R*. So Super-Jones will not *learn* anything about these color experiences. Yet this seems quite wrong. Surely when Super-Jones is first introspectively aware that he is having an experience with phenomenal content *R* he will make a significant discovery.

Super-Jones will make a discovery, sure enough. When, for the first time, he becomes aware, via introspection, that a particular experience of his (call it '*f*') has *R*, he will come to know what *f* is like. He did not know that at any earlier time because he did not know until then what it was like to undergo an experience having *R*. And he did not know what it was like to undergo an experience having *R* because, before the operation, neither had he undergone an experience having *R* nor had he identified any experience as having *R* solely on the basis of introspection. So after the operation, Super-Jones does learn things about his color experiences, for he acquires knowledge as to what they (both token and type) are like. But according to the physicalist, he does not acquire knowledge of any new

147

facts. Rather by introspection he acquires a new way of knowing certain facts he already knew by other means.

In closing this section, I shall show very briefly that physicalism is consistent with the empiricist thesis that some linguistic terms cannot be fully understood by persons who have not experienced their referents. Consider again 'R'. Empiricists would maintain that Jones before the operation does not fully understand 'R'. Yet he clearly has some understanding of 'R'. He can formulate causal descriptions that R uniquely satisfies, and he has no difficulty in identifying occasions on which R is present in Smith's experiences. So what does Jones lack? The obvious answer is that Jones, unlike Smith, does not know what it is like to have an experience with R. *This* is why he does not fully understand 'R'. But according to the analysis I have given, Jones does not know what it is like to have an experience with R (at least in part) because he has not experienced R (or any phenomenally similar quality). The physicalist, then, can certainly accept the following empiricist thesis. Full understanding of the meaning of a rigid name for a phenomenally simple quality presupposes experience of that (or some phenomenally similar) quality.

III

Central to my argument so far has been the following claim. A person who knows what it is like to have a visual experience with phenomenal quality Q does not thereby know any further fact than a person who has all the relevant physical information. It may be suggested that this claim leads to certain problems that my discussion does not yet fully answer. Suppose, for example, that a supernatural being has created an entire material world just like our material world but that he still has to decide what it will be like for the humans in this world to have Q experiences. According to my defense of physicalism, since this being knows all the physical facts, before making any decision, she already knows *all* the experiential facts. So counterintuitively, she cannot really have anything left to decide about human experiences after all. Alternatively, consider again the case of Super-Jones. How, it may be asked, can this remarkable individual *really* learn anything about color experiences, on my account, when he gains his sight? Admittedly, as I say, Super-Jones will acquire new epistemic access to what he already knows. But contrary to my claims, he will not thereby learn anything, for surely to learn something is to acquire *genuinely new* knowledge.

In my view, the first of these apparent difficulties, like others of its ilk, rests upon an illegitimate appeal to imaginability of the sort I criticized in Section I. That is to say, the described counterfactual situation is classified as possible presumably because intuitively it seems imaginable. But the fact that it seems to us that we can imagine a supernatural being who has created a physical world in every respect like ours and yet who remains in a position to decide what it will be like for humans in that world to have Q experiences, say, does not entail that we have succeeded in imagining any such thing. Perhaps the physical world we imagine is not exactly like ours (have we, for example, really imagined all the relevant neural details?). Alternatively, perhaps we have imagined the right physical world and even a being who has created it, but one who *erroneously* believes that there is still something she can decide about what human experiences are like.

This reply does not strike me as counterintuitive (especially when it is seen against the background of my earlier discussion of imaginability). Furthermore, there is, I suggest, separate reason to think it correct; for if, as is widely accepted, the physical facts determine all the facts, then, whether or not there are any non-physical facts, necessarily once the physical facts are fixed all the phenomenal facts are automatically fixed too. So after the creation of a complete physical realm, the supernatural being is *not* in a position to choose which subjective experiences the inhabitants of that realm undergo.

Let us now take up the second problem. Does Super-Jones really learn anything, on my account, after he has the operation? The earlier analyses (1c) and (2) entail that before the operation Super-Jones does not know what certain experiences, token and type, are like, whereas after the operation he does. Given the following common-sense definition,

(3) x discovers at time t what an experience E (token or type) is like = df (i) x does not know, before t, what E is like; (ii) x knows at t what E is like,

together with (1c) and (2), it should be clear that, on my approach, Super-Jones makes a discovery: He discovers what certain experiences are like. Hence, in one sense of the term 'learn', he does indeed learn something. Of course, as I have repeatedly emphasized, if physicalism is true, then he does not learn any new facts. But this presents no real difficulty. I maintain that discoveries can be made even when no new facts are discovered. This, it seems to me, is an independently plausible position. Consider, for example, the case of a man who, by experiment, *finds out* how to balance a pencil on the end of his nose. This man obviously discovers something, but what he discovers is not a new fact. I claim that, in this respect, Super-Jones and he are in the same boat.

On my view, then, a conceptual distinction can be drawn between discovering a new fact and discovering what a new experience is like. This is not to say that no discoveries of the latter type are ever discoveries of the former type. On the contrary, in typical cases a person who finds out what a certain experience is like comes to know a fact about that experience that he did not know before. My point is that (1c), (2), and (3) do not *require* for their truth that a new fact be discovered. Thus, there will be possible cases, such as that of Super-Jones, in which the conditions laid down in (1c), (2), and (3) are satisfied, thereby ensuring that a discovery is made, even though, *according to the physicalist*, no new fact is uncovered.

I believe that the above critical examination renders the argument from knowledge entirely ineffective. Since I know of no other arguments that succeed in establishing that there are facts about our sensory experiences that cannot be captured in the physicalist's net, I see no reason to suppose that the subjective qualities of experience pose any special problem for physicalism.

7

The propositional attitudes of folk psychology

My concern in this chapter is to defend an operator theory of the propositional attitudes of folk psychology. My discussion is divided into four sections. In Section I, I introduce and explain the motivations for two widely accepted alternatives to the operator view. In Section II, I discuss some of the problems these alternatives face. In Section III, I introduce my own theory, and I argue not only that it is well motivated, but also that it avoids the problems adumbrated in Section II. Finally, in Section IV, I show how my operator view can be applied to *de re* and *de se* attitudes.

I

The two most popular metaphysical theories of the propositional attitudes of folk psychology are the sentence token view and the abstract proposition view. According to the former view, statements of the type

(1) x believes (desires, hopes, remembers, etc.) that P

are to be analyzed as

(1a) $(\exists y)[y$ is a token of a sentence that means that P, and x stands in the relation of believing (desiring, hoping, remembering, etc.) to $y]$.[1]

The sentence tokens quantified over in statements of type (1a) are held to be identical with concrete configurations of neural events or states. These tokens are held to be believed or desired or re-

---

1 See, e.g., Hartry Field, "Mental Representation," *Erkenntnis*, 13 (1978): 9–61; W. Lycan, "Toward a Homuncular Theory of Believing," *Cognition and Brain Theory*, 4 (1981): 139–60. I might add that Fodor is often taken to accept an analysis of statements of type (1) along the lines of (1a). However, in several places, Fodor denies that his account of belief is an analysis. See, e.g., Fodor, "Propositional Attitudes," *Monist*, 61 (1978): 501–23.

membered in virtue of their functional roles. That is to say, a given token t, which means that there is going to be a snowstorm, say, is classified as an object of belief, for example, if, and only if, (very roughly) it is of a type that tends to cause its owner to act in a way that would maximally satisfy his or her desires, whatever they might be, if it were true that there is going to be a snowstorm. Similarly, a given token t', which means that the house plants bloom, say, is classified as an object of desire if, and only if, (very roughly) it is of a type that tends to cause its owner to act in a way that would bring it about that the house plants bloom, if his or her beliefs, whatever they might be, were true. Both of these preliminary accounts make use of intentional notions. However, *taken together* they can form part of a general functionalist theory of mental concepts that reduces the mental – in one fell swoop – to the nonmental.

The sentence token view sketched above involves no explicit commitment to abstract propositions. But propositions can still enter in the analysis of what it is for a given sentence token to mean that such and such is the case. Thus, it is a mistake to suppose that a sentential approach to the attitudes *automatically* avoids propositions.

Turning now to the abstract proposition view, we can distinguish two main variants. Historically, advocates of this view held that belief and other folk psychological attitudes involve direct relations of intuitive awareness connecting minds to abstract propositions. Today, it is usually supposed that the relevant relations of believing, desiring, and the like are both indirect and functional. For example, it is said that a person, Jones, believes the proposition that megadoses of vitamin C prevent cancer, say, if, and only if, (very roughly) Jones is in a state that standardly causes him to act in a way that would maximally satisfy his desires, whatever they might be, if the proposition that megadoses of vitamin C prevent cancer were true.[2] This crude preliminary account parallels the functionalist sketch given for the sentence token view with two differences: There is no commitment to the existence of any mental sentence tokens, and there is now explicit reference to a proposition.

It should be noted that contemporary versions of the abstract proposition view do not usually eschew mental tokens altogether.

2 See, e.g., Robert Stalnaker, *Inquiry* (Cambridge, Mass.: MIT Press, 1984).

After all, it is standardly supposed that for a person to be *in* a state there must be a token of the state that the person undergoes. Given this supposition, statements of type (1) become doubly relational as follows:

(1b) $(\exists y)[y$ is a token, and x stands in the relation of believing (desiring, hoping, etc.) to y, and y stands in a further relation to the proposition that $P]$.

So according to the above view, belief tokens *might* (sometimes) turn out to have a linguistic structure, but they are certainly not required to do so.

Now, both the sentence token and the abstract proposition theories are motivated initially by the general thought that folk psychological attitudes (hereafter FPAs) such as belief *must* be relational, since existential generalization applies to the syntactic objects of those attitudes. For example,

Jones believes that gorillas are more intelligent than chimpanzees

entails

There is something Jones believes.

But what motivates adherence to one of these two views in particular? Proponents of the sentence token account usually point to the following major considerations.

To begin with, it is noted that there are parallels between the objects or contents of speech acts and the objects or contents of belief, desire, and so on. For example, I may say what I believe. Furthermore, the object of believing, like the object of saying, can have semantic properties. We may say, for example,

(2) What Jones believes is true

and

(3) What Jones believes entails what Smith believes.

The explanation the sentence token theorist offers for these parallels is that the object of belief is the same sort of entity as what is uttered in speech acts (or what is written down). The sentential view of FPAs also seems supported by the following argument. The ability to think certain thoughts appears intrinsically connected with the ability to think certain others. For example, the ability to think that John hits Mary goes hand in hand with the ability to think that

Mary hits John, but not with the ability to think that English butlers are polite. Why is this? The ability to produce or understand certain sentences is intrinsically connected with the ability to produce or understand certain others. For example, there are no native speakers of English who know how to say 'John hits Mary' but who do not know how to say 'Mary hits John'. Similarly, there are no native speakers who understand the former sentence but not the latter. These facts are easily explained if sentences have a syntactic and semantic structure. But if sentences are taken to be atomic, these facts are a complete mystery. What is true for sentences is true also for thoughts. Thinking thoughts involves manipulating mental representations. If mental representations with a propositional content have a semantic and syntactic structure like that of sentences, it is no *accident* that one who is able to think that John hits Mary is thereby also able to think that Mary hits John. Furthermore, it is no *accident* that one who can think these thoughts need not thereby be able to think thoughts having different components – for example, the thought that English butlers are polite.[3]

Consider next the inference from

(4) Rufus believes that the round object ahead is brown

and

(5) The round object ahead is the coin Rupert dropped

to

(6) Rufus believes that the coin Rupert dropped is brown.

This inference is strictly parallel to the inference from

(7) Rufus uttered the sentence 'The round object ahead is brown'

and (5) to

(8) Rufus uttered the sentence 'The coin Rupert dropped is brown.'

If the objects of belief are sentence tokens, we should *expect* the former inference to be invalid just as the latter is.

Another motivating factor is the thought that, since the pattern of causal interactions among FPAs often mirrors various inferential

---

3 The above argument is presented by J. Fodor and Z. Pylyshyn in their "Connectionism and Cognitive Architecture: A Critical Analysis," *Cognition*, 28 (1988): 3–71.

relations among the sentences that are ordinarily used to specify the objects of those FPAs, it is natural to suppose that FPA objects have logical form. For example, corresponding to the inference from

(9) All dogs make good pets

and

(10) All of Jane's animals are dogs

to

(11) All of Jane's animals make good pets,

we have the fact that, if John believes that all dogs make good pets and he later comes to believe that all of Jane's animals are dogs, he will, in all likelihood, be caused to believe that all of Jane's animals make good pets. Generalizing, we can say that a belief of the form

(12) All F are G

together with a belief of the form

(13) All G are H

typically causes a belief of the form

(14) All F are H.

This generalization concerns belief alone. But other generalizations link different FPAs. For example, a desire of the form

(15) Do A

together with a belief of the form

(16) In order to do A, it is necessary to do B

typically generates a desire of the form

(17) Do B.

Now these generalizations categorize FPAs according to the logical form of their objects. They therefore require that the objects of FPAs have logical forms. But the primary possessors of logical form are sentences. Hence, the objects of FPAs are themselves sentences.

The final consideration I shall mention is that of coherence with recent work in cognitive psychology. Some FPAs, memory, for

155

example, have been scrutinized in depth by cognitive psychologists. Philosophers have sometimes taken the empirical theories proposed by these psychologists to be theories of the *essential* nature of the relevant FPAs. Since such theories frequently appear to invoke sentential or quasi-sentential representations, it is often inferred that anything other than a sentence token approach is empirically implausible.

As for the abstract proposition theory, there are, so far as I am aware, three major motivating considerations.[4] First, it is noted, as it was earlier, that the objects of belief are parallel to the objects of saying. The explanation now offered, however, is that saying is usually the expression of belief. One who says that such and such is the case has certain beliefs and intentions, and the content of what is said *derives from* the contents of those beliefs and intentions held within the whole speech community. On this approach, the sentence token theorist is deemed to have read too much into the parallel between believing and saying. The object of a belief is not, or should not be, modeled on *what is uttered* in saying. Rather the parallel is between *what is said by* uttering a given sentence and what is believed; and this parallel does not require that the object of a belief have any syntactic structure.

A second motivation of some importance is a desire to avoid the *chauvinism* implicit in the sentence token theory. According to sententialists, the *form* in which beliefs, desires, and other FPAs are represented is essential to them: FPAs *must* involve tokens having a sentential structure. Advocates of the proposition theory insist that this imposes much too strong a constraint on the size of the domain of possible believers. Maybe *our* beliefs are represented in our heads in the form of sentences in a language of thought, but why should all beliefs necessarily be so represented in *all* creatures? For example, couldn't belief tokens take the form of graphs, maps, pictures, or indeed some other form dissimilar to any of our public forms of representation? To answer this question affirmatively is, propositionalists maintain, to see the need for some other entity to be what is believed (or desired or whatever), an entity that can bear truth and falsehood and that can serve as the common object of the FPAs of many different people.

A final consideration derives from the explanation of rational

4 These considerations are mentioned in Stalnaker, *Inquiry*.

action. According to propositionalists, it is essential to the role of beliefs in such explanations that their contents divide alternative possibilities into those that make the beliefs true and the desires satisfied, and those that do not. But the specific form in which the contents of belief and desire are represented is not essential to explanations of rational action. There is therefore nothing in a functionalist approach to belief and desire that requires the essential involvement of any linguistic representational tokens. Rather, as I noted above, what is supposedly required is that belief and desire contents distinguish among alternative possibilities. This requirement is met if such contents are taken to be ways of determining truth values, given the facts, that is, functions from possible worlds to truth values. And functions of this sort are what many contemporary advocates of the abstract proposition theory take to be propositions.

So much, by the way of background, for the two most popular theories of the nature of FPAs and the factors that motivate them. I shall now discuss some of the problems these theories face.

II

To begin with, it seems to me that the argument of Chapter 1 against the token identity theory creates serious difficulties for the sentence token theory (and also for the abstract proposition theory insofar as it countenances FPA tokens); for the problem of finding a single temporally extended neural token that is more suited than any other for identification with a given mental token is particularly acute in the case of tokens of belief, desire, and other FPAs. After all, tokens of belief, for example, often have relatively long lifetimes; they also often seem to have imprecise temporal boundaries. And where in folk psychology many different effects are traced to a single belief as the cause, according to recent work in cognitive psychology, these effects may actually have more than one cognitive cause.[5]

A further difficulty often raised for the sentence token theory concerns the semantics of sentences in the head. On one popular

5 For a defense of this last claim concerning cognitive psychology, see, e.g., Marvin Minsky, "K-Lines: A Theory of Memory," in *Perspectives on Cognitive Science*, ed. D. Norman (Norwood, N.J.: Ablex, 1981).

analysis of meaning, a sentence 's' means that P if, and only if, a convention exists among a population of speakers that 's' should be used to mean that P.[6] Sentence meaning, thus, is tied to speaker meaning plus the appropriate conventions. Speaker meaning, in turn, is analyzed via the beliefs and intentions of the speaker, and conventions are explained via patterns of beliefs and intentions of members of the population of speakers. Now it should be clear that *this* analysis of sentence meaning cannot be used to explain the meanings of sentences in the head; for not only are there no conventions of any sort associated with such sentences, but also there is an obvious problem of circularity. On another recent proposal, the causal theory of reference is invoked. The basic idea here seems to be that sentence meaning is to be analyzed via Tarskian truth-conditions, and the word–world relations of reference and satisfaction embedded in these conditions are then to be analyzed via Kripke's causal theory.[7] This account, as it stands, is open to the charge of incompleteness, since it focuses only on what was earlier called 'truth-theoretic meaning'. Putting this point to one side there is also the following difficulty. According to Kripke's causal theory of reference, terms refer in virtue of causal connections that are themselves partly intentional. The fact that 'Aristotle' refers to Aristotle, for example, is to be explained via an initial evidential causal interaction that 'introduced' the original users of 'Aristotle' to Aristotle, and later a social causal transmission of 'Aristotle' from one speaker to another. Any further specification of the latter causal connections seems to involve at least that persons pass on the name 'Aristotle' in the same way as the persons from whom they learned the name. It appears, then, that if a causal theory of reference is to form part of the foundation of a reductive analysis of the meaning of sentences in the head, much more work must be done in order to show how this theory can be spelled out *without* the use of intentional concepts.

Another related problem for the sentence token theory concerns the *syntax* of sentences in the head. Syntax, as we normally conceive it, is a conventional matter. Within the community of speakers, certain conventions are maintained that govern how words can be

6 See, e.g., H. P. Grice, "Meaning," *Philosophical Review*, 66 (1957): 377–88; idem, "Utterer's Meaning and Intention," *Philosophical Review*, 78 (1969): 147–77; Stephen Schiffer, *Meaning* (New York: Oxford University Press, 1972).
7 See Field, "Mental Representation."

combined into sentences. No such conventions exist, however, for mental sentences. So it is not immediately clear what it means to say that tokens of FPAs have a syntactic structure.

One way in which the sentence token theorist can reasonably respond to the above objections concerning semantics and syntax is to maintain that the objects of belief are really quasi-sentences, that is, items that in certain respects are like sentences but in other respects are dissimilar. The task, then, will be to spell out how these quasi-sentences are to be conceived.

A rather different objection to the sentence token theory is that it is guilty of representational chauvinism. This objection was mentioned earlier in the context of motivating the abstract proposition theory, so I will not restate it here. Insofar as it is simply *assumed* that tokens of FPAs *must* represent in the manner of language, then, it seems to me, the objection from chauvinism has considerable power, especially given alternative possible, and according to some cognitive psychologists actual, ways in which mental tokens represent the world (assuming *arguendo* that there are such tokens).[8] Of course, if the advocate of the sentence token theory were able to *demonstrate* that FPA content must be linguistic, the objection from chauvinism would lose its force. But I know of no such successful demonstration.

A further problem with the sentence token theory concerns the analysis of the assertion in (1a) that the inner sentence token y, to which person x is related, means that P. Just what is the logical form of the claim that y means that P? There are, I think, three general possibilities. One is that this claim requires that y express the abstract proposition that P. Another is that it requires that y stand in some appropriate relation to the ordinary, public sentence 'P'. And a third is that the claim has an operator analysis of the sort presented in the next section. The first of these possibilities enmeshes the sentence token theorist in the same problems, or at least many of the same problems, as the abstract proposition theorist. The second possibility has the disadvantage of making belief contexts explicitly metalinguistic. The third possibility undercuts much of the motivation for the sentence token analysis of belief

8 See, e.g., the accounts of mental representation to be found in connectionist psychological theories. See also my discussions of nonsentential representation in "The Picture Theory of Mental Images," *Philosophical Review*, 97 (1988): 497–520, and *Mental Imagery* (London: Routledge & Kegan Paul, forthcoming).

statements; for if predicates of the type 'means that P' are admitted to have a logical form of the sort assigned by the operator theory, it is hard to see why predicates of the type 'believes that P' should be given a radically different logical form.

A final problem with the sentence token theory is that, in my view, it involves gratuitous metaphysical complexity in its postulation of inner sentence tokens. Such tokens, I maintain, are not needed in order to understand how it is that statements "about" beliefs and other FPAs can be true. Hence, by Occam's razor, they should be eliminated.

The same problem arises for the abstract proposition theory. In this case, both tokens of FPAs and abstract propositions are posited, and neither are needed if the alternative operator theory I shall present shortly is espoused.

Another objection to the abstract proposition theory focuses on the nature of propositions. Recent advocates of the theory have responded to the charge that propositions are "creatures of darkness" by identifying them with functions from possible worlds to truth values or equivalently with sets of possible worlds in which the value of the function is "true." Propositions, conceived of in this way, do at least have the virtue of reasonably clear identity conditions. But these identity conditions themselves generate a serious problem for the abstract proposition theory; for the possible-worlds elucidation of propositions entails that, if the proposition that P is necessarily equivalent to the proposition that Q, then the former proposition is identical with the latter. Hence, on the abstract proposition theory, if a person believes that P, he or she automatically believes that Q. And this result seems unacceptable.[9] Surely, for example, I can believe that all brothers are male siblings without believing that all ophthalmologists are eye doctors. The situation with mathematical beliefs is even more counterintuitive. It seems undeniable that I can believe that $7 + 5 = 12$ without possessing all true mathematical beliefs. But the proposition that $7 + 5 = 12$ is necessarily equivalent to every true mathematical proposition, so that really there is only one such proposition.

9 For a detailed discussion of this problem, see M. J. Cresswell, *Structured Meanings: The Semantics of Propositional Attitudes* (Cambridge, Mass.: MIT Press, 1985); also Stalnaker, *Inquiry.*

Hence, in believing that $7 + 5 = 12$, I must also believe that $793 - 132 = 661$, that $18 \times 19 = 342$, and so on.

One standard reply to the problem mathematical beliefs present for the proposition theory is to argue that such beliefs really relate persons to contingent propositions about the link between overt, public mathematical sentences and the one necessary proposition. Thus, to believe that $7 + 5 = 12$ is to believe the contingent proposition that '$7 + 5 = 12$' expresses the necessary proposition. Since this contingent proposition is not necessarily equivalent to the proposition that '$793 - 132 = 661$' expresses the necessary proposition, one can believe that $7 + 5 = 12$ without thereby automatically believing that $793 - 132 = 661$.

This reply faces a further objection, however. Suppose a Frenchman has a belief that he expresses by uttering the sentence 'Sept et cinq sont douze'. If I have a belief that I express by uttering the sentence 'Seven plus five equals twelve', then, unless the contexts of utterance are atypical, it seems intuitively reasonable to say that we have the same mathematical belief. But according to the above reply, my belief must be different from that of the Frenchman.

A second strategy is to adopt the Fregean view that propositions are structured entities having as constituents the meanings or senses of the terms composing the sentences embedded in contexts of the form 'that P'. This view evidently handles the above problem of mathematical beliefs. But it immediately faces a significant problem of its own, for synonyms are not always intersubstitutable *salva veritate* in belief contexts. Suppose, for example, that when asked about Jill and John's whereabouts, Paul says sincerely that they have gone to Paris for a dozen weeks. Suppose also that Paul is under the misapprehension that a dozen is twenty items, not twelve, so that he expects Jill and John to return twenty weeks later. Then it seems reasonable to say both that

(18) Paul believes that Jill and John have gone to Paris for a dozen weeks

is true and that

(19) Paul believes that Jill and John have gone to Paris for twelve weeks

is false. However, (19) results from (18) by the substitution of terms that are ordinarily classified as having the same meaning.

One possible reply the proposition theorist might make to this problem is to argue that 'twelve' and 'a dozen' do not really have exactly the same meaning. The difficulty now is that it is far from clear which expressions *do* have the same meaning. Moreover, for any two expressions that *are* synonymous, there might be someone who believes that they differ in meaning. So a case parallel to that in (18) and (19) could still be constructed.

A further difficulty is that we often allow substitutions of expressions in belief contexts even though the expressions clearly have different meanings or senses. Suppose, for example, that Paul is convinced that 'the Dorset strangler' and 'the murderer of five children in Bath' refer to the same individual. Then if Paul hears of another murder, Paul's attitude might be described as

(20) Paul believes that the Dorset strangler strikes again

or alternatively as

(21) Paul believes that the murderer of five children in Bath strikes again.

Now, the fact that in this case one definite description freely substitutes for another having a different meaning does not entail that the context is transparent, that is, that any coreferential singular term can be inserted in place of either description without change of truth value.[10] Suppose that Paul's oldest friend, Neil, is, in fact, the Dorset strangler. Paul has not the slightest idea that this is so, and indeed he considers Neil incapable of any sort of violence. Then the statement

(22) Paul believes that Paul's oldest friend strikes again

is false. So 'Paul's oldest friend' cannot be substituted *salva varitate* for 'the Dorset strangler' in (20). It appears, then, that there are nontransparent belief contexts that do not conform with the Fregean view.

I have now presented a number of objections to the two most popular theories of FPAs. But I have not as yet shown that the arguments for these theories are unpersuasive. I turn next to this task in the context of the development of my own position.

---

10 See Catherine Z. Elgin, "Translucent Belief," *Journal of Philosophy*, 82 (1985): 74–91.

Terms for FPAs such as 'belief', 'desire', and 'memory' are verbal nouns. In this respect, they are of a type with the term 'sensation'. Generally, conversion of a verbal noun to a verb converts its adjectival modifiers to adverbs. Thus, transforming 'belief' to 'believes' transforms 'dogged', for example, to 'doggedly'. Transformations of this sort suggest an operator theory of FPAs in which statements about FPAs are assigned a logical form like that assigned earlier to statements about bodily and perceptual sensations. From this perspective, it is a fundamental error to assume that a statement such as

(23) Nigel has a dogged belief

asserts a relation to obtain between Nigel and a belief token. Rather (23) is to be analyzed as

(23a) Nigel believes doggedly

or formally

(23b) $[\mathbf{D}]Bn$,

where 'n' denotes Nigel, '$\mathbf{D}$' is a predicate operator abbreviating 'doggedly', and 'B' is a predicate abbreviating 'believes'. Statement (23), then, like

(24) Nigel has a throbbing sensation,

is really only about *one* concrete entity, not two. A parallel treatment can be given for statements that assign a definite representational content to FPAs. For example,

(25) Nigel has the belief that marsupials are vegetarians

can be analyzed as

(25a) Nigel believes that-(marsupials are vegetarians)-ly.

In (25a), the predicate operator 'that-(marsupials are vegetarians)-ly' is assumed to be syntactically structured. It consists of an operator 'that', which operates on the sentence 'Marsupials are vegetarians'. We have already met operators that operate on other symbols, thereby forming predicate operators, so (25a) introduces nothing radically new. Formally, let us abbreviate 'that' by '$\mathcal{T}$', and let us abbreviate sentences by capital letters other than 'S' from the end of the alphabet (reserving also 'P' and 'Q' for use as sentence variables). Then if 'V' symbolizes 'Marsupials are vegetarians', we can regiment (25a) as

(25b) $[\mathcal{T}V]Bn$.

As with the earlier formalizations, there are two possible ways of spelling out the formal semantics for (25b). On one proposal, '$\mathcal{T}$' will express a function that maps the meaning of the sentence 'V' (or alternatively the proposition expressed by 'V') onto the function expressed by '$\mathcal{T}V$'. This function will then map the property of believing onto the property expressed by '$[\mathcal{T}V]B$'. On the other proposal, '$[\mathcal{T}V]B$' will be assigned a set S. This set will be a subset of the set assigned to 'B', since '$[\mathcal{T}V]$' is a standard operator; and (25b) will be true if, and only if, Nigel belongs to S. On this account, then, (25b) is semantically unstructured within the truth theory. Statement (25b) does not have a simple overall meaning, however; for as we have seen, there is more to meaning than is revealed in formal, truth-theoretic semantics. The first of these two proposals seems to me unsatisfying, since it is as complex metaphysically as the proposition theory and it also faces the very same problems of substitutability.[11] The second proposal is, I suggest, much more promising. Let me begin my discussion of this proposal by addressing some questions.

It may be wondered why there is any need to introduce syntactic complexity into the predicate operators that are used to regiment the 'that' clauses in belief sentences. In the case of (25), for example, why should it not simply be analyzed as

(25c) $[\mathbf{M}]Bn$,

where '$\mathbf{M}$' is the unstructured operator 'that-marsupials-are-vegetarians-ly'? There is, I think, one major reason. Any theory that treats the content-specifying predicate operators as syntactically unstructured will have to introduce infinitely many syntactic primitives, one for each of the infinitely many belief sentences. So Davidson's objection from learnability (the one discussed in Chapter 3) will now very much apply. By contrast, once the predicate operators are taken to have embedded sentences, there is no diffi-

11 See pp. 160–2.

culty in grasping how it is that we manage to understand FPA predicates. Let me explain.

The infinitely many generalizations involving FPA predicates can be generated recursively, via instantiation, from a finite number of quasi-analytic generalization schemata, *only if* these schemata contain sentence variables within the FPA predicates. Consider, for example, the following schemata:

(26) For any person x, if x believes that-P-ly truly then P.

(27) For any person x, if x believes that-P-ly falsely then not-P.

(28) For any person x, if x desires that-P-ly and x believes that-(P, only if Q)-ly then, ceteris paribus, x desires that-(Q)-ly.

(29) For any person x, if x believes that-(P)-ly then, ceteris paribus, x is disposed to assent to 'P' or to some appropriate paraphrase of 'P'.

(30) For any person x, if x believes that-(P)-ly then, ceteris paribus, x is disposed to utter 'P' or some sentence that is an appropriate paraphrase of 'P'.[12]

Replacement of the sentence variables 'P' and 'Q' by sentences in (26)–(30) yields folk psychological generalizations. Infinitely many sentences can replace 'P' and 'Q', so infinitely many generalizations can be generated. No recursive generation of these generalizations would be possible if FPA predicates contained syntactically unstructured predicate operators.

Now, in order to understand a belief predicate one has not encountered before one must understand the predicate 'believes' and the relevant content-specifying operator. One will understand this operator provided that one understands what the sentence embedded in it ordinarily means (i.e., what it means when it is located outside of an FPA predicate), and one grasps that the operator must be used in such a way that the generalizations generated by the appropriate instantiation of the schemata (generalizations having the given sentence as a component) come out true. One will understand the predicate 'believes' provided that one grasps that this and other parallel predicates, for example, 'desires', must be used in such a way that the generalizations generated by any instantiation of the relevant schemata must come out true under any proper assignment of extensions to FPA predicates.[13]

---

12 For a discussion of what counts as an appropriate paraphrase in these contexts, see the end of the present section.

13 Or at least must come out by and large true. I ignore this qualification here and below for ease of exposition.

The general idea, then, is that if one knows the ordinary meanings of sentences embedded in 'that' clauses within FPA predicates and one also knows the meanings of the other vocabulary that occurs in FPA generalizations outside of FPA predicates, then so long as one grasps the role played by the generalization schemata in constraining the assignment of extensions, one thereby comes to know the correct use of potentially infinitely many FPA predicates.[14] There is, moreover, no difficulty in learning or grasping the schemata themselves, for they are finite in number.

Of course, I am not suggesting here that any competent user of FPA predicates must be able to state the generalization schemata upon request. Rather, as I noted earlier, knowledge of schemata and their instances may be tacit.[15] I might also add that three of the schemata I state above, namely (28), (29), and (30), are very rough and ready. They can be tidied up by the addition of further qualifications,[16] but as with earlier schemata, it seems to me unlikely that the ceteris paribus clauses can be eliminated altogether. This might be problematic, were my view the standard functionalist one that there are psychological properties or states whose essential nature is revealed in explicit reductive functional definitions. But as I have repeatedly emphasized, I reject this view.[17] On my account, there is no need for the generalization schemata to be specific in every last respect. It suffices that they be specific enough to satisfy the requirement that they yield generalizations that come out true under at least one collective assignment of extensions to FPA predicates.[18]

The second question I want to address concerns the relationship my proposal bears to the currently popular indicator theory of belief content developed by Dennis Stampe, Robert Stalnaker, and others.[19] Should my view be seen as being committed to an alternative

14 I am in agreement here with Terence Horgan, "Attitudinatives," *Linguistics and Philosophy*, forthcoming. For a more detailed discussion of Davidson's learnability argument in the context of FPA predicates, see ibid.
15 See, e.g., pp. 97–8.
16 For example, the appropriate causal language.
17 See, e.g., p. 97; also Chapter 5, note 36.
18 If there is more than one collective extension assignment that makes the generalizations of folk psychology come out true, then alternative assignments should be compared with respect to naturalness. For a discussion of naturalness and its relevance to the issue of indeterminacy of interpretation, see Chapter 3, note 26 and Chapter 5, Section IV.
19 See Stalnaker, *Inquiry*; Dennis Stampe, "Toward a Causal Theory of Linguistic

account of belief content, or could it be supplemented by the indicator theory?

Let me begin by briefly sketching the basic indicator theory. Suppose we have an object that changes in ways that, under normal conditions, systematically correlate with certain changes in its environment. Suppose also that these changes in the object take place because of the environmental changes. Then it seems reasonable to say that the object (under normal conditions) is a reliable indicator of its environment. Consider, for example, the pointer on a car speedometer. Assuming that the speedometer is working properly, the position of the pointer correlates in a systematic manner with the speed of the car, and for any given pointer position p and correlated speed s, the pointer occupies p because the car is moving at s. In these circumstances, the pointer position p indicates that the speed of the car is s. There is, then, a definite representational content that attaches to the pointer position. Furthermore, this content obviously presents no difficulty for a physicalist point of view.

Advocates of the indicator theory maintain that the representational content of beliefs is to be conceived in a similar manner. I believe that there is a red object ahead, for example, just in case I am in a belief state x such that, under optimal conditions, if I were in x then there would be a red object ahead, and in these conditions, x would be brought about in me as a result of there being a red object ahead.

One interesting objection to this view is that it ignores the holistic character of belief.[20] What one believes on any given occasion typically depends in part on what else one believes. Consider, for example, the case of a simple perceptual belief such as the one just mentioned. If I mistakenly believe that things that look red to me are really green then, even when there is something red ahead and that something looks as if it is red to me, the belief I will form is that there is something *green* ahead. This problem can be eliminated, it may be suggested, only by citing the *contents* of certain background beliefs in one's specification of the optimal conditions for believing that there is something red ahead. But this specification

Representation," *Midwest Studies in Philosophy*, 2 (1977): 42–63; also Fred Dretske, *Knowledge and the Flow of Information* (Cambridge, Mass.: Bradford, 1981).
20 See Brian McLaughlin, "What Is Wrong With Correlational Psychosemantics," *Synthese*, 70 (1987): 271–86.

will undercut the proposed reductive, naturalistic analysis of the given belief content, since the parallel analyses of the contents of the background beliefs will themselves need to cite other contents and so on.

The above objection seems to me to present a significant difficulty for the indicator theory. Now, the view that the physicalist needs an analysis of the sort that the indicator theory provides, that is, an explicit, reductive definition of what it is that makes a belief have a certain content, presupposes that there are beliefs and also that there are properties of the type, having such and such a content, that beliefs have. The problem for the physicalist is to give some account of these properties which shows that they lie within his or her metaphysical scheme. Since I deny that there are any beliefs or properties of the given type, I deny that any reductive definition or analysis is needed. So my operator theory is compatible neither with the indicator theory nor with any other theory that attempts to analyze the *nature* of belief content. This is not to say that my theory cannot incorporate any of the insights of the indicator theory. For example, it seems reasonable to hold that two of the generalization schemata relevant to perceptual belief predicates are along the following lines:

(31) For any person x, if x is a normal perceiver in standard conditions and there is a (real) F object before x's eyes then, ceteris paribus, x senses F-ly.

(32) For any person x, if x senses F-ly and x believes that x senses F-ly and x also believes that x is a normal perceiver in standard conditions then, ceteris paribus, x believes that there is a (real) F object present.

These schemata together link perceptual belief predicates to external 'input conditions'. In this limited respect there is a point of contact with the indicator theory.

Another question regarding the proposed operator theory of FPAs concerns its apparent incompatibility with the fact that existential generalization applies to the syntactic objects of the attitudes. This fact, I noted earlier, motivates the general view that FPAs *must* be relational. My reply is that there is really no incompatibility. If (25), for example, is formalized as (25b), the inference to

(33) There is something Nigel believes

is validated via existential generalization to

(33a) $(\exists P)[\mathcal{T}P]Bn.$

I take the existential quantifier in (33a) to be substitutional, since the substitution instances of the variable 'P' are sentences, not singular terms. Hence, I deny that (25b) is committed to the existence of any object of belief.

It is perhaps worth noting that, on my proposal, the inference from (25) to

(34) Nigel has a belief

need not be handled in the same way. Instead, (34) can be regimented as

(34a) $Bn,$

and (34a) follows from (25b) by operator detachment. The situation here, I might add, is rather like certain others not involving FPAs. For example, on the predicate-operator view, the inference from 'Nigel sings at midnight' to 'Nigel sings' can be justified by operator detachment. But the inference from 'Nigel sings at midnight' to 'There is a time at which Nigel sings' is justified by existential generalization on the singular term embedded in the operator 'at midnight'.

The above difference between (34) and (33) disappears on another version of the operator theory that treats 'believes' as part of an operator 'believes that', which operates on the sentence it precedes to form a predicate.[21] On this account, if we symbolize 'believes' by '$\mathcal{B}$' and abbreviate 'believes that' by '$\mathcal{B}(\ )$', where '$\mathcal{B}(\ )$' applies to any sentence 'P', thereby forming a complex predicate, we can regiment (25) as

(25d) $\mathcal{B}(V)n.$

Now (33) and (34) are *both* regimented as

(33b) $(\exists P)\mathcal{B}(P)n,$

and (33b) follows from (25d) by substitutional existential generalization.

I have no real objection to this account. For example, it is, I think, evident that the earlier response to the question of learnability

---

21 See W. V. O. Quine, *Word and Object* (Cambridge, Mass.: MIT Press, 1960), p. 216; also Terence Horgan, "Attitudinatives."

will still apply. I am somewhat inclined to prefer the first proposal, since it provides a somewhat more unified treatment of psychological statements generally. But the difference between the two proposals is not great. Both proposals introduce operators on sentences, and both also introduce predicate operators. In the case of the second proposal, predicate operators are needed in the analysis of statements involving terms such as 'dogged'. For example, the earlier statement

(23) Nigel has a dogged belief

is analyzed as

(23c) $(\exists P)[\mathbf{D}]\mathcal{B}(P)n$.

Before proceeding further, I want to emphasize that the nature of the disagreement between the operator theory and either the sentence token view or the abstract proposition theory is fundamentally metaphysical. I assume that the two latter theories are committed metaphysically to entities that the operator theory avoids. I maintain that the arguments summarized in Section I do not provide any strong reason for preferring either the sentence token view or the abstract proposition theory to the operator theory. I also maintain that none of the problems adumbrated in Section II present any difficulties for my position. I want now to substantiate the claims expressed in the last two sentences, beginning with the former.

Consider first the assertion that there are parallels between the objects or contents of speech acts and the objects or contents of belief, desire, and the like. Here the operator theorist can grant that there is a close parallel between predicates of the type 'believes that P' and predicates of the type 'says that P'. This is because, on the operator theory, a statement such as

(35) Nigel says that marsupials are vegetarians

is analyzed in exactly the same way as the corresponding belief statement (25). The clause 'that marsupials are vegetarians' is treated as a predicate operator containing the sentence 'Marsupials are vegetarians'. Alternatively, 'says that' is taken to be an operator that operates on this sentence. Of course, on the preferred semantics there will not really be any entity that is the object of either saying or believing. Nonetheless, given (35) as a premise, I may certainly infer

(36) Nigel says something,

just as earlier, given (25), it was permissible to infer (33).

As for the claim that what is believed can have the semantic property of truth, this will also present no difficulty. On the operator theory, a statement such as

(37) Nigel believes that there are pandas in California and what Nigel believes is true

can be analyzed as

(37a) Nigel believes that-(there are pandas in California)-ly truly.

Here 'truly' is an iterated predicate operator, which can be detached in the standard manner. Alternatively, (37) can be analyzed as

(37b) Nigel believes that (there are pandas in California) truly,

where 'believes that' operates on the sentence in parentheses and 'truly' is a predicate operator. A further possible analysis consistent with the general operator approach is to rewrite (37) as

(37c) Nigel believes that there are pandas in California and thereby Nigel believes something that is true.

Then, using the generative connective $\overset{g}{\rightarrow}$ and the substitutional sentence quantifier '$(\exists P)$', we can regiment (37c) as

(37d) Nigel believes that-(there are pandas in California)-ly $\overset{g}{\rightarrow}$ $(\exists P)$[Nigel believes that-(P)-ly & 'P' is true]

or alternatively as

(37e) Nigel believes (there are pandas in California) $\overset{g}{\rightarrow}$ $(\exists P)$[Nigel believes (P) & 'P' is true].

In these analyses the predicate 'is true' is used, but again there is no need to acknowledge a property of truth.

In the case of belief entailment the situation is similar. Consider, for example, the earlier statement

(3) What Jones believes entails what Smith believes.

How is this statement to be analyzed? The obvious analysis is

(3a) $(\exists P)(\exists Q)$[Jones believes that-(P)-ly & Smith believes that-(Q)-ly & 'P' entails 'Q'].

Essentially the same analysis will be offered if 'believes that' is treated as an operator on sentences.

171

Turning now to the argument that appeals to the intrinsic connections among some thoughts, for example, the thought that John hits Mary and the thought that Mary hits John, it seems to me that the operator theorist can say the following. Taken literally, the question as to why certain thoughts are intrinsically connected is unanswerable, since it falsely presupposes that there are thoughts. Taken as a question about the connections between certain psychological predicates, the answer is to be found in the generalization schemata that govern the application of such predicates. So far, in the schemata I have adumbrated, the only variables present have been sentence variables. This will not be the case for all FPA schemata, however. Consider, for example, the schema

(38) For any person x, if x thinks that-(yRz)-ly then x has the capacity to think that-(zRy)-ly.

This schema yields true instances upon replacement of the variables 'y' and 'z' by singular terms and of 'R' by a specific relational term. It does so, moreover, as a matter of the meanings (conceptual roles) of its component vocabulary. Thus, the predicate 'thinks that John hits Mary' is intrinsically connected with the predicate 'thinks that Mary hits John' via meaning ties. These meaning ties guarantee that one who thinks that John hits Mary can also think that Mary hits John.[22]

The next point concerns the inference from the statements

(4) Rufus believes that the round object ahead is brown

and

(5) The round object ahead is the coin Rupert dropped

to

(6) Rufus believes that the coin Rupert dropped is brown.

According to the operator theory, this inference is not formally valid. Moreover, the inference is not semantically valid either, for it cannot be justified, by reference to any of the meaning-giving generalization schemata.

What of the claim that FPA objects have logical form? This claim

---

22 Schema (38) attributes a capacity to person x. It may be wondered how talk of capacities is to be analyzed. For a brief discussion of this issue, see Chapter 8, Section II.

was advanced earlier on the grounds that certain folk psychological generalizations categorize FPAs according to the logical form of their objects. One such generalization is that a belief of the form

(12) All F are G

and a belief of the form

(13) All G are H

typically cause a belief of the form

(14) All F are H.

From the perspective of the operator theory, there are no beliefs. So there are no true generalizations of this sort. Instead, there are true generalizations generated by schemata such as the following:

(39) For any person x, if x believes that-(all F are G)-ly and x believes that-(all G are H)-ly then, ceteris paribus, x believes that-(all F are H)-ly.

The generalizations corresponding to (39) (and other schemata) do not require for their truth that there be objects of belief or other FPAs no matter how categorized. So the argument for the conclusion that FPA objects have logical form rests on an assumption about FPA generalizations that can reasonably be rejected.

The final consideration on my list of factors motivating the sentence token theory was that of coherence with work in cognitive psychology. This consideration seems to me to carry very little weight. For one thing, as I noted earlier, some recent cognitive theories avoid even the appearance of any commitment to linguistic mental representations.[23] For another, in the next chapter, I shall argue that even those cognitive theories that assume the general digital computer model of mind are not committed metaphysically to such representations. Third, it seems to me that empirical theories of FPAs do *not* yield universal *necessary* truths about FPAs and hence that their commitments do not have any relevance to the logical analysis of FPA sentences.

Consider, for example, Saul Sternberg's work on short-term

---

23 I have in mind here connectionist theories. For a good summary of connectionist views, see D. McClelland, J. Rumelhart, and the PDP Research Group, *Parallel Distributed Processing*, Vol. 1 (Cambridge, Mass.: MIT Press, 1986), pp. 77–109.

memory.[24] In Sternberg's experiments, subjects were shown randomly generated lists of six or fewer numbers. The lists were visually displayed for roughly one second. Two seconds after each list disappeared, a trial digit appeared. Subjects were asked to pull one lever if the digit was on the list and another lever if it was not. Sternberg discovered that the mean response time varied linearly with the length of the memorized list and that for any given list the response times were the same whether or not the trial digit was on the list. The hypothesis Sternberg formed to explain these results was that, in short-term recall of lists, our minds scan serially across each list, in each case going to the end before responding *even if* the test digit matches one of the earlier numbers on the list.

It seems reasonable to suppose that short-term memory does not *have* to work in this way in all possible creatures even though it does in fact work this way in us. For example, there could be creatures who engage in "self-terminating" serial searches that lead to a response as soon as a match is discovered between the test digit and a number on the list. The reponse times of these creatures would be different from ours (they would vary with the location of the test digit on the list), but it would hardly follow that the creatures did not have the capacity to remember recently seen symbols.

It seems to me, then, that theories about how given cognitive capacities, describable in folk terms, work are really theories about how those capacities are *realized* in some actual population or other. The upshot is that the commitments of theories in cognitive psychology, in my view, have no direct bearing on the proper regimentation of FPA sentences.

Turning now to the two factors not yet discussed, factors alleged to support the abstract proposition theory, it is, I think, clear that these factors are compatible with my approach. After all, the operator theory avoids chauvinism just as much as the abstract proposition theory does. Furthermore, the claim that belief and desire contents must distinguish among alternative possibilities can be reconstructed within the operator theory as the claim that people believe and/or desire in ways that are so defined that in certain alternative possible situations the persons thereby have true beliefs

24 See Saul Sternberg, "High-Speed Scanning in Human Memory," *Science*, 153 (1966): 652–4.

(i.e., believe truly) and/or satisfied desires (i.e., desire satisfied-ly), whereas in others they do not. This claim, I might add, does not presuppose that possible worlds exist either unless, of course, all talk of possible situations ultimately involves a metaphysical commitment to possible worlds.[25]

The general conclusion I reach is that the FPA features usually adduced in defense of the two most popular theories do not, in fact, support those theories over the rival view I have elaborated. I want next to return to the problems raised in Section II.

It should be obvious that all the problems confronting the sentence token theory and all but one of the problems confronting the abstract proposition theory dissolve, once the operator theory is accepted. The one problem requiring discussion is that of substitutability in belief contexts. I propose to approach this problem by raising another that is closely related. Consider the sentence

(40) Nigel has at least two false beliefs.

How is this sentence to be regimented? One possibility is to analyze (40) as

(40a) $(\exists P)(\exists Q)$[Nigel believes that-(P)-ly falsely & Nigel believes that-(Q)-ly falsely & 'P' $\neq$ 'Q']

or, if preferred, as

(40b) $(\exists P)(\exists Q)$[Nigel believes (P) & Nigel believes (Q) & 'P' is false & 'Q' is false & 'P' $\neq$ 'Q'].

This will not work, however; for it seems clear that two different sentences sometimes express a single belief. Suppose, for example, that Nigel is described on some given occasion as believing falsely that Deborah has just turned fourteen years of age. Nigel *might* equally well be described as believing falsely that Deborah has just turned 14 years of age. Or consider the pair of sentences (20) and (21), and the surrounding discussion in Section II.

My preliminary suggestion is that such counterexamples are best handled by analyzing (40) as

(40c) $(\exists P)(\exists Q)$[Nigel believes that-(P)-ly falsely & Nigel believes that-(Q)-ly falsely & 'P' is not an appropriate paraphrase of 'Q'].

---

25 I deny that this is so, but I cannot pursue the regimentation of modal discourse here.

More generally, I maintain that two sentences can be intersubstituted *salva veritate* in a nontransparent belief context if, and only if, one of the sentences is an appropriate paraphrase of the other.[26] Now the earlier discussion of the problem of substitutability in Section II showed that synonymous sentences are not always intersubstitutable *salva veritate* in nontransparent belief contexts. It also showed that necessarily equivalent sentences are not always so substitutable either. So appropriate paraphrase, as I understand it, is not to be explicated in terms of either synonyomy or necessary equivalence. What, then, is the criterion for appropriate paraphrase?

There is, I think, no answer to this question, no general criterion for deciding when one sentence is an appropriate paraphrase of another. What counts as an appropriate paraphrase is, I suggest, a somewhat flexible, context-relative matter. If two sentences are logically equivalent and differ only very minimally in logical form, as, for example, in the case of

(41) John is tall and John is handsome

and

(42) John is handsome and John is tall,

then in almost any communicative context one will be counted as an appropriate paraphrase for the other. But if two sentences lack this very intimate logical connection, then whether one is classified as an appropriate paraphrase of the other varies with the context. For example, our grounds for saying that 'the murderer of five children in Bath' is substitutable *salva veritate* for 'the Dorset strangler' in the earlier sentence

(20) Paul believes that the Dorset strangler strikes again

is Paul's conviction that these descriptions designate the same individual. Our grounds for denying that 'Paul's oldest friend' is substitutable *salva veritate* is Paul's conviction that his oldest friend is incapable of any sort of violence. Here, then, our criterion for counting 'the murderer of five children in Bath strikes again', but

26 This proposal is also made by Catherine Elgin in her "Translucent Belief." Although the proposal I make is restricted to nontransparent belief contexts, it can be extended to transparent belief contexts. See Elgin, ibid., p. 87. I should add that the comments that follow on appropriate paraphrase are influenced by Elgin's discussion, although I reject her overall analysis or explication of belief sentences.

not 'Paul's oldest friend strikes again', as an appropriate paraphrase for 'the Dorset strangler strikes again' appeals to Paul's convictions in the given context and so takes the believer as the final authority.

Other criteria are also employed. Suppose, for example, that Paul sincerely utters the sentence

(43) Doctor Lee is a heart specialist

in the context of a casual conversation with some friends. Paul might be reported later by these friends as having said that Doctor Lee is a cardiologist or as having expressed the belief that Doctor Lee is a cardiologist on the grounds that it is widely known that 'cardiologist' and 'heart specialist' are coextensive. In this case, then, the criterion for an appropriate paraphrase appeals to common knowledge. But this common knowledge does not *have* to be knowledge that Paul himself has. For example, Paul, for one reason or another, might never have come across the word 'cardiologist' even though he fully understands 'heart specialist'. There are, then, certain circumstances in which we can reasonably ascribe to people beliefs that they do not recognize as theirs.

The conclusion I draw is that it is a mistake to view belief ascription as rigid: There is no straightforward, context-independent criterion that lays down once and for all the limits on substitution in (nontransparent) belief sentences. Fortunately, the operator theory is not committed to there being any such criterion.

I hope that I have now said enough to show that the operator theory of FPAs is an attractive view that coheres well with the operator theory of sensations and that *overall* is more promising than either the sentence token theory or the abstract proposition theory.

IV

In this section, I present an account of how the operator theory can be applied to the task of analyzing *de re* and *de se* belief statements.[27] I begin with the formal semantics of *de re* belief. Consider the statement

(44) Julia believes of Rupert that he is handsome.

27 Although I focus on the case of belief, I intend my discussion to generalize to all FPAs.

On the operator theory, there are two ways of viewing this statement. One possibility, first suggested by W. V. O. Quine,[28] is to take 'believes' to be part of a variable-binding operator, which, when applied to the open sentence 'y is handsome' and the variable 'y', produces a dyadic relative term, 'believes y (y is handsome) of'. Statement (44), then, is true just in case the ordered pair consisting of Julia and Rupert satisfies this relative term. In the case of a more complex *de re* belief statement, for example,

(45) Julia believes of Rupert and Mary that the former loves the latter,

a corresponding analysis will be given. Thus, 'believes' will here be part of a variable-binding operator that, when applied to the open sentence 'y loves z' and the variables 'y' and 'z', produces a triadic relative term, 'believes y, z (y loves z) of'. Thus, (45) is true if, and only if, the ordered triple consisting of Julia, Rupert, and Mary satisfies 'believes y, z (y loves z) of'. Analyses of the same sort will be given for yet more complex cases.

The other possibility is to take 'that' in (44) to be part of a variable-binding operator that, when applied to the open sentence 'y is handsome' and the variable 'y', produces a further operator 'that y (y is handsome) of'. This operator then operates on the singular term 'Rupert' to form a predicate operator 'that y (y is handsome) of Rupert', which, in turn, operates on the predicate 'believes' to form a complex predicate. Formally, this proposal can be implemented as follows. Let '$\bot y(Hy)$' abbreviate 'that y (y is handsome) of'; further, let '$\bot y(Hy)$' directly precede any singular term it operates on, thereby forming a predicate operator; also let 'r' and 'j' symbolize 'Rupert' and 'Julia', respectively; and, as before, let 'B' symbolize 'believes'. Then (44) can be regimented as

(44a) $[\bot y(Hy)r]Bj$.

The formal semantics for (44a) runs parallel to that presented in Chapter 4 for statements that locate bodily sensations in limbs.[29] Thus, the set assigned to the predicate '$[\bot y(Hy)r]Bx$' will depend on (i) the set assigned to 'Bx', (ii) the kind of operator '$\bot y(Hy)r$' is, and (iii) the referent of 'r'. Since '$\bot y(Hy)r$' is standard, we require that the set assigned to '$[\bot y(Hy)r]Bx$' be a subset of the set assigned

28 See his *Word and Object*, p. 216.
29 See pp. 81–2.

178

to 'Bx'. As before, we also require that for any objects o and o' (in the domain of our interpretation for the formal language), if 'r' designates o then o' belongs to the set assigned to '$[\perp y(Hy)r]Bx$' if, and only if, the ordered pair $<o, o'>$ belongs to the set assigned to '$[\perp y(Hy)z]Bx$', where the latter expression is a *binary* structured predicate with free variables 'x' and 'z'.

Given these semantics, existential generalization on the name 'r' in (44) will be valid, as will detachment of the operator '$\perp y(Hy)r$'. There is one important respect in which, on the present account, the formal semantics of *de re* belief statements is more complex than that of statements that locate bodily sensations. Consider again (45). The present version of the operator theory analyzes (45) as

(45a) Julia believes that y, z (y loves z) of Rupert and Mary.

In (45a), 'that y, z (y loves z) of Rupert and Mary' is a predicate operator within which there are *two* different singular terms. How, then, is the formal semantics of (45) and other *de re* belief statements that introduce three or more objects of beliefs to be spelled out?

The general approach I favor is as follows. Let us introduce variable-binding operators of the general type 'that $y_1, y_2, \ldots, y_n$ (y_1 bears n-adic relation R to $y_2, \ldots, y_n$) of' or, fully symbolized, '$\perp y_1 y_2 \ldots y_n (R y_1 y_2 \ldots y_n)$'; and let us permit each such operator to precede n singular terms, 'c_1','c_2',$\ldots$,'c_n', thereby forming a predicate operator. Suppose now we have a predicate '$[\perp y_1 y_2 \ldots y_n (R y_1 y_2 \ldots y_n) c_1 c_2 \ldots c_n]Bx$' of arbitrary complexity. Suppose we also have another $(n + 1)$-adic predicate that is the same except that each singluar term 'c_1', 'c_2',$\ldots$, 'c_n' has been replaced by a variable 'z_1', 'z_2', $\ldots$, 'z_n'. The set S^* assigned to '$[\perp y_1 y_2 \ldots y_n (R y_1 y_2 \ldots y_n) c_1 c_2 \ldots c_n]Bx$' will depend on the set S assigned to 'Bx' and on the referents of 'c_1', 'c_2', $\ldots$, 'c_n'. The former dependence is straightforward enough: S^* must be a subset of S. But how is the latter dependence to be specified? Generalizing on the earlier approach, I suggest we say that for any objects o_1, $o_2, \ldots, o_n$ and any further object o, if 'c_1', 'c_2',$\ldots$, 'c_n' designate $o_1, o_2, \ldots, o_n$, respectively, then o belongs to the satisfaction set assigned to '$[\perp y_1 y_2 \ldots y_n (R y_1 y_2 \ldots y_n) c_1 c_2 \ldots c_n]Bx$' if, and only if, the ordered $(n + 1)$-tuple $<o_1, o_2, \ldots, o_n, o>$ belongs to the satisfaction set assigned to '$[\perp y_1 y_2 \ldots y_n (R y_1 y_2 \ldots y_n) z_1 z_2 \ldots z_n]Bx$'. Truth conditions can now be stated for arbitrarily complex *de re*

179

belief sentences: A sentence '$[\perp y_1 y_2 \ldots y_n (R y_1 y_2 \ldots y_n) c_1 c_2 \ldots c_n] Ba$' is true if, and only if, a is a member of S^*.

Of course, the above formal semantics does not give us a full account of the meaning of *de re* belief sentences. But as I have repeatedly emphasized, semantics of its type were never intended to capture meaning as a whole. An important element in the meaning of *de re* belief predicates and operators is the role they play in folk psychological generalizations, just as it was for the earlier belief predicates and operators. In the *de re* case, one of the relevant generalization schemata might go roughly as follows

(46) For any person x and for any person y, if x desires that z (z is ψ) of y, and x believes that z (in order for it to be the case that z is ψ, it must be the case that P) of y, and x believes that z (z can bring it about that P) of x, then, ceteris paribus, x will bring it about that P.[30]

This schema generates folk psychological generalizations upon replacement of 'P' by sentences and 'ψ' by action verbs. As before, generalizations generated via instantiation of schemata such as (46) must come out true (or by and large true) under a correct extension assignment for FPA predicates.

I turn now to the analysis of *de se* belief statements, that is, sentences such as 'He believes that he himself is a millionaire' and 'I believe that I am about to be attacked'. It is tempting to suppose that ascriptions of belief *de se* are trivially equivalent to ascriptions of belief *de re* about oneself. There are, however, well-known and decisive counterexamples to this view. Suppose I am looking at a mirror and that I do not realize I am doing so. Suppose also that I see a person in the mirror, namely myself, and I believe of the person I am seeing that his trousers are on fire. I do not yet believe that *I* am wearing trousers that are on fire, although very shortly I will do so.[31]

How, then, are *de se* belief sentences to be analyzed? As far as

---

30 It would be more accurate to revise (46) so that "x believes that z (z can bring it about that P) of x" is *de se* with respect to x instead of *de re*. I ignore this complication since I have not yet discussed the canonical regimentation of *de se* belief sentences.

31 This example is due to David Kaplan. A similar example is given by Roderick Chisholm in his "Logic of Believing," *Pacific Philosophical Quarterly*, 61 (1980): 31–49.

canonical regimentation goes, the simplest strategy is to analyze a sentence such as

(47) I believe that I am wearing trousers on fire

as either

(47a) I believe that-(I am wearing trousers on fire)-ly,

where 'that-(I am wearing trousers on fire)-ly' is a predicate operator, within which 'that' is a further operator on the embedded indexical sentence, or as

(47b) I believe (I am wearing trousers on fire),

where 'believe ( )' is an operator on the same indexical sentence. Sentence (47a) [or (47b)] will be true just in case the person referred to by 'I' satisfies the set assigned to the belief predicate.

Now, as with other belief predicates, the predicates in (46a) and (46b) have a meaning that is tied to their role in folk psychological generalizations. It seems reasonable to claim that the role such predicates play in folk psychological generalizations is markedly different from the role played by belief predicates within which there are no indexical sentences embedded. This will explain why I can satisfy the nonindexical predicate 'believes that the person I am seeing is wearing trousers that are on fire' without satisfying the indexical predicate 'believes that I am wearing trousers that are on fire'. It will also explain why my coming to satisfy the latter predicate is associated with a striking change of behavior. It seems to me, then, that there is no difficulty in extending the operator theory to *de se* belief ascriptions.

In this chapter, I have tried to show that there is a defensible operator theory of FPAs that goes naturally with an operator theory of sensations and that avoids the pitfalls and deficiencies of certain other accounts. In the next chapter, I articulate an important extension of the operator theory outside the realm of folk psychology.

181

8

The metaphysics of cognitive psychology

My aim, in this chapter, is to present an interpretation of the research program of cognitive psychology that eschews any metaphysical commitment to mental representations. I begin by summarizing the subject matter, assumptions, and general methodology of cognitive psychology. Next I consider various arguments that purport to show that quantification over mental representations within cognitive psychology is ineliminable. I try to show that none of these arguments is compelling. Finally, I turn to a discussion of arguments against the existence of mental representations. I reject some of these arguments but maintain that others are sound.

I

The distinctive questions of cognitive psychology are "how" questions pertaining to the exercise of our cognitive capacities. Cognitive psychologists try to explain how we remember, how we understand, how we form mental images, how we perceive, and so on.[1] The basic assumption shared by these psychologists is that the mind is a *representational* system: Persons, in exercising their cognitive capacities, are to be viewed as having mental representations that are typically subpersonal and that are transformed or operated on in various ways.[2] In calling these representations (and

---

1 In contrast, the framework of folk psychology typically deals with "why" questions pertaining to our manifest behavior. For example, 'Why did you read Maurois's biography of Balzac?' Answer: 'Because I believe that Maurois is a first-rate biographer and I wanted to know more about Balzac's life'.

2 See, e.g., Ned Block, "Mental Pictures and Cognitive Science," *Philosophical Review*, 92 (1984): 499–542; Fred Dretske, *Knowledge and the Flow of Information* (Cambridge, Mass.: Bradford, 1981); Jerry Fodor, *The Language of Thought* (New York: Cromwell, 1975); idem, *Representations* (Cambridge, Mass.: MIT Press, 1981); Barbara Von Eckardt, "Mental Images and Their Explanations," *Philosophical Studies*, 53 (1988): 441–60.

operations) typically subpersonal, what is meant is that they are usually inaccessible to introspection.[3]

Now, in appealing to subpersonal entities, cognitive psychologists are effectively decomposing our cognitive capacities into their more basic components. One important feature, then, of the explanations of cognitive psychology is that they are typically *decompositional*. Another important feature is that they are *functional* rather than neural. A useful analogy here may be found in the explanations of computer science. Suppose that I have a computer that produces the output 1 when I input 1, the output 8 when I input 2, and the output 27 when I input 3. One way to explain how the computer produces these outputs for the given inputs is to specify all the complex electrical and mechanical goings on that connect the two. Another kind of explanation – one at the level of software rather than hardware – is that the computer is running a particular program so that given as input any number N it performs the operation $N \times N \times N$. Any further account of how the computer performs the operation $N \times N \times N$ will break it down into simpler operations that themselves can be decomposed until such simple operations are reached that they can be explained only by reference to the physical structure of the computer. It is at this point that the software and hardware explanations ultimately come together. The same is true for the explanations of cognitive psychology and neurophysiology. Cognitive psychologists offer explanations at the level of the mind's program, so to speak; these nonphysiological explanations appeal to operations and representations and their causal relationships. Ultimately there must be a fit with neurophysiology, however. That is to say, if the explanations cognitive psychologists offer are correct, the structures and operations they posit must finally be decomposable into structures and operations so simple that (i) they cannot be explained in functional terms and (ii) they can indeed be physically realized in us given our particular physical makeup.

The methodology employed by cognitive psychologists is that used in science generally. Cognitive psychologists establish facts concerning the cognitive capacity they wish to understand and they propose theories that, if true, would explain why those facts obtain.

3 The term 'subpersonal' is Daniel Dennett's. See his "Ascription of Content," in *Content and Consciousness* (London: Routledge & Kegan Paul, 1969), pp. 93–6.

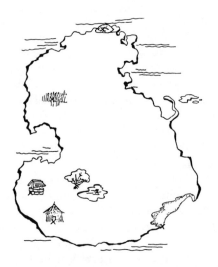

Figure 1

The salient facts are established by experiments on our exercise of the relevant cognitive capacity. Consider, for example, the facts Sternberg uncovered by his experiments on short-term memory (facts I cited in Chapter 7) and Sternberg's proposed theory.[4] Alternatively, consider Stephen Kosslyn's map-scanning experiment on mental imagery.[5] This experiment required subjects to study a map (see Figure 1). When the subjects had become familiar enough with the map to be able to draw it, they were asked to form a mental image of it and then to focus in on one particular object in the image, and this request was repeated for different objects. It was found that, the farther away an object was from the place on the image presently being focused on, the longer it took to focus on that new object. For example, shifting attention from the tree part of the image to the hut part took longer than shifting attention from the tree part to the lake part.

Kosslyn has taken this experiment to support both the idea that mental images can be scanned and the idea that mental images can have parts of which their subjects are unconscious. The latter idea

4 See pp. 173–4.
5 See S. Kosslyn, T. Ball, and B. Reiser, "Visual Image Scanning," *Journal of Experimental Psychology: Human Perception and Performance*, 4 (1978): 47–60.

is suggested by the fact that when the subjects focused on one part of their images they were not aware of imaging other parts. Yet independent experiments on the time it takes to produce images showed that their scanning times were much too fast for them to be generating a new image each time they focused in on a new object.

The general conclusion Kosslyn draws from this and related experiments is that the data structures underlying our experience of imagery are quasi-pictures in the head, which persons can construct and scan.[6] There has been much debate in cognitive psychology, of course, about whether this conclusion is licensed (and also about the distinctive features of quasi-pictorial data structures). Many cognitive psychologists maintain that Kossyln's experiments can be explained without rejecting the widely held claim that we (or our minds) always process information via the manipulation of quasi-linguistic data structures.[7] The question of who is right on this issue need not concern us here. It suffices to note that Kosslyn's program is inconsistent with any characterization of cognitive psychology that commits its workers to the thesis that our cognitive activity is always analogous to the symbolic operations and data structures found in digital computers.[8]

So much for the basic framework of cognitive psychology. It is time now to take up the question of whether cognitive psychology

---

6 For a summary of the experimental data that Kosslyn takes to support this conclusion, see his *Image and Mind* (Cambridge, Mass.: Harvard University Press, 1980).

7 See, e.g., Zenon Pylyshyn, "The Imagery Debate," in *Imagery*, ed. Ned Block (Cambridge, Mass.: MIT Press, 1981), pp. 151–206; idem, *Computation and Cognition* (Cambridge, Mass.: MIT Press, 1984).

8 This is not to say that Kosslyn's program is inconsistent with the digital computer model of the mind, for digital computers contain both symbolic and quasi-pictorial data structures. This point is not widely appreciated by philosophers, and it has led to some bad misunderstandings of Kosslyn's view (by, e.g., Block, "Mental Pictures"). For a defense of these claims, see my "Picture Theory of Mental Images," *Philosophical Review*, 97 (1988): 497–520.

I might add that there is, of course, a program within cognitive psychology that *is* inconsistent with at least some aspects of the digital computer model, namely the program of parallel distributed processing. See D. McClelland, J. Rumelhart, and the PDP Research Group, *Parallel Distributed Processing*, Vols. 1 and 2 (Cambridge, Mass.: MIT Press, 1986). For a discussion of the nature of representation in parallel distributed processing, see my "Representation in Pictorialism and Connectionism," *Southern Journal of Philosophy*, 27 (supplement containing proceedings of Spindel Conference on Connectionism, 1988).

is really committed to the existence of mental representations, as is almost universally supposed.

II

A variety of arguments can be constructed from the brief summary given above for the view that there are mental representations. To begin with, it can be urged that any representational account of the mind requires a metaphysics that includes mental representations; for if there are no such representations, surely the mind cannot be representational.

I find this argument unpersuasive. The claim that there are no mental representations is consistent with the claim that representational talk in cognitive psychology is true; for statements putatively about mental representations may be reconstructed as statements about persons or their brains. Consider, for example,

(1) James's brain presently contains a representation the content of which is that a cat is ahead.

On my view, (1) is to be analyzed as

(1a) James's brain presently represents that a cat is ahead.

Sentence (1a) can be formalized within the framework of my general operator theory in the following way. Let 'P' abbreviate 'presently'; let 'Rx' be the predicate 'x represents'; let '$\mathcal{T}$' abbreviate the operator 'that', which operates on the sentence 'A cat is ahead' to form the predicate operator 'that-(a cat is ahead)-ly; let 'W' symbolize 'A cat is ahead', and let 'Bxj' abbreviate 'x is a brain of James'. Then (1a) becomes

(1b) $(\exists x)\{Bxj\ \&\ (y)(Byj \supset y = x)\ \&\ [\mathbf{P}][\mathcal{T}W]Rx\}$.

The '$\mathbf{P}$' and '$\mathcal{T}W$' in (1b) iterate; they also obey the standard operator detachment rule. An alternative way of regimenting (1a) is to take 'represents that' to be an operator that operates on the sentence 'A cat is ahead', thereby forming a predicate. These two regimentations run parallel to those proposed in Chapter 7 in connection with belief sentences. On either analysis, the only entities to which (1a) is metaphysically committed are James and his brain.

As far as the meaning of 'represents' in the above analysis is concerned, it seems to me that we can appeal, as before, to the various generalization schemata in which this term figures. Some of these schemata will reflect the technical, theoretical contexts in which 'representation' is used in cognitive psychology, whereas others will provide a link between 'representation' and ordinary folk psychological terms such as 'belief' and 'desire'. For example, two of the latter schemata might be as follows:

(2) For any person x, if x believes that-(P)-ly, then (x believes that-(P)-ly *and thereby* x represents that-(P)-ly).

(3) For any person x, if x desires that-(P)-ly then (x desires that-(P)-ly *and thereby* x represents that-(P)-ly).

It may be wondered how the technical generalization schemata from cognitive psychology are to be formulated within the framework of the operator theory. I shall take up this question later. For now, let us turn to the operator 'that-(a cat is ahead)-ly' in our analysis. In my view, this operator is to be handled in the same general way as the term 'represents', with one minor difference: Since the sentence 'A cat is ahead' is a perfectly ordinary common or garden-variety sentence that occurs inside and outside of everyday propositional attitude contexts, it seems plausible to say that its meaning is given in the *folk psychological generalizations* that are generated by replacing the sentence variable 'P' by the sentence 'A cat is ahead' in the appropriate generalization schemata.

Now the interpretation I have proposed for (1) is at odds with the widely accepted literal interpretation, according to which (1) is to be understood as

(1c) $(\exists x)[x$ is a mental representation & x is presently contained in James's brain & x has the content that a cat is ahead].

I reject (1c) in part because mental representations, if they exist, will surely be physically realized in our brains by neural events or states or processes or conditions. And from my perspective, there are no neural entities of these types. I shall return to this point [together with other reasons for rejecting (1c)] later. For the moment, it suffices to note that, since (1a) is a cogent alternative to (1c), it does not follow that minds cannot be representational unless there exist mental representations or data structures.

Perhaps it will be objected that the single example I have discussed is not enough to make out my case. Other representational statements, it may be suggested, are more problematic. Consider, for example, the many statements from cognitive psychology that putatively refer to mental representations but that specify the contents of those representations using just an 'of' clause. How are these statements to be analyzed? Furthermore, what account is to be given, on my view, of representation retrieval from, and storage in, long-term memory? Don't at least these aspects of representation processing require the existence of mental data structures?

Let us take these questions one by one, beginning with the first. Consider the statement

(4) James has a mental representation of a bat.

Since 'representation' is a verbal noun, upon conversion to the verb 'represents' its modifiers become adverbs. Hence (4), on my operator theory, is regimented as

(4a) James mentally represents a-bat-ly.

It may be wondered how the operator 'a-bat-ly' in (4a) is to be understood. My reply is that there is no reason to take this operator to mean anything different in the present context from what it means in application to experiential verbs such as 'senses', 'images', and 'hallucinates'. Since the application in this context was discussed in Chapter 5, no new elucidation is required.

I readily admit that what I said earlier does not suffice to explain the meaning of each and every operator of the type 'an-F-ly' that may be appended to the term 'represents'. After all, if the given F is not a perceptible object, the earlier folk psychological generalizations will not be appropriate. It should be noted, however, that there will remain other generalizations that *are* appropriate, namely those making up the cognitive theory or theories that introduce expressions of the type 'of an F' in (putative) application to representations, whether or not Fs are perceptible. In this case, the relevant theoretical generalizations will be generated from schemata via instantiation of the variable 'F' by general terms.

Turning now to the issue of the storage of representations in long-term memory and their subsequent retrieval, my basic proposal is that the phrases 'stored in long-term memory' and 'retrieved from long-term memory' can be analyzed via predicate operators. The general idea here is that predicate operators can be introduced to handle both the cognitive centers in the flow chart models of cognitive psychologists and also the operations that are performed on mental representations at such centers. So talk of the long-term memory center, for example, is reconstructed via the use of the operator 'long-term-memory-ly'. Similarly, talk of a representation's being stored in a given center or retrieved from it is taken upon analysis to involve the operator 'storingly' or 'retrievingly'. Thus, the statements

(5) James stores the representation that there is a mouse in the house in long-term memory

and

(6) James retrieves the representation that there is a mouse in the house from long-term memory

can be analyzed as

(5a) James storingly represents that-(there is a mouse in the house)-ly long-term-memory-ly

and

(6a) James retrievingly represents that-(there is a mouse in the house)-ly long-term-memory-ly,

respectively. These analyses, at least at first glance, seem a little odd. But properly understood they are not.

To begin with, we should note that there are plenty of ordinary statements that concatenate adverbs in the manner of (5a) and (6a). Consider, for example,

(7) James intentionally screamed loudly.

Second, we should grasp that the idea behind (5a) is simply that, if James stores a representation in long-term memory, he represents in a certain way – the stored-in-long-term-memory way. James represents in this way provided that, under a correct assignment of extensions to cognitive psychological predicates (i.e., an assignment that makes the theoretical generalizations involving such predicates come out true or by and large true), the complex predicate in (5a) is assigned a set to which James belongs. This account is, I suggest, not far removed from the standard metaphysical account. On the latter view, (5) will be true just in case James has a mental data structure that represents that there is a mouse in the house and that is itself stored in long-term memory. The data structure will be classified as stored in long-term memory if, and only if, it is initially deposited and later available for subsequent retrieval, if,

189

and only if, that is, it plays a certain functional role specified by the theoretical generalizations.

In the case of (6a), similar reasoning is used. If James retrieves a representation from long-term memory, he is representing in a certain complex way, a way markedly different from the stored-in-long-term-memory way, though related to it.

Given these analyses, the entailment from (5) or (6) to

(8) James has a representation the content of which is that there is a mouse in the house

is preserved, since (8) becomes

(8a) James represents that-(there is a mouse in the house)-ly,

and (8a) follows from (5a) or (6a), in each case via detachment of both (standard) operators.

The upshot, then, is that talk in cognitive psychology of the retrieval and storage of representations need *not* commit us metaphysically to the existence of mental representations. We can make sense of such talk with an ontology that includes no more than persons, brains, and sets of such.[9]

I want now to return to the question of how the cognitive psychological generalization schemata are to be formulated. If, as I suggested above, talk putatively about cognitive centers can be analyzed via the use of predicate operators and if, as I also suggested above, talk putatively about cognitive operations of one sort or another can be analyzed in like manner, then we should have no difficulty in stating generalization schemata that are consistent with the general operator theory. The variables in the schemata will take general terms and/or sentences as their instances, and the predicate 'represents' will be modified by assorted operators. As for the cognitive theories themselves, each of these theories will consist of the infinitely many generalizations generated by the appropriate schemata.

The next argument I want to take up is one that lends indirect support to the view that cognitive psychology is committed to the existence of mental representations by attacking the alternative ap-

---

9 I assume here, of course, my more austere semantics for predicate operators. On the richer semantics, the ontology would include persons, brains, functions, and properties.

proach I have sketched out. Barbara Von Eckardt, in a response to some of my views, states the attack as follows:

The result of adverbializing the theoretical claims of cognitive psychology will be twofold: (a) all sentences will be about persons and their properties, and (b) properties will be properties of the whole person. Thus, any reference to sub-personal components or processes will be eliminated. But this restriction, in effect, undercuts the major explanatory strategy of cognitive psychology which, roughly speaking, attempts to explain the properties of the whole person in terms of properties of his or her parts. More specifically, the strategy is to explain whole person capacities (such as the capacity to understand spoken utterances, the capacity to remember what we perceive etc., the capacity to recognize faces) in terms of the ordered exercise of the sub-capacities of a person's (sub-personal) functional components. But such an explanation simply cannot be provided if we are not allowed to include such sub-capacities and sub-components in our ontology.[10]

I do not agree with Von Eckardt that the decompositional nature of explanations in cognitive psychology presents a problem for my operator theory. To begin with, not all sentences of cognitive psychology *have* to be taken to be about whole persons on my account. We can easily take some of these sentences to be about parts of persons and places (or better space–time regions) within those parts as, for example, with 'There is a space time region r such that Smith's brain represents that so and so is the case at r'.[11] Second, even without any reference to parts of persons, explanations of whole-person capacities in terms of a number of subcapacities can be analyzed in a relatively straightforward manner on the operator approach via the use of the generative sentential connective *'and thereby'*. To understand how this analysis proceeds let us consider a specific capacity, say, the capacity to recognize *spoken* utterances. This capacity takes as inputs stimulations to one's auditory system and yields as outputs beliefs concerning one's present auditory experiences. Cognitive theories decompose this capacity into a number of different subcapacities. For instance, it might be supposed that there is a subdoxastic physical-feature-analyzing capacity that takes the auditory stimulations as inputs and yields as outputs subdoxastic representations concerning the acoustic features of these stimulations. It might also be supposed that there is a phonological-

---

10 Von Eckardt, "Mental Images and Their Explanations," p. 456.
11 In this sentence, 'at r' is to be interpreted as a predicate operator that modifies 'represents'.

feature-analyzing capacity that takes as inputs the above subdoxastic representations and yields as outputs subdoxastic representations concerning phonological features of the auditory stimulations. Of course, further subcapacities would be needed to fill out the theory, but these need not concern us here.[12]

The explanation sketched above is initially transformed on my theory as follows. Creatures who can recognize spoken utterances have a subdoxastic physical-feature-analyzing capacity together with a phonological-feature-analyzing capacity (plus certain other capacities), *and thereby* they have the capacity to recognize spoken utterances. This explanation appears to refer to capacities. But in reality it does no such thing. In my view, a creature c has a subdoxastic physical-feature-analyzing capacity just in case (in first approximation) it is true that if c receives a signal s with so and so acoustic features then c will represent subdoxastically that s has so and so acoustic features. Similarly, c has a phonological-feature-analyzing capacity just in case (in first approximation) it is true that if c represents subdoxastically that a signal s has so and so acoustic features then c will represent subdoxastically that s has such and such phonological features.

My suggestion, then, is that one can specify cognitive capacities by stating special laws linking the appropriate inputs with the appropriate cognitive outputs. Cognitive outputs, in turn, are specified by sentences that state the kind of cognition involved and its content. The formal regimentation of these sentences will make use of both operators like 'subdoxastically' and operators like 'that-(s has acoustic feature F)-ly'.

Now, since each capacity has an input and an output, we can also say, on my view, that in exercising a given cognitive capacity a creature receivingly represents that-(so and so is the case)-ly and then outputtingly represents that-(such and such is the case)-ly. Thus, in the instance of the subdoxastic physical-feature-analyzing capacity, for example, we can say that the creature c receives a signal s with so and so acoustic features *and thereby* c outputtingly represents that s has those features. In speaking here of the creature c as representing in the way I call 'outputtingly', it may appear that I am suggesting that c is conscious that signal s has the given acoustic

12 In the next three paragraphs, I am indebted to an unpublished discussion by Terence Horgan entitled "Purging the Language of Thought."

features. No such suggestion is intended, however, since c is representing *subdoxastically*. Perhaps it would be more accurate, then, in the above case to say that c *acoustically*, outputtingly represents that s has so and so acoustic features. The use of the adverb 'acoustically' indicates that the output has limited availability, as it were. What is outputted from the acoustic analyzing capacity is available only as input for various other subdoxastic capacities that the former capacity is linked with. In similar fashion, it may be potentially less misleading to speak of c acoustically representing receivingly instead of just representing receivingly. And we can similarly modify our characterizations of c in connection with other subdoxastic capacities.

Finally, I should stress that I take the complex predicates I have introduced above – for example, predicates of the type 'acoustically, receivingly represents that P' – to have implicit definitions of the same general sort as the earlier definitions of folk psychological propositional attitude predicates such as 'believes that P'. The difference between the former predicates and the latter resides merely in the background theories by reference to which the predicates are defined.

It may perhaps now be suggested that the view I have taken of cognitive psychology is threatened by the following simple argument. There are certainly data structures or representations in digital computers. Our minds (according to many cognitive psychologists) frequently, if not always, store information in the same way as digital computers. Hence, there must be representation in minds.

My response to this argument should come as no surprise. I deny the first premise. Although it is true to say that digital computers are so designed that information is stored inside them, typically in patterns of electrically charged and uncharged states in a central grid, this talk need not be taken to imply that there really exist certain states or events or conditions that in various combinations function as representations. In keeping with my earlier analyses, I propose that such talk can be analyzed so as to refer to just the grid itself (and various space–time regions the grid occupies). Consider, for example, the statement

(9) The charged states of the grid at places p_1 and p_2 together with the intervening uncharged state at place p_3 carry the information that the code word is 'boomerang'.

On my analysis, (9) becomes

(9a) The grid is charged electrically at p_1 and at p_2 and the grid is uncharged electrically at p_3, and thereby it represents that-(the code word is 'boomerang')-ly, and moreover p_3 intervenes between p_1 and p_2.

This analysis can be clarified further by formalization. Let 'g' name the grid, and let 'C' and 'R' abbreviate the predicates 'is charged' and 'represents', respectively. Let '$\mathscr{A}$' be the operator 'at'. This operator precedes singular terms for space–time regions, thereby forming predicate operators, for example, '$\mathscr{A}p_1$'. Operators of this sort were discussed at length in Chapter 4. Let 'E' abbreviate 'electrically', and let '$\mathscr{T}$' and 'W' abbreviate 'that' and "the code word is 'boomerang'," respectively. Finally, let 'I' abbreviate the three-term relational expression '_____ intervenes between _____ and _____ ', and let '$\overset{g}{\rightarrow}$' symbolize 'and thereby'. Statement (9a) is now regimented as

(9b) $\{([\mathscr{A}p_1][E]Cg \ \& \ [\mathscr{A}p_2][E]Cg \ \& \ \sim[\mathscr{A}p_3][E]Cg)\overset{g}{\rightarrow}[\mathscr{T}W]Rg\} \ \& \ Ip_3p_1p_2$.

In (9b), there are iterated predicate operators in the three conjuncts preceding the generative connective '$\overset{g}{\rightarrow}$'. These operators can be permuted within each conjunct without restriction, since it is necessarily true that the grid is charged electrically at place p just in case the grid is charged at p electrically.

The metaphysics associated with the semantical interpretation of (9b) includes the grid and the relevant space–time regions together with various sets. There is obviously no commitment, however, to any state that carries information. Now, what goes for (9) goes mutatis mutandis for other related statements – for example, statements about pulses of electricity carrying information (here we may speak of the grid pulsing electrically in the appropriate places and thereby representing in various ways).

I can now hear it objected that my discussion above is unpersuasive because it cannot give any account of the fact that digital computers process information via the manipulation of *symbols*. This requires a little explanation. On the standard view, the computer is taken to manipulate formulas made up of just two basic elements, 1 and 0. These formulas make up the machine code or the machine language, and they are held to be represented or tokened in the machine itself as either combinations of charged and uncharged states of each element of the "active memory" or as combinations of pulses and no-pulses in the various pathways of the central processing unit. The computer manipulates given formulas via banks of logic gates, each of which takes a 1 or a 0 at each input port and gives a 1 or 0 as an output, where the output is determined solely by the input and the structure of the given gate. Since formulas from propositional logic can be encoded in the machine language, and since furthermore certain combinations of logic gates will process these formulas so that the outputs are truth-functional combinations of the input formulas, the computer can perform a variety of logical operations. How, it may be asked, can we make sense of any of this, if we deny that there really are any charged or uncharged states and any pulses of electricity? For without these concreta, there are no symbolic tokens for the computer to manipulate.

My reply should not be difficult to anticipate. Strictly speaking, the general supposition that digital computers manipulate symbolic tokens is false. This need not prevent us from agreeing, however, that there is a sense in which the various claims made above are true; for talk of the manipulation of symbols can be analyzed in a way that eschews reference to or quantification over symbolic tokens. For example, suppose that in a given computer a the formula 101 is inputted at one of the input pathways (call it i) to logic gate l and that the formula 100 is outputted at another pathway (call it o). Then, on my view, a *symbolizes* 101-ly at i and a *symbolizes* 100-ly at o. How will a symbolize 101-ly at i? Well, a symbolizes 101-ly at i (assuming that a is a typical digital computer) just in case there are three times t_1, t_2, and t_3 such that a pulses electrically at i at t_1, a does not pulse electrically at i at t_2, and a pulses electrically at i at t_3, where t_1, t_2, and t_3 are minimally differing times so ordered that t_1 is before t_2 and t_2 is before t_3.[13] This account can be extended mutatis mutandis to the claim that a symbolizes 100-ly at o.

Consider now the assertion that the above computer a is processing information via its transformation of the formula 101 into the formula 100. This assertion will be true, I maintain, if, and only if, there is a gate g in a such that (a symbolizes 101-ly at one of the input pathways to g and a symbolizes 100-ly at an output pathway from g) *and thereby* a represents that so and so is the case.

The view sketched here can also be applied to an account of how the computer performs various truth-functional operations. The

13 This account runs parallel to the standard metaphysical account, according to which 101 is tokened in the input channel i just in case *there is* a pulse of electricity in i followed by a no-pulse followed by a further pulse in i.

195

basic requirements in the case of conjunction, say, are these: (i) The computer *a* symbolizes *F*-ly at some input pathway *i* to some logic gate *g*, where *F*-ly is a binary mode, that is a mode of the same type as 100-ly and 101-ly; (ii) *a*, by symbolizing *F*-ly at *i*, represents that something *P* is the case – in other words, *a* inputs *F*-ly at *i*, *and thereby a* represents that-(*P*)-ly; (iii) likewise, *a* inputs *G*-ly at some other input pathway *i'* to *g*, where *G*-ly is another binary mode, *and thereby a* represents that-(*Q*)-ly; (iv) *a* symbolizes *H*-ly at an output pathway *o* from *g*, where *H*-ly is some third binary mode, *and thereby a* represents that-(*P* and *Q*)-ly. It is obvious that this analysis can be applied mutatis mutandis to other truth-functional operations allegedly performed by the computer.

The overall conclusion I draw, then, is that there is nothing about the manner in which digital computers process information that is inconsistent with my general metaphysical view. This conclusion licenses the rejection of the widely held position that computation, be it by machines or minds, requires the existence of a system of representations, a medium, if you will, in which the computation is carried out.[14] Thus, arguments that use this position either as an explicit or as an unstated premise (e.g., Jerry Fodor's argument that since in the common-sense psychological theory of a rational agent the expected utilities of various courses of action are computed, there must be linguistic tokens comprising an inner language of thought)[15] are no longer compelling.

It is convenient at this stage to turn to another objection to my view, namely that if mental representations are eliminated from the ontology associated with cognitive psychology, no clear distinction can be drawn between cognitive theories that appear to introduce pictorial representations and cognitive theories that appear to posit linguistic or descriptional representations only.

Some philosophers may be tempted to respond to this objection that, even given the existence of mental representations, there is no really clear account of the difference between pictorialist and descriptionalist theories.[16] What I shall try to show is that the difference between these theories is no *less* clear on my view than it

14 See, e.g., Fodor, *The Language of Thought*; idem, *Representations*; Pylyshyn, *Computation and Cognition*.
15 See Fodor, *The Language of Thought*.
16 I try to develop such an account in my "Picture Theory of Mental Images." See also my *Mental Imagery* (London: Routledge & Kegan Paul, forthcoming).

is on a literal interpretation of their metaphysical commitments. To this end, I want to take up two different explanations (which are prominent in the literature) of the pictorial–descriptional dichotomy. Consider first the claim that one important respect in which pictorial, or better 'quasi-pictorial', mental representations differ from linguistic, or 'quasi-linguistic', representations is that the former carry information in analog form, whereas in the latter information is digitalized. The central idea here, at least on one well-known account, is that a picture of, say, a cat on a mat carries not only the information that a cat is on a mat, but also *other* information about, for example, the shape of the mat and the relative size of the cat and the mat, information that is not analytically or nomically 'nested' in the former information.[17] By contrast, the sentence 'A cat is on a mat' carries the information that a cat is on a mat together with information that follows from it, for example, the information that there is a cat, but no *further* information. This distinction can be captured perfectly well within my operator approach. On my view, a statement such as

(10) Paul has a mental representation that carries the information that a cat is on a mat in analog form

is analyzed as

(10a) Paul mentally represents that-(a cat is on a mat)-ly and he does that analogly

or

(10b) Paul analogly mentally represents that-(a cat is on a mat)-ly.

Now (10b), on the above account, will be equivalent to the following statement:

(10c) Paul mentally represents that-(a cat is on a mat)-ly *and thereby* there-is$_{substitutional}$ some P such that (i) Paul mentally represents that-(P)-ly and (ii) it is neither analytically nor physically necessary that anything that represents that-(a cat is on a mat)-ly also represents that-(P)-ly.

In (10c), the variable 'P' takes sentences as its substitution instances. On the alternative operator view, which treats 'represents that' as an operator on sentences, essentially the same analysis is offered.

In the case of the statement

---

17 For detailed elaboration of this idea, see Dretske, *Knowledge and the Flow of Information*.

(11) Paul has a mental representation that carries the information that a cat is on a mat in digital form,

I propose to introduce the predicate operator 'digitally' instead of the operator 'analogly'; furthermore, (11) will be equivalent to the following statement:

(11a) Paul mentally represents that-(a cat is on a mat)-ly, but it is not the case that the conditions specified in (10c) also obtain.

I do not mean to suggest, in presenting (10c) and (11a), that there are no other ways of spelling out the distinction between representing analogly and representing digitally. A cursory look at the literature reveals any number of explanations of the analog–digital distinction.[18] Still I see no reason to suppose that alternatives to the explanation I have briefly given will be any harder to reconstruct within the operator framework.

A second (and very different) respect in which pictorial representations are sometimes held to differ from linguistic representations concerns the manner in which spatial relations are represented. Consider, say, a picture of a man standing to the left of a tree. In this picture there will be a part p_1, which represents a man, and a part p_2, which represents a tree, but there will be no further part that represents the relation of being to the left of. Rather this relation will be represented by the juxtaposition of the parts p_1 and p_2. By contrast, the sentence 'A man is to the left of a tree' not only has parts that represent a man and a tree but also has a further part, namely 'is to the left of', which represents the spatial relation of being to the left of. Now, it has been suggested that this difference between pictorial and linguistic representations can be applied to the task of explaining how quasi-pictorial mental representations differ from quasi-linguistic mental representations; for although it seems implausible to assert that mental representations sometimes represent by having component parts whose spatial relationships in the brain exactly duplicate the spatial relationships of the parts of the objects represented (as would have to be the case if some of these representations were literal pictures in the brain), still it may be that mental representations sometimes represent spatial rela-

18 See Block, "Mental Pictures"; John Haugeland, "Analog and Analog," *Philosophical Topics*, 12 (1981): 213–26; Kosslyn, *Image and Mind*; Roger Shepard and Lynn Cooper, *Mental Images and Their Transformations* (Cambridge, Mass.: Bradford, 1982); Pylyshyn, "The Imagery Debate."

tionships via relations of one sort or another among their parts. The thought, then, is that one respect in which quasi-pictorial mental representations differ from quasi-linguistic representations is that the former represent spatial relations among the parts of the objects represented via relations among their parts, whereas the latter represent such spatial relations via further component parts.[19]

Can the distinction this account draws between quasi-pictorial and quasi-linguistic representations be preserved within the confines of my operator theory? I think it can. In the case that Smith has a mental quasi-sentence which means that a man is to the left of a tree, I hold that Smith quasi-sententially represents that-(a man is to the left of a tree)-ly. According to my version of the above account, the following are *necessary* conditions for it to be true that Smith represents in this way: (i) Smith has a representation of a man, that is, Smith represents a-man-ly; (ii) Smith has a representation of a tree, that is, Smith represents a-tree-ly; (iii) Smith has a representation of the relation being to the left of, that is, Smith represents left-ly.[20] In the case that Smith has a mental quasi-picture of a man to the left of a tree, I hold that Smith quasi-pictorially represents in the combined (a-man-ly-to the left of-a-tree-ly) manner. In this case conditions (i) and (ii) still pertain. However, (iii) is no longer included in the list of necessary conditions. This is because, in the quasi-pictorial case, 'to the left of' is an operator on the predicate operators 'a-man-ly' and 'a-tree-ly', whereas 'left-ly' in (iii) is a predicate operator itself. The suggestion, then, is that the distinction between representational parts and representational relations among such parts can be preserved by appealing to the difference between predicate operators and operators on predicate operators in representational contexts.

I turn now to another argument for the existence of mental representations. Jerry Fodor has urged that there are any number of explanations in cognitive psychology that require the postulation of mental representations:

There is a well-known and very robust psycholinguistic phenomenon known as the "frequency effect." What it comes to is that if I flash a letter sequence on a screen and ask you to reply as rapidly as you can whether

19 This view is to be found in Block, "Mental Pictures." It is also endorsed by Kosslyn, *Image and Mind.*
20 I want to emphasize that these conditions are *not* intended to be jointly sufficient for Smith to quasi-sententially represent that-(a man is to the left of a tree)-ly.

it constitutes a word you know, then (for cases where the correct response is "yes") the speed of your response will be proportional to the relative frequency with which tokens of the word occur in corpora of your language: relatively high frequency words (like "find") elicit faster responses than relatively low frequency words (like "crib"). This phenomenon persists when boring variables (like word length, etc.) are controlled for.

Now here is one story about the frequency effect. There is, in your head, a mental lexicon: a list of such of the words in your language as you know. When you are asked whether a letter string is a word you know, you search for the letter string in this mental lexicon. If you find it, you say "yes"; if you fail to find it, you say "no." And: the words in the mental lexicon are listed in order of their frequency and they are searched in the order in which they are listed. . . .

I'm not, at present, primarily interested in whether this story is true, only in whether it can be told without attributing properties to (hence quantifying over) mental representations. I admit to not seeing how. Notice, for example, that we can't get the force of the explanation merely by attributing to the subject the belief that (e.g.) "find" is a high frequency word and that "crib" is not. For though it is doubtless true that subjects have such beliefs, it isn't assumptions about the beliefs that the subject has, but rather assumptions about the ways in which his mental representations are arranged and processed, that do the work in the theory. You need the notion that recognizing a word involves being related in a certain way to a mental representation of the word in order to make the story go. And that notion is an aspect of the representational theory of the mind.

You aren't, of course, required to like this explanation of the frequency effect. You are at liberty to discharge its ontological commitments by showing that the explanation is false or by finding some other explanation that is less prodigally committed. But what strikes me as simply irresponsible – though it is, alas, a standard philosophic practice – is to reject the mental representation construct without bothering either to disconfirm or to reconstruct the explanations it occurs in. . . .

I think the best kind of ontological argument is the kind I've just given: we need this construct to do our science.[21]

I think that the story Fodor tells of why the frequency effect obtains can be reconstructed without quantifying over mental representations. Hence, I am not persuaded that Fodor has succeeded in producing an example of a psychological explanation that really does turn ineliminably upon the postulation of mental representations. The basic claims of the preferred explanation are these:

(12) You have a list of mental representations of words that you know.
(13) When you are asked whether a string of letters is a word, you conduct a search through your list of mental representations of words.

21 Fodor, *Representations*, pp. 27–9.

(14) The more frequently you retrieve a mental representation of a word, the nearer to the beginning it is located on your list.

Consider first claim (12). From an adverbialist perspective, what (12) says is that for each of the words you know you mentally represent in some way with respect to that word, and further that for any such ways of representing, F-ly and G-ly (each with respect to a different word), either you represent in the combined F-ly-listed before-G-ly manner or vice versa. This requires some unpacking, but the underlying thoughts are simply that talk of representations can be analyzed in terms of talk of ways of representing and that talk of relations among representations can be analyzed in terms of talk of complex ways of representing having other ways of representing as components. These thoughts run parallel to those earlier in the book. For example, in Chapter 5, talk of afterimages was replaced by talk of ways of imaging or sensing, and talk of relations among afterimages (e.g., 'Jones has a red afterimage spatially separated from another red afterimage') was replaced with talk of persons imaging in more complex ways [e.g., 'Jones images (redly–spatially separated from–redly)-ly'].[22]

On the above account, (12) can be formalized as follows. Let 'Wx', 'Kxy', '$R'xy$', and 'Rx' mean 'x is a word', 'x knows y', 'x represents with respect to y', and 'x represents', respectively; let 'a' name you, let '**M**' be the predicate operator 'mentally', and let '$\mathscr{L}$' be a two-place operator on predicate operators that abbreviates 'listed before'. Then we have

(12a) $(x)\{(Wx\ \&\ Kax) \supset (\exists\mathbf{O})[\mathbf{M}][\mathbf{O}]R'ax\}\ \&\ (\mathbf{O})(\mathbf{O'})\{((\exists x)(Wx\ \&\ Kax\ \&\ [\mathbf{M}][\mathbf{O}]R'ax)\ \&\ (\exists y)(Wy\ \&\ Kay\ \&\ x \neq y\ \&\ [\mathbf{M}][\mathbf{O'}]Ra)) \supset ([\mathbf{O}\mathscr{L}\mathbf{O'}]Ra \lor [\mathbf{O'}\mathscr{L}\mathbf{O}]Ra)\}.$[23]

Given this regimentation, (12) is metaphysically committed to no more than you and the words you know. So (12), as I interpret it, is *not* committed to mental representations.

Consider now statement (13). I maintain that what (13) says is that, when you are asked whether a string of letters s is a word, you represent in some way, F-ly, with respect to that string, and

---

22 I talk above as if there are ways of representing and imaging. This is not really true, of course, on the austere semantics I am advocating for adverbial discourse.

23 In this formalization, the operator quantifiers are substitutional. Also, the predicate operators preceding '$R'ax$' modify the dyadic predicate '$R'xy$'. For a discussion of the semantics of such operators, see Chapter 3, note 25. For my views on operators of the type to which '$\mathscr{L}$' belongs, see Chapter 5, Section III.

there are already various ways in which you represent with respect to the words you know, and moreover you now represent in these ways one after another in the inspecting manner ('inspectingly') until you represent in a way, G-ly, such that you also represent in the combined F-ly-is found to match-G-ly manner. This is a little awkward, admittedly. But the account I have given is intended to run parallel to an account of (13) that requires you to inspect your mental representations of words one by one until you find a representation that matches the one associated with the string of letters you hear. Now (13) can be regimented in much the same fashion as (12).[24] Once again, then, there is no metaphysical commitment to mental representations. There is, moreover, no special problem associated with understanding either 'inspectingly' (which is a predicate operator) or 'is found to match' (which is an operator on pairs of predicate operators). The view I take here is that the meanings of these operators are no harder to grasp than the meanings of the corresponding terms that appear in the mental representations account. In that account, the relational terms 'inspects' and 'is found to match', the former connecting a person and a representation and the latter connecting different representations, evidently do not mean what they mean in ordinary public contexts. After all, we have no inner eyes with which to inspect items in our minds or to check to see if different items match. Rather these terms within the context of a theory of cognitive psychology are implicitly defined by the cognitive generalizations composing that theory. Much the same is true, on my account, for the corresponding operators: Their meanings are given in various cognitive generalization schemata from which the relevant theoretical generalizations can be generated.

Consider finally statement (14). In my view, (14) can be reconstructed as saying that for any ways of representing, F-ly and G-ly (each with respect to a different word), if you mentally represent F-ly in the retrieving manner (retrievingly) more often than you mentally represent G-ly retrievingly, then you mentally represent

24 As with (12), my comments above about there being ways of representing are to be regimented formally by means of a substitutional quantifier having a component variable, the substitution instances for which are predicate operators. Thus, (13), like (12), does not require that there *really* be any such entities as ways. What is true here for (13) is true also for the analysis of (14) proposed in the next paragraph.

in the combined F-ly-listed before-G-ly manner. I assume that there is no need to introduce further discussion of the operators 'retrievingly' and '(F-ly-listed before-G-ly)-ly'. As to the expression 'more often than', I am inclined to take it as a non-truth-functional sentential connective. Of course, truth conditions will ultimately have to be supplied for this connective. I will not attempt to spell out these truth conditions here. I merely note that if the only satisfactory account turns out to be the obvious one, which introduces quantification over numbers and which compares numbers of times, my proposal will have to countenance numbers. I am hopeful that some other account can be developed. But even if numbers are needed, my proposal is certainly no more complex metaphysically on this score than an analysis that postulates mental representations; for if there are such representations, talk of the relative frequency of their retrieval itself seems committed to numbers.

I conclude that Fodor has not made out his case. The example he gives of a psychological explanation is not one that requires the existence of mental representations. In showing that Fodor is mistaken with respect to this one case, I am *not* claiming that I have thereby *proved* that mental representations are not ultimately needed in any psychological explanation. However, I hope it is clear by now that the operator theory has a richness and general flexibility that allow it to deal with many different prima facie problematic contexts. Before I turn to another topic, I shall further illustrate the power of my approach by showing how it applies to another psychological explanation from a context that is very different from the one reconstructed above.

Psychologists interested in understanding mental imagery have invented many fascinating experiments. Earlier in this chapter I briefly sketched a map-scanning experiment devised by Stephen Kosslyn. The experiment I take up now is similar.

Consider the pairs of block figures shown in Figure 2. Are the figures in (A) congruent? What of those in (B) and (C)? In an experiment designed by Shepard and Metzler, subjects were shown sixteen hundred pairs of block figures and asked whether or not they were congruent.[25] As the angular separation of the figures in

25 Some pairs were rotations in the plane of the page, some were rotations perpendicular to the page, and some could not be made to match by any rotation. R. N. Shepard and J. Metzler, "Mental Rotation of Three-dimensional Objects," *Science*, 171 (1971): 701–3.

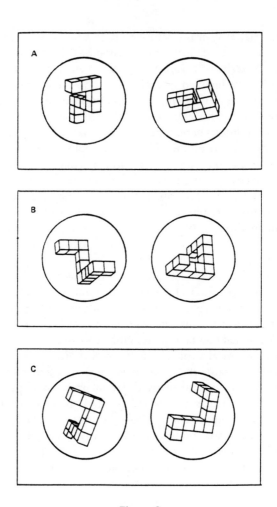

Figure 2

each pair increased, so, in linear proportion, did the length of time each subject typically needed to respond. When asked how they reached their answers, subjects reported imagining one figure rotated so as to superimpose the other. Some psychologists (including Shepard and Metzler) claim that this experiment suggests that people can rotate mental images, and at fixed speeds. This, in turn, suggests that mental images are quasi-pictures, or so it is often supposed.

The explanation pictorialists give of this experiment requires further unpacking. If we permit ourselves to indulge in the fantasy that mental images are spatially extended geometrical figures that bear definite angular separations from one another and that are capable of real rotation, we can immediately explain the results of the experiment. But, of course, the pictorialist, in claiming that the subjects are rotating mental images, is not asking us to indulge in this fantasy. On the standard interpretation of the pictorialist's view, mental images are taken to be neural entities having features that represent spatial extension and angular separation. Further, image rotation is taken to be a neural process that transforms images bit by bit so that they represent objects at gradually changing angles. The explanation the pictorialist is, in fact, proposing, then, goes something like this: When a person imagines one figure f_1 rotated so as to superimpose another f_2, he has an image of f_1 and an image of f_2 that share a feature K representing the angular separation of f_1 and f_2. As the person rotates the former image at fixed speed so as to superimpose the latter, K systematically and smoothly changes so as to represent decreasing angular separations of f_1 and f_2. Thus, the time t it takes to imagine one figure rotated so as to superimpose another increases linearly with increasing angular separation of the figures because, with greater angular separations, K has to go through more changes as the images are rotated so as to superimpose, and t, given a fixed rotational velocity, increases linearly with increasing changes in K.

I have discussed the merits of this explanation elsewhere.[26] What I wish to show here is that the above pictorialist explanation does not ultimately require the existence of mental images or quasi-pictorial data structures.

Consider first the claim that when a person imagines the figure f_1 rotated so as to superimpose the figure f_2, he rotates an image of f_1. On my view, such a person images rotatingly with respect to f_1. But what does this involve? Let us see first what is involved on the version of the operator theory that introduces properties and functions of various sorts. Initially the person images f_1 at a certain

---

26 See my "Debate about Mental Imagery," *Journal of Philosophy*, 81 (1984): pp. 678–91. For my more recent views on this experiment, see *Mental Imagery*. For an argument that the explanation Kosslyn gives of his well-known map-scanning experiment can be reconstructed without reference to or quantification over mental quasi-pictures, see my "Debate about Mental Imagery."

angular separation from f_2, and as time passes he images f_1 at ever decreasing angular separations from f_2. At the beginning of image rotation, then, the person images in the combined G-ly-at angular separation A from-H-ly manner, where G-ly and H-ly are ways of imaging with respect to the figures f_1 and f_2, respectively, and 'at angular separation A from' expresses a function that maps these ways (functions) onto the way (function) expressed by '(G-ly-at angular separation A from H-ly)-ly'. As image rotation takes place, that is, as the person images rotatingly, there is a sequence of properties of the type imaging (F-ly-at angular separation so and so from G-ly)-ly that the person instantiates. Thus, corresponding to the relational feature K of images that appeared in the original account, we now have a two-place function or rather a series of such functions, each expressible by an operator on predicate operators. We also have ways of imaging F-ly and G-ly corresponding to the two mental images. There is, I might add, no difficulty in explaining what it is to image in the complex way described above: Since pictorialists hold that the representations involved in imagery are of the same type as those involved in perception, one who images (F-ly-at angular separation A from-G-ly)-ly represents in the way that normal perceivers represent as a result of viewing with the eyes in standard conditions figure f_1 at the appropriate angular separation from f_2. The final pictorialist explanation, then, becomes this: Since with greater angular separations between the two figures, the person will inevitably instantiate through time one after the other a greater number of properties of the above sort as he images rotatingly, it will take longer for him to decide if the figures are congruent for figures with wider separations. It is assumed in this explanation that the person is imagining rotatingly *at fixed speed*, that is, that he instantiates each appropriate imaging property in the sequence for the same period of time.

Now the account I have sketched above can be restated without difficulty within the metaphysical confines of the operator theory I have been advocating. Instead of talking of the imager as instantiating various imaging properties, we can classify him as belonging to various sets, namely the satisfaction sets of linguistic predicates of the type 'images (F-ly-at angular separation so and so from -G-ly)-ly'. And instead of appealing to a function as the representational analog of the relational feature K of images, we can simply deny that any representational *entity* is needed. Given these changes, the

206

explanation goes through along the lines indicated. It appears, then, that we can make sense of the pictorialist's account of image rotation without assuming either that there are mental images or that there are such processes as image rotation.

In this section I have considered a wide variety of arguments for the claim that cognitive psychology is inevitably committed to the existence of mental representations. I have tried to show that these arguments are not decisive. But I have not as yet presented any positive arguments for denying the existence of mental representations within cognitive psychology. Rather I have contented myself with sketching out an alternative metaphysical interpretation. In the next section, I try to show that this interpretation is preferable to the standard literal one.

III

I shall begin by taking up some well-known arguments against positing mental representations in cognitive psychology that seem to me flawed. Having done this, I shall present some arguments that I find convincing. I proceed in this way so as to make it clear that my own account does not rest on a shaky foundation.

One standard objection to positing either descriptional or pictorial mental representations is that, if we opened up some brave volunteer's head and peered inside his skull, we would not see hidden there any tiny pictures or any little book with sentences written in the person's native tongue. Instead, we would find only the gray matter composing his brain.

In the case of pictorial mental representations, this objection would be decisive, if such representations were held to be just like ordinary pictures; for it is surely essential to any public object's being classified as a (realistic) picture that it be perceptible and that it look like the object or objects it pictures. This is not to say, of course, that any public picture must exactly resemble what it is a picture of. A black and white photograph of an orange, for example, will not have the same color as the orange. Still there must be a significant resemblance for the one object to be a picture of the other.

Pictorial mental representations, however, are not to be conceived of as being just like ordinary pictures. Rather they are to be thought of as representations that are *in certain respects* analogous or similar to public pictures, although in other respects they are very different. Although the relevant similarities here are a matter of some dispute, it is quite clear that none of the cognitive psychologists who posit (or seem to posit) pictures in the head conceive of these representations as actually *looking like* what they represent – hence, the use of the term 'quasi-pictorial' in cognitive psychology to characterize the appropriate representations.

In the case of linguistic or descriptive mental representations, the same kind of reply applies. Sentences in the head are not just like any spoken or written sentences. Hence, we should not expect to be able to see familiar linguistic representations when we open up our volunteer's head. In general, we will be in a position to classify something we see as a linguistic token of a language L only if we already know what items count as basic sign designs within L and also what combinations of items count as well-formed strings of sign designs in L. Since we do not yet know anything about the structure or elements of an inner neural language, we will inevitably fail to notice parts of such a language when we conduct our cerebroscopic examination. But to argue on this basis that there are no inner linguistic representations is to commit the fallacy of arguing from ignorance.

It should also be stressed that cognitive psychologists in speaking of inner linguistic representations are really speaking of representations that are similar in *some* important ways to public linguistic representations. For this reason, it is less misleading to use such qualified terms as 'quasi-linguistic' and 'quasi-sentential'.

Another argument against the existence of mental representations is this: The research program of cognitive psychology is based on the computer model of information processing. But the representations manipulated by digital computers have a conventional syntax and semantics via their connections with the decisions and beliefs of programmers. By contrast, the mental representations we allegedly manipulate have no conventional syntax or semantics. Hence, the computer model is not really appropriate for understanding the mind, and the program of cognitive psychology itself rests on a mistake. Since mental representations are part and parcel of this program, they too should be repudiated.

Two points can be made by way of reply to this argument. First, as I argued in Section I, mental representations are not *necessarily* part of the metaphysical baggage carried by cognitive psychology.

Second, as I noted above, the representations most often posited (or rather apparently posited) by psychologists are *quasi*-linguistic. Hence, there is no more reason to take these representations to be just like the representations in a digital computer than there is to take them to be just like the representations of English or French. Of course, there remains the question of just what it is that makes a representation quasi-linguistic. But that is a different issue.

A third objection to positing mental representations is what Ned Block has called the "paraphernalia objection."[27] If there were any inner mental pictures, there would have to be inner eyes to scan them, inner flashlights to illuminate them, and inner hands to rotate them. Similarly, if there were any inner mental sentences, there would have to be inner scissors and glue to transform these sentences into other sentences, and again there would have to be inner eyes and flashlights for the purpose of reading. Since there obviously are no paraphernalia of this sort, it is concluded that there are no mental representations either.

It seems to me that this argument is no more persuasive than the previous ones. Once it is grasped that the terms 'picture' and 'sentence' in application to mental representations do not have their ordinary literal meanings, there is no longer any reason to think that mental representations can be rotated or scanned with an eye or cut up into parts in any literal sense. So, for example, as I noted earlier, cognitive psychologists who claim that pictorial mental representations can be rotated are in reality claiming that such representations can be transformed so that they *represent* objects at changing orientations. Similarly, the claim that pictorial mental representations can be scanned is really the claim that they can be transformed so as to *represent* objects whose position in the field of view moves from the left side of the viewer to the right. It is also worth pointing out that, if a digital computer can manipulate sentential or linguistic representations without an inner eye or inner hands, there is no reason to think that we or our brains cannot do likewise.

The argument I have just considered naturally leads into another argument that seems to me more worthwhile. If, as has been suggested, terms like 'pictorial', 'sentential', 'is rotated', 'is scanned' are not to be taken to have their ordinary, literal meanings within

27 See his "Mental Pictures."

cognitive psychology, then why even suppose that these terms are really functioning as predicates? Admittedly they *seem* to be predicates, and in ordinary, public contexts they certainly are predicates. But once it is conceded that these terms, within cognitive psychology, have peculiar meanings, it is surely unreasonable to insist that they *cannot* belong to a peculiar logical category, that they *must* belong to the logical category of predicate. The point I wish to make, then, is simply that the specialized character of the terms 'pictorial', 'is rotated', and the like viz-à-viz their meanings should also make us suspicious of any formal account of the logical role of these terms that automatically takes them to occupy their obvious literal grammatical category, especially when, as we have already seen, there is another viable formal account.

There are several arguments that should move us from suspicion to outright rejection of the literal interpretation of cognitive psychology. First, Occam's razor counts against the postulation of mental representations and mental operations. Since we have an alternative interpretation of cognitive psychology that is metaphysically simpler than the standard account, the introduction of mental representations and operations is entirely gratuitous. Hence, such entities should be eliminated from our ontology. This conclusion, I might add, is also supported by reflection on the fact that mental representations and operations, if they existed, would be realized physically by neural events (or states or conditions) and neural processes; for part of the thrust of this book has been that there are no such entities, that causation is not a relation between concrete tokens.

Second, considerations of overall theoretical unity count against the claim that cognitive psychology is committed to the existence of mental representations and operations. If, as I have argued, folk psychology is best understood within the general framework of the operator theory and if, as I have also argued, cognitive psychology *can* just as well be understood within the same framework, then it is surely unreasonable to interpret cognitive psychology in any other way. Consider, for example, the operator theory of phenomenal visual experience. To couple this theory, which systematically regiments talk of phenomenal sensations, images, and so on in terms of talk of persons who sense, image, and so on, with a theory that posits underlying visual representations of a pictorial (or sentential) sort is to enter into a very strange marriage. For one thing, 'mental

210

representation' is a verbal noun phrase like 'visual sensation'. Thus, if the latter is best taken to function as a verb–adverb phrase, so too, it seems reasonable to suppose, is the former, *unless* some compelling argument can be given against such an interpretation. For another thing, it would be rather odd to insist that, in folk psychological causal statements about visual experience, the term 'causes' *always* functions as a sentential connective, whereas in the corresponding contexts in cognitive psychology, 'causes' is frequently a two-term relational expression whose relata are singular terms designating events. Yet if we accept both the operator theory of phenomenal visual experience and the standard interpretation of cognitive psychology, this is just what we will have to hold.

A further argument against the postulation of mental representations within cognitive psychology derives from the considerations brought forward in Chapter 1. It seems to me that there will likely be, in some instances at least, many different equally eligible neural candidates for identification with a given mental representation (or a given mental operation on a representation for that matter). Admittedly the decompositional structure of the explanations of cognitive psychology will make the problem of multiple possible neural realizations (within a single individual at a single time) less severe than it is in folk psychology for folk mental events. But it is, I think, wishful thinking to suppose that cognitive theories will always 'bottom out' in the neurophysiological hardware in just the way that is required by a simple literal interpretation of the metaphysical commitments of those theories (assuming *arguendo* that there are neural events, processes, etc.). For a defense of this claim, the reader should return to the arguments of Chapter 1. What follows, I suggest, is that it is a mistake to suppose that every mental representation (or operation) is identical with some neural event or condition or process (assuming again that there are such neural tokens). And what we should conclude from the failure of the token identity theory here is that there are no mental representations (or operations), that the literal interpretation of the metaphysical commitments of cognitive psychology is mistaken.

There is one final argument I want to bring against the existence of mental representations. If, as I am happy to accept, cognitive psychology is a worthwhile and fruitful research program, the better of two alternative interpretations of its associated metaphysical commitments is the one that makes its theories least vulnerable to future empirical refutation (assuming, of course, that the interpretations are equally good in other respects). Now, it should be clear from what has already been said that we *could* make future neural discoveries that would falsify given cognitive theories on their standard literal interpretation but that would *not* falsify those theories on my operator interpretation. For example, we could discover that in some given creature c there is more than one way of mapping the events apparently posited by some cognitive theory T onto the neural events. This discovery would falsify T on its standard literal interpretation (assuming that T is meant to apply to c and other creatures of its type). But it would not falsify T on my operator interpretation, for T does not now really posit token events at all. It should also be clear that every discovery that falsified given cognitive theories on my metaphysical interpretation would falsify those theories on the standard interpretation. This is because if it turns out that there is no way of assigning extensions to the cognitive predicates of a given theory T, say, so that the generalizations of T come out true (or by and large true) in application to c and other creatures of c's type, then the problem with T, on a *literal* interpretation of its commitments, will be that it posits mental representations for which there are *no* eligible neural candidates for identification (rather than too many), that is, no neural tokens that play the functional roles associated with the representations by T. It follows, then, that the standard, literal interpretation is not the best. Hence, the metaphysical account of cognitive psychology that posits mental representations and mental operations should be rejected.

In this chapter, I have tried to develop an account of the metaphysical foundations of cognitive psychology that overall is preferable to the standard account. The general metaphysical theory of mind, of which the view elaborated in the present chapter is part, has great systematic unity and great simplicity. The constructions it invokes may seem strange. But I hope I have shown that they are syntactically and semantically well founded and that the theory as a whole is a worthwhile alternative to the usual approaches.

Index

absent qualia argument, 135
abstract proposition theory of the propositional attitudes, 151–3, 156–7, 170; objections to, 157, 160–2
adverbial analysis of sensory experience, 55, 57–9, 102
adverbs, *see* predicate operators
afterimages, 109, 122, 123, 124–6
analog–digital distinction, 197–8
appropriate paraphrase, 165, 175–7
argument from knowledge, 138–48

belief (*see also* conceptual role, of belief predicates and operators; folk psychological generalizations, relationship to the meanings of psychological predicates; functionalism, with reference to the propositional attitudes), 151–81; *de re*, 177–80; *de se*, 180–1; holistic character of, 167–8

Cartesian dualism, 9; *see also* psychophysical event dualism
causal connective, 36–9
causal role of mental, 11–12, 29–30, 35–8
causal theory of reference, 158
causation, 13–19, 210; analysis of causal statements, 35–43; and context relativity of "the cause", 13–19; and general laws, 14–18; *see also* supervenient causation
central nervous system, 20
ceteris paribus clauses, 71–2, 96n, 166; *see also* conceptual role; folk psychological generalizations
chauvinism, 156, 159
Chisholm, R., 53
Churchland, P., 33

cognitive capacities, 182; decomposition and analysis within the operator theory, 191–3
cognitive psychology, 23–5, 155–6, 173–4; explanations of, 183, 191–3; generalization schemata within, 190; methodology, 183–5; relationship to neurophysiology, 183
colors, 129–30
compositionality, 60–1, 63, 68–74; *see also* folk psychological generalizations, relationship to the meanings of psychological predicates
conceptual role (*see also* formal semantics, relationship to the theory of meaning; folk psychological generalizations, relationship to the meanings of psychological predicates; functionalism; meaning), 70–4, 95–8; of belief predicates and operators, 164–6, 180–1; of psychological predicates and operators generally, 96; of sensory predicates and operators, 95–6, 127–9
Cornman, J., 59

Davidson, D., 14–18, 26, 35, 52, 67, 69, 71–4, 107
Dennett, D., 33–4
Descartes, R., 9
descriptionalism, 196; *see also* quasi-linguistic mental representations
digital computers, 193–6; and the manipulation of symbols, 194–6; as a model for understanding the mind, 208–9

eliminative materialism, 2, 33–4
emergence of mental states, 31–2

213